Scimitar into Stanley

Scimitar into Stanley

One Soldier's Falklands War

Roger Field

Pen & Sword
MILITARY
AN IMPRINT OF PEN & SWORD BOOKS LTD.
YORKSHIRE - PHILADELPHIA

First published in Great Britain in 2022 by
Pen & Sword Military
An imprint of
Pen & Sword Books Ltd
Yorkshire – Philadelphia

Copyright © Roger Field 2022

ISBN 978 1 39907 234 2

The right of Roger Field to be identified as Author of this work has been asserted by him in accordance with the Copyright, Designs and Patents Act 1988.

A CIP catalogue record for this book is available from the British Library.

All rights reserved. No part of this book may be reproduced or transmitted in any form or by any means, electronic or mechanical including photocopying, recording or by any information storage and retrieval system, without permission from the Publisher in writing.

Printed and bound in the UK by CPI Group (UK) Ltd, Croydon, CR0 4YY.

Pen & Sword Books Limited incorporates the imprints of Atlas, Archaeology, Aviation, Discovery, Family History, Fiction, History, Maritime, Military, Military Classics, Politics, Select, Transport, True Crime, Air World, Frontline Publishing, Leo Cooper, Remember When, Seaforth Publishing, The Praetorian Press, Wharncliffe Local History, Wharncliffe Transport, Wharncliffe True Crime and White Owl.

For a complete list of Pen & Sword titles please contact

PEN & SWORD BOOKS LIMITED
47 Church Street, Barnsley, South Yorkshire, S70 2AS, England
E-mail: enquiries@pen-and-sword.co.uk
Website: www.pen-and-sword.co.uk

Or
PEN AND SWORD BOOKS
1950 Lawrence Rd, Havertown, PA 19083, USA
E-mail: Uspen-and-sword@casematepublishers.com
Website: www.penandswordbooks.com

It was John Quincy Adams (6th US President) who is credited with saying, 'I am a warrior, so that my son may be a merchant, so that his son may be a poet.' In my family we skipped a generation as my daughter works in television and my son is a sculptor. Long may this situation last!

To my two grandsons, Elki and Oliver.

Contents

Preface ix
Acknowledgements xiii
Map xv

Chapter 1: *Queen Elizabeth 2.* Southampton Docks, 12 May 1982   1
Chapter 2: *QE2* – Sailing   9
Chapter 3: Sailing South   21
Chapter 4: Stiff Upper Lips   25
Chapter 5: Africa   29
Chapter 6: Tropical Torpor   37
Chapter 7: Active Service   47
Chapter 8: Towards Grytviken, South Georgia   53
Chapter 9: Grytviken to Bomb Alley   58
Chapter 10: Ashore   64
Chapter 11: Tractors at Darwin   69
Chapter 12: The Power of Command   80
Chapter 13: 'Bloodied but Unbowed'. Wazzock!   87
Chapter 14: Playing with the Paras   102
Chapter 15: Berets on, Helmets off – the Fog of War   117
Chapter 16: The Battle of Wireless Ridge   126
Chapter 17: The Fog of Victory   148
Chapter 18: The Spoils of War   157
Chapter 19: Windsor   165

Postscript 177
Appendix The Guards Magazine *article* 183

Preface

'If any particular group deserves special praise for what was done that night (the Battle of Wireless Ridge), then it must be the tanks of The Blues and Royals. Their mere presence had been a remarkable boost to morale during all the attacks that had taken place, and the speed and accuracy of their fire, matched by their ability to keep up with the advancing Paras, had been a severe shock to the enemy. Lance Corporal of Horse Dunkeley's tank, which Captain Field had taken over following the injury to its commander, had alone fired forty rounds from its 30mm gun.'

2 Para Falklands; The Battalion at War, Major General John Frost CB, DSO & Bar, MC (Commanding Officer, 2 Para at Arnhem, September 1944)

It is forty years since that night on Wireless Ridge. A world ago, it seems.

Decades ago, I remember an aged great-aunt telling me that when she looked in her mirror she saw an old woman, whilst inside she felt like a young girl. While I sort of understood what she was saying, on a deeper level I did not. How could I? These days, I fully understand. There is an ancient African proverb: 'When an old man dies, a library burns.' My generation of Falklands veterans is ageing, memories fading, dropping ever faster off our proverbial perches; the attrition rate ever increasing. If I don't tell my story soon it will be too late, and I at least think it is a tale worth telling because, sometimes by accident, at other times by dint of volunteering, I found myself in some interesting places from the outset of the war right through to its very end.

What's more, I kept a diary; detailed during the voyage south when, come evening, as the luxury cruise liner *Queen Elizabeth 2* ploughed her majestic way through the calm seas and warm breezes of the tropics, it required little effort to settle down in my cabin, iced cocktail in hand, and record the day's events and frustrations. Everything changed once I went ashore. From then on I was too tired, cold and busy to even think about writing up the day's events, although I did jot down operational briefings and make the occasional cryptic observation in the pocket notebook all soldiers carry.

Come 16 June, two days after the fighting ended, safe again in a nice warm house in Port Stanley, already getting bored although mighty relieved to be alive, I knew that I had been part of momentous events. Now, however, my diary served a different purpose. I needed to get my experiences on paper before they dimmed or became confused by time; or, given some of what I witnessed, that I later got to wondering whether I had been imagining things.

I wrote my journal fast and turned each page; no editing or revising; no looking back. Once back home, I stuck everything from the Falklands in a drawer and, probably like most who were there, resolved to get on with my life and forget about it.

I have just read my Falklands diary and looked at my files for the first time since 1982. Over 12,000 words of diary – so quite a detailed account of a very short war, and whilst those long-ago scribblings are raw and unpolished, I doubt many Falklands accounts get much fresher, even all these forty years later.

My diary, letters home (my parents kept mine to them) and documents stashed in my long unread files give an unvarnished view of, first, setting sail on a luxury cruise aboard the legendary *QE2*, and then the war I fought. These entries are in bold in the book. I have added occasional extra words in [square brackets] to give context – the edit I might have done at the time, but did not. I explain the inevitable military shorthand/jargon in (round brackets).

So why, apart from advancing years, now?

Even on 16 June, writing up my journal, I knew that I had experienced a rather singular war. Most in the Task Force had one 'job'. I ended up with three. Once home, I was told to write an article for the *The Guards Magazine* (see Appendix). I entitled it, 'A Vignette of the Falklands as a Watchkeeper, Infanteer and Armoured Car Commander' – my three jobs. On 1 December 1982, as the 'senior detachment commander' of my regiment, The Blues and Royals, Prince Philip hooked the South Atlantic Medal on to my chest at the Household Division, Falklands Parade at Buckingham Palace.

'I read your article,' he said as he did so, giving me a cheery smile. 'Sounds as if you had an interesting war.'

'Write a book,' my chums said.

That presented a problem. My experiences on the front line were of ordinary soldiers and their officers doing exceptional things under horrendous conditions; something I could happily write about. However, some of my experiences working on the staff at HQ 5th Infantry Brigade were far less happy.

The British Army teaches many things, and loyalty – '*omerta*' (the South Italian Mafia code of silence) at its most extreme – is high on that list; loyalty both to one's regiment and to individuals within it, at least to outsiders. This policy of silence is also called 'not rocking the boat' – an expression a fellow veteran used when cautioning me against including one less than complimentary story in the book.

However, an account that left out my worm's-eye view of the failings of HQ 5 Brigade would be a false account. It would also be a dull account. So I didn't write it. Then I learned that Brigadier Wilson, the architect to my mind of so much that went 'wrong' – although, of course, plenty went 'right', otherwise we would not have won the war and in such fine style! – had died. And that somehow made it all right for me to tell my story.

'Never apologize, never explain' is a useful political maxim. But I am no politician, so I am going to, if not apologize, then at least offer a brief explanation. I strongly suspect that family and friends – certainly – and fellow soldiers who knew, worked with and doubtless liked Brigadier Wilson will not recognise the picture I paint of him in this book. One former colleague who worked with him as a colonel told me he was always amiable, and certainly he was always friendly towards me. But friendly and amiable do not necessarily make for an effective war leader.

'A bit cruel, don't you think?' queried one ex-soldier who pre-read my story. And that may well be the case. All I can say is that this is my view based on what little I saw of him – but that little was often close-up and made a deep impact. Others may consider my depiction of him as near-traitorous. However, when I did a bit of background research on the war, it transpired that there was plenty that I did not know about certain events within HQ 5th Infantry Brigade, even though I had been 'in the room' or as good as 'around the corner' at certain times. Little of it was 'good'. My researches also led me to realize how little loyalty I felt towards that headquarters and its Brigadier. I was attached to them for less than two months. I started second-guessing them from Day One. I quickly decided they were more than capable of getting me killed. I escaped them at the first opportunity. They had to send a helicopter to fetch me back when the fighting was over.

I never saw them again once I got home. So, bugger *omerta*; this particular leaky Brigade boat has needed 'rocking' for decades.

And, if that causes upset for some, as I am sure it will, then I am sorry for those hurt feelings.

But, and then again, why throughout millennia of military memoir-writing has it been deemed acceptable for senior generals to opine on, and often 'diss' their subordinates and fellow generals, but near-treason for a lowly subordinate to do something similar in reverse?

As to my story, 'they' say that each person's view from trench, turret or radio set is different. That sounds right to me.

This, therefore, is what I saw, or thought I saw, through the fog and confusion of order, counter-order, lack of any orders, and battle. Any mistakes or misunderstandings or unfairnesses are all my own.

The Cotswolds
December 2021

Acknowledgements

Writing this memoir has been a pretty selfish undertaking as it involved little more than my contemporaneous diaries and letters home, plus my memory. Add in a couple of books – checked for specifics and not read in their entirety – and that has been that. So no list of sources and no list of contributors.

With two massive exceptions. Worried that I might be committing heresy, getting the 'flavour' of the times wrong, or 'going too far', I asked for help from two friends who served in the same peacetime army as I. Both resigned as captains. Neither served in the Falklands. Neither was in my regiment. In fact, neither even served with me. But they know the British Army I joined in 1974 very well indeed, and both are highly intelligent individuals. So, a huge thank you to Jeremy Harbord and Robert Elwell for the time and effort you put in to helping me make this as 'edgy' as you deemed reasonable, whilst ensuring that I did not overstep the mark.

And, finally, a big thank you to Henry Wilson of Pen and Sword for taking on my book at the eleventh hour. He was a Brigadier once, and I said to him, after he'd read it and said he wanted it, words along the lines of 'I'll wager you'd have hated to have had me as one of your troop leaders.'

'Not a bit of it,' he replied. 'You'd have been rather fun . . .'

I hope you have fun reading this too . . .

Map

The Saddleback
SADDLEBACKS
Beagle Ridge
Jameson's Stream
Turner's Stream
Drunken Rock
Murrell River
Furze Bush Pass
Drunken Rock Pass
Lower Pass
PHASE 1
PHASE 2
PHASE 3
PHASE 4
MT LONGDON
Mt Longdon
3 PARA
ROUGH DIAMOND
WIRELESS RIDGE
APPLE PIE
BLUEBERRY PIE
Islet Pt
HEARNDEN W
Wireless Ridge
Moody Brook Camp (derelict)
Moody Valley
Moody Brook
Two Sisters
COMANDOS
Water filtration plant (big white building)
Wind Pumps
ESRO Building (position approx)
British Ant
Seaplane Slip and Hangar
Race Co
Felton Stm
SCOTS
TUMBLEDOWN
Tumbledown Mt
GUARDS
Mt William
Sapper Hill
453
Mt Harriet
Pumping Station
MULLET CREEK
Pony's Pass
Ford
Mullet Creek Stream
WEST END
SAND BAY
Narrow Point
PORT HARRIET
Port Harriet House
SEAL POINT
PORT HARRIET POINT
Rodeo Pond

SAS & SBS ATTEMPT

Chapter 1

Queen Elizabeth 2. Southampton Docks, 12 May 1982

'Rush to wait. Wait to rush.' (Officer mutilation of the proud motto of the Royal Military Academy Sandhurst: 'Serve to Lead')
   —'Berets On. Berets Off.' (All ranks variant of the above)

Today's the day. It's finally here. After weeks of 'Will I? Won't I?' I definitely will. Sail to the Falklands, that is. Whether I get to fight is another matter.

It's 9.00 am when the bus that brought us from Aldershot pulls up on the *QE*'s quay at Southampton docks. The ship sails at 4.00 pm and there'll be a full-on send-off: families, politicians, top brass, press, what have you. I watched the TV as the SS *Canberra* left Southampton on 9 April, so I have some idea what a jamboree it will be. Right now it's deep focus and all business.

Gather kit; make sure I leave nothing behind. This is a pedantic exercise, obsessive almost. I've got a lot of kit: canvas webbing with my fighting stuff in it; SMG (Stirling sub machine gun); large mountaineering rucksack (Bergen) with second-line kit; suitcase and 'kit bag' with third-line spares for the boat, and for the six months we've been told we can expect to garrison the Islands.

I've been packing and repacking for days now. Leave something out, leave something on the bus, and nobody is coming along to give it to me tomorrow. The *QE2* isn't making any U-turns.

Bergen and webbing on back, a bulging case in each hand, shooter across my shoulder, I struggle across the quay and join the Scots Guards filing up the main gangplank.

In front and looming above us, the *QE2* is so large that she fills the dock. Like a floating block of flats laid on its side. There's lots of the expected bravado and 'couldn't-care-less-ness' from the soldiers. They josh and joke with one another, just as countless generations of secretly fearful soldiers have doubtless done before us, standing on quays, waiting to board ships to take them to distant shores to fight brutal wars. Whilst it makes me feel part of a continuum, it does not console. History also teaches that many of those tough, trained, joshing, joking young warriors never came home.

Fortune has smiled. A fellow Brigade watchkeeper is a chum of mine, Nick Schrayne of the 13th/18th Royal Hussars. We've been on the bus together, chatting away, making light of what is coming. We join the queue together. I also have chums amongst the Scots and Welsh Guards who will be on the ship. This could turn into quite a jolly trip, as long as we ignore what is at the other end of it.

Step off the concrete of the quay and on to the wooden gangplank. I try to memorize the exact moment I step from the hard, safe, solidity of land to the slight movement of the sea; the actual point of no return. I look suitably stern and soldier-like, not least because there are already a few photographers about and I don't want my photo in tomorrow's newspapers looking as if I'm struggling to carry all this stuff. My family would forgive and forget; my regiment would not. Anyway, I've been a soldier for eight years now and am well-practised at looking suitably officer-like.

Up the broad gangplank.

Standing at the very top, checking each of his guardsmen on board, making sure they are all fully equipped and looking fit for purpose, is the impeccably tailored, genuinely grim and soldierly-looking Regimental Sergeant Major Mackenzie, Scots Guards. 'Ronnie' Mackenzie was my company sergeant major when I was training to be an officer at Sandhurst. He very soon rumbled me as one of the less, shall we say, reverential and more exuberant cadets. I've been on the wrong end of a bawling-out from him more than once. And here he is, as good as being forced to welcome me on board as I'm mixed in with his soldiers.

I look at him. He looks at me.

'Good morning, Mister Mackenzie,' says I, keen to overcome any awkwardness – RSMs are always called 'Mister'; a genuine sign of respect used by officers of all ranks for those few who reach the top of the NCO (non-commissioned officer) tree.

He hesitates. 'Oooh nooo,' he says in his thick, slow Scottish burr. 'Now I've seen it all . . .'

My warrior's façade is well and truly punctured.

Step into the ship. We are allocated a room number and deck. Nick and I are sharing. Good.

There is a note for us. We are to report to the Brigade Ops Room on the Quarter Deck when we are settled in. All very efficient.

We are directed up the stairs and not down into the bowels of the ship, where I feared we, as mere radio 'watchkeepers' and not full-time members of the brigade staff, might find ourselves. I lead the way, Nick following. Up more stairs, then down a corridor covered with taped-down hardboard, doubtless to stop us vulgar lot ruining the expensive carpet underneath.

I open the door of our cabin. Hallelujah! I can scarcely believe it. A full-on stateroom.

It takes a nanosecond for me, blocking the door, to sweep the room and evaluate. Two large, luxurious-looking queen- (as it turns out) sized beds. Two narrow, fold-up cot-type beds set up on the floor. Far double bed, the best one, nearest the windows, already with a mountain of kit on it. Taken. But no kit on the near double.

Advance. Sit on bed. Add suitcases. Mine.

Poor old Nick, one step behind, will spend the next three weeks on a camp bed. His only solace is that he gets to choose which one. Julian Stanley, Royal Marines, the fourth to join us in the room, ends up with the one nearest the door; the one we will bash into when we enter the cabin late and in the dark. That's the army way. First come, first served, and no whingeing

With nothing else to do I tell Nick I have a plan. Down we go to the main lounge deck, where I seek out the rather frazzled Chief Steward.

'What's the booze situation?' I ask him.

Answer: red and white wine, champagne and beer. These will be charged to us at little or no profit, much as if we were in our own officer's mess.

'Spirits?'

No, they have all been unloaded.

'Mixers? Like tomato juice?'

They, too, have been removed, for some strange reason.

We thank him and let him get back to his proper job. We are on the *QE2*, one of, if not *the* greatest luxury liner afloat. We have the perfect set-up with our cabin, plus outside private balcony with seating area and sun loungers, plus all-important fitted fridge. The tropics demand cocktails.

As the rest of 5th Infantry Brigade continue to troop across the quay to the gangplank, Nick and I slip furtively – we do not want to be questioned by some humourless high-up who might get it into his head that we are deserting, or some such stupidity – down to the bottom, bow end of the ship where, the Chief Steward has told us, there's a narrow, crew-only gangplank. Down it we go. Stride purposefully back across the dock and out through a side gate. Taxi to the nearest Oddbins, and £80 each later – quite a lot of money back then – we emerge with boxes full of vodka, Galliano, malt whisky and champagne, plus cocktail mixers: orange and tomato juice, and consommé (for Bullshots – upgraded Bloody Marys, the consommé being particularly good for hangovers).

Back to the ship. Back up the crew gangplank. Stock fridge. We are tropics-ready.

We meet our other two cabin mates: Adam Drummond, a Grenadier Guard, and Julian Stanley, the Royal Marine. He certainly looks the part; green beret, impressive moustache and gives the impression of one who enjoys eating a glass as an after-dinner party trick. Outwardly at least, he's a hairy-arsed 'bootneck'. In contrast, Adam and I are Household Division, Nick is 'line' cavalry. We are clean-shaven, use glasses to drink from – elaborate cocktails as Julian will discover – and wear blue berets. To a marine that makes us 'crap hats', because the colour of the hats (berets) we wear are, to him, 'crap' compared to his treasured green. We blue-beret wearers could not give a stuff about this beret colour fixation and just ignore it. But, we soon discover, Julian's a happy soul who fits in admirably. He's just relieved to have made the trip – most of his fellow Marines are on the first wave – and he doesn't want to miss out, even if he did end up with the worst bed in the room.

There are two other watchkeepers, making us six in all. Their names, to my utter shame, now elude me, although it is probably because they are in another cabin and I see very much less of them. But, sitting here in our glorious stateroom that first day – £56,000 per person to hire for a 3-month voyage, we are told – surrounded by a happy gang of like-minded campers, were it not for the fact that we are heading towards a war in one of the most inhospitable places on earth, I'd say that everything in the garden is looking peachy.

And now the big moment is here: leave-taking. The offices and buildings opposite have been filling with families and top brass. The gangplank is empty of soldiers. I'd have dearly liked a girlfriend here to wave me off; someone to write to and think about over the long months to come. However, my love life has been more than chaotic of late – a long-term relationship that ran into the sands not that long ago. Lengthy overseas postings have an evil reputation for exposing fault lines, especially when you are young and intent on living life to the utmost. Unexpectedly asked at the eleventh hour if I'd like to 'go down south', a new, gently blossoming relationship found itself with only days to flower. Or not. A last night in

London with her, which I had had high hopes for, descended instead into 'Will I? Won't I?' confusion until, with time running out in the early hours, I had to say goodbye and hightail it back to Windsor before I missed my transport to Southampton this morning. Not exactly the romantic send-off for the bold, departing warrior that every soldier shipping out to war hopes for; but then again, real life is rarely a happy Hollywood movie.

Not that I blame her for her confusion. Were I her friend, and had she come to me for relationship advice, I'd have cautioned her strongly against a new relationship with someone heading 8,000 miles into a combat zone. And for how long? If, indeed – and this is not beyond the bounds of possibility – he ever comes back.

My mother might like to recount how, when my father shipped out to North Africa in 1941/2, he said to her on getting the news; 'You will wait for me, won't you?'

To which she as good as replied, 'You've got to be joking.'

So, they married. Which was lucky for him as he didn't make it home until 1945. But that was then, and all the bold young men were shipping out to war. And this is now, and only the tiniest handful of us are heading off.

At least my parents are coming to wave me off. I told them they didn't need to, but they insisted. I am secretly delighted, although I'm already wondering how I will spot them in the ever-growing crowds, and it is close to cast-off time.

In the sort of move that only the British regimental system can dream up, the band of the Scots Guards are at one end of the quay and the band of the Welsh Guards – both bands in their finest parade scarlet – at the other; each facing their own men on board. Each band is giving it welly, playing their own medley of music, seemingly determined to drown out the other; *Men of Harlech* versus *Scotland the Brave*; Welsh drums beating, Scottish pipes wailing, the British regimental system at its very competitive worst. A dog's dinner of competing noise where our cabin is located, roughly in the middle.

My diary describes what happens next: '**What a send off; tremendous cheering, the soldiers being their normal delightfully crude selves. Sadly officers cannot shout 'Drop 'em' to the enthusiastic girl who constantly waggles her rather superb boobs much to everybody's delight, even her husband's. Nott (the Minister for Defence) appears. Silence.**

I remark that if only his Press Secretary were to get the wife to waggle her boobs as he waves, the resultant cheer might just save his obviously faltering political career. The man looks like a loser.'

Then, mere minutes before we are about to sail, I spot my parents. We wave to one another. Rather formally, as if it is the first day of term and we are standing outside school surrounded by fellow pupils and parents, all equally scared to show any spontaneity or affection lest it expose us to future ridicule. No wonder 'foreigners' think we Brits are so buttoned-up and cold as a nation, when in fact we're just trying not to appear weak and emotional. Then again, I suspect we will be needing lashings of British 'stiff upper lip' before this jaunt is over.

As I wave, and then wonder what to do next, everything changes. Up until now it has all been surface bombast and gaiety, going through the motions as we laugh at and cheer the girl who removes her bra and gestures to a crane driver to swing it over to her delighted husband on the ship. This, however, is the reality of going to war. Waving goodbye to the people you love. Who love you. They knowing, you knowing, that this may be for the final time. I am totally deflated. Depressed even. **'Let's go. Everybody wants off. Finally we do.'**

Now the gangplank is removed. Then dock workers start lifting the massive mooring ropes, each as thick as a man's thigh, and, as if by magic, the two bands combine, note-perfect. Their music soars up from below. Whether they play *Rule Britannia* before *Land of Hope and Glory*, or the other way round, I do not remember. I do remember us all singing our lungs out as water begins to appear between the boat and the quay and we pull away. My parents shrink to mere dots in moments, their faces a blur in the crowd. When I say there is hardly a dry eye on the ship I mean it. No one acknowledges it. We do not look at each other. Far too embarrassing. But we are all feeling it now. Grown warriors in their battle kit? With tears in their eyes as they sing? I still cannot hear those two songs, usually on television at the Last Night of the Proms, without those same tears, the ones that are in my eyes now, welling up from the Lord alone knows where even as I write this.

And, my diary tells me, just how jingoistic, nationalistic, all this is: **'What a send off, it really makes one incredibly proud to be English.'**

That send-off – the bands playing, the crowds cheering, the gurning politicians and generals but, more importantly, the concern and love of my already-disappearing-into-the-distance parents – is no different from

Queen Elizabeth 2. Southampton Docks, 12 May 1982

archive footage I have seen of previous generations of British soldiers being waved off to war; bands playing, families waving, soldiers proud to be going.

And what is wrong with that? Far better than, and the polar opposite to, the experience of a five-years-older-than-me generation of American teenagers forced to go to war in Vietnam, many – probably most – wondering why they were going; taunted by shouts of 'Baby-killers!' and furious that Uncle Sam was stealing what should have been their golden years, their youth.

But not 5th Infantry Brigade. We volunteered to join our army. **'Suddenly there is a realisation that must have been felt by countless generations of soldiers going to do battle that there is more than just you in this, there is a nation who count on you and wishes you well . . . for the first time, I understand what is meant by "England expects".'**

Determined to be gay – in the old fashioned, military sense of the word – Nick and I pop the cork on that bottle of champagne we bought at Oddbins and **'the sadness is gone. My parents are no longer visible, just a cheering throng. Hoots and whistles from the other ships in the dock. All around me laugh joyously as *QE2* thunderously replies.'**

And then something extraordinary; something that I've never heard remarked on before. It affected me deeply at the time and does to this day. Champagne drunk – a bottle does not last long between six thirsty soldiers – the others drift back into the cabin and start unpacking, getting to know one another; only Nick and I have met before. I stay outside. I have a small sailing boat and know the Solent shoreline well, but I can barely believe what I am seeing. **'The beaches are thronged for miles. Fifteen minutes later and the beaches are still full of people; distant speck as we must be to them.'**

The sheer number of people needed to form this unbroken black line along the shore, people who have come to wave us off knowing that we will not be able to see them but have made the pilgrimage in any event, is beyond my calculation. And still we sail and still the line snakes along the beaches. It is truly humbling. **'The send-off at the dock was a very personal thing; this is almost more impressive in its way . . . Truly we are carrying Britain's hopes.'**

It is only when our well-wishers merge into the warm afternoon murk and we turn due south and head out to sea that I finally go back inside.

We were told when we boarded to make ourselves known at the Brigade HQ Ops room, and now the time has come. This will be our first proper meeting with HQ 5 Brigade and, I'm guessing, given the need for us watchkeepers to get up to high military speed from a standing start – none of us have worked with 5 Brigade before – they will have a brutal induction programme ready for us and, doubtless, a mass of jobs needing doing. I anticipate being kept very busy on the journey south.

The Ops Room, the Brigade's communications centre, is still being set up in what used to be the Card Room on the Quarter Deck. There's lots of activity, soldiers toing and froing, but of what they are up to we have no idea. When we enquire we are told that there are no instructions for us. Yet.

So, with nothing better to occupy us we tune in, as soldiers are wont to do, to the already churning rumour machine. The news is not particularly encouraging. Our glorious departure was, we are shocked to discover, an exercise in smoke and mirrors. Only one of *QE2*'s three steam turbines is working. They plan to get the second running overnight and then fix number three on the voyage south. We will heave to, out of sight of land, while the engineers get their spanners out. If they cannot fix whatever is wrong, tomorrow may see us limping back into Southampton for repairs. Also, another downer, some numpty has turned a stopcock in the wrong direction and a load of brown effluent has disgorged itself into the indoor swimming pool rather than out to sea. So, *adios* to lounging by the pool – although I recently read that 'they' got it cleaned pretty quick-sticks. Not that they told us. They clearly didn't want to share the pool with 3,000 swim-happy soldiers. Bastards.

It's not all bad news. We officers will be eating extremely well in the Queen's Grill, the First Class restaurant, and there's to be a film tonight. I've had it fixed in my mind for decades now that it was the 1953 film, *The Cruel Sea*, they screened that first night; a Second World War tale of submarine sinkings and death beneath huge, icy seas on the murderous North Atlantic convoys. Just what someone with a suitably gallows sense of humour *would* show a ship full of soldiers heading to war in the South Atlantic; spine-stiffening, sphincter-loosening stuff.

However, my diary tells me I'm wrong: '**We had an excellent dinner with a good red wine, followed by the only hint of war to date – a film called** *Enter the Ninja*. **Plenty of death there, also a bouncy Susan George slinking around to the cheers of the boys.**'

Perhaps they showed us *The Cruel Sea* on another occasion. I hope so.

Chapter 2

QE2 – Sailing

'Bullshit baffles brains' – another much loved army saying.

On *QE2* that first morning I awake and stretch in my luxury queen-sized bed in our luxury cabin. I note the lift and roll of the ship. We are poling along at a fair old lick. Up. Look out of the window. No land to be seen. The grease monkeys have sorted out the problem and, in the words of Rod Stewart, 'We are sailing.'

I can guess at what time I awoke that first morning as I have a copy of 'Daily Routine Orders, Operation Corporate' (the formal military name for the re-invasion of the Falkland Islands). This tells me that each shipboard day works as follows:

Reveille	0600 hrs
Breakfast	0700–0800 hrs

First works parade 0830 hrs (this, in my regiment, is called 'first parade' and takes place on the vehicle park. Soldiers, and officers, are first all checked off as being present, outwardly sober and correct and are then given their tasks for the day. On *QE2*, with no parade square or vehicle park to assemble on, each regiment or sub-unit has its own assembly point. For us watchkeepers it is the Brigade Ops room.)

Lunch 1200–1300 hrs

Second Works parade 1345 hrs. Note the leisurely 45-minute gap between the end of lunch and starting work for the afternoon; plenty of time for a quick bit of 'Egyptian PT' (sleep).

Dinner 1700–1800 hrs SNCO's and ORs (senior non-commissioned officers and other ranks)

1900–2000 hrs Offrs (Officers). I have no idea how it works today but, back then, the soldiers liked to eat a whole lot earlier than us officer lot. They call their large evening meal 'tea'. We call ours dinner.

There is a logic behind the name. I started my army career as a trooper in basic training and know for a gnawing-hole-in-my-stomach fact that by 10.00 pm we squaddies were desperate for a second meal, or dinner; this explains the timeless proliferation of fast-food outlets near military bases. Tea in the cookhouse was 'dry' and, as the name implies, there was always a large steel urn of tea steaming away.

Bar Facilities (I kid you not) **1830–2300 hrs**. In other words, and rather wonderfully, a full four and a half hours of Brigade-sanctioned drinking time.

These timings, taken from this Daily Routine sheet, tell me that on 13 May I leap from my bed, all keenness and determination, at about 0740 hrs.

This for me is a lie-in. At Windsor, where I am stationed, I need to be up between 0600 and 0630 – depending where in London I have bedded down for the night – to beat the traffic and be on first parade, spick and spruce, at 0830. And when I was stationed at Bovington, in Dorset, I had to be starting my car by 0500 to guarantee being on parade 120 miles away at 0800. Doing that a couple of times a week, or every night at Windsor – after a night of 'fun', otherwise why bother? – explains the rationale behind those nannying motorway signs: 'Tiredness Can Kill'. How I wasn't remains a mystery

If our cabin is splendid, our en suite marble-tiled bathroom is palatial. Two colour-coordinated marble washbasins, one crapper and one combination bath and shower. We four can, *in extremis*, all 'ablute' simultaneously. All being experienced soldiers with plenty of time in the field between us, there's no 'Hurry up in the shower! Who's nicked my soap?' to worry about.

So, with breakfast finishing at 0800, we four can just about, as the army expression goes, 'Shit, shower, shave' within twenty minutes, and still be in time to enjoy our Weetabix and full English before appearing with the required five minutes to spare, for 0830 'First Parade' in the Ops Room.

Julian, our tough Marine, might have been up early that first morning getting in some extra press-ups, but if my memory serves me correctly, in no time we four are legging it down to breakfast at the last possible moment.

I am agog to see what Brigade HQ is like. My Foot Guards chums have been telling me about the 'cake and arse' party that was Exercise Welsh Falcon, the two-week 'work-up' training for this trip south that

5 Brigade conducted on Sennybridge in Wales in mid/late April. The Guards battalions, the captains who are my chums, some of whom I was at Sandhurst with, others who I have got to know as we bump into one another socially, are not happy. Nor, apparently, are their majors. As I am attached to Brigade HQ, some are wary of me. However, I am Blues and Royals and Household Division like them. I hope those I know will put in a good word for me.

Regardless of the muttering, I want to believe in the Brigadier. After all, he's won an MC (Military Cross) for bravery, and they are almost as rare as hen's teeth in our 1980s peacetime army, an army where I come across colonels and majors with no campaign medals whatsoever on their chests. MCs have to be earned. That gives me confidence in him. But I also know from my reading of history that, at the beginning of the Second World War, some of the biggest duffers as generals were the highly decorated young thrusters of the First War. The question I should have asked is: how does an MC awarded on the mean streets of Northern Ireland qualify someone to command a brigade on an amphibious operation in the sub-Antarctic? The answer, as I will soon discover, is that it does not.

The Scots and Welsh Guards joined 5th Brigade just before the exercise started, replacing 2 and 3 Para, who were seconded to 3rd Commando Brigade, now sailing south. That Welsh exercise was the first time they all worked together – a near-guaranteed recipe for the semi-balls-up I gather it turned into. However, and rightly, nobody is interested in excuses. We are going to war. Brigade HQ is either fit for purpose or it is not. If it is not, then they will get people killed; probably unnecessarily.

That first morning, Brigade HQ is abuzz with activity. Brendan Lambe, the Brigade Major, is here. I met him last week and my jury is still firmly out.

It was only on Thursday, 6 May that my commanding officer told me that I was going for certain. He tells me I am to report tomorrow to Brendan at HQ 5th Infantry Brigade in Aldershot. He will brief me on what is expected of me. I also need to go to 5 Brigade stores to collect the extra 'Arctic/Antarctic' gear that will be essential to survival in the sub-Antarctic. We don't stock any at our regimental stores in Windsor, and there's no time to order any in. My standard issue war-in-Europe kit is clearly not fit for purpose.

Friday, 7 May, I drove to 5th Infantry Brigade HQ – Aldershot Garrison is like a small town – and introduced myself to Brendan as instructed.

'**Come to a watchkeeper's conference on Monday and collect your kit,**' he told me. He's very busy, obviously, and equally obviously hasn't got time to talk to me.

'Shouldn't I pick up my kit right now as I'm already here?' I countered.

To which eminently sensible suggestion Brendan, my diary tells me, '**demurred**'.

I start smelling a rat. Years of 'fine' British schooling, followed by time spent being endlessly buggered about by the army, make me wary of all authority. My watchword has long been, 'Hope for the best, but expect the worst'. Then, when the worst almost inevitably happens, I will not be surprised, or disappointed. I may even be prepared.

It takes a nanosecond to work out what has probably happened. I must be the very last person to collect my Arctic kit. The rest of 5 Brigade were probably issued theirs weeks ago. I'll bet the shelves are nearly empty. Although why Brendan is being unhelpful is puzzling.

I don't like it. He should be trying to help. After all, if they haven't got any Arctic kit here for me now, what chance will they have of issuing it to me later? Since my earliest army days I've had it drilled into me that if I forget to bring something I only have myself to blame. It's a lesson I've always heeded. I've never been caught short before. I don't intend to start now.

So, refusing to take 'No' for an answer, '**I insisted. The Brigade Major looked surprised – it was curious his attitude of come back and do it later. I realised that the BM was very surprised to see me.**' [He must have forgotten he had invited me to come.]

He relented, dismissed me, and I drove off to find the Brigade stores. Little surprise: it had been pretty much picked clean. What followed could have come from an Edwardian end-of-pier farce, complete with the obligatory pair of pantomime dames:

'**I met two delightful, good natured, mid-sixties females, slightly peeved at missing their tea break and no more idea of the importance of correctly fitting equipment in the South Atlantic than I did of working in a clothes store in Aldershot.**

'Sorry, we've only got left fitting (waterproof) over-boots. Ha ha.'

Despair from me. I felt that if I was going to war I should be getting the best, not two women who could not conceive of a world where to get wet feet was to live like that and without hope of drying out. And so it went on. Arctic hat:

'Only got small.'

'Oh, doesn't he look funny?'
I stand over 6′ 2″ and have a large head.'

Always well-mannered, I nevertheless explained to these well-meaning but hopeless 'civvies' a few facts of military life in an emphatic enough way for one of them to suggest an alternative 'Regimental' store which, she thought, might be better stocked. Back into my car.

There I chanced upon two charming, bored privates who were only too keen to help. They had a pile of boxes that they were about to send to Southampton. They dug them open and found me some kit that fitted. But not everything I needed. I ended up going to war with thermal underwear three sizes too large. Although I did end up with a pair of correctly sized rubber over-boots and a cold-weather hat. Thank God

'Monday found me at the watchkeepers' meeting and seeing others who had tried to get their kit on the Monday – as suggested to them by the Brigade Major – and failed.'

After that 'Welcome to 5 Brigade' introductory balls-up, my fellow Antarctic-kitless watchkeepers are also looking at Brendan in a somewhat leery way.

That, however, was last week's SNAFU (situation normal all fucked up). What matters now is what comes next. In the Ops Room we have modern Clansman radios, tables for them to sit on and comfortable chairs for us. The radios will be monitored by us at all times during the trip south. There will always be a Royal Signals guy in attendance in case anything techie needs doing. Nobody wants an officer fiddling with a radio . . .

I am tasked to the 'Forward' G (Operations) net to the battalions when we go ashore. I seem to remember I am paired off with Nick. He'll be on duty whilst I am asleep, and vice versa. There is a 'Rear' net that will report back to Divisional HQ. Adam (I'm pretty certain, although I may be wrong) is on that.

We are further split into 'Main' and 'Tac'. I will be Tac. Tac moves forward whilst the Brigadier remains at Main. When Tac is up and working, the Brigadier and his staff will join us and we become Main. The others follow and we become Tac again, ready for the next move forwards. That, at least, is the theory.

I offer a silent prayer of thanks. At least I will have the more interesting job in what I suspect will be a very dull role. If someone had told me I was to be on 'Rear', ordering up extra pairs of socks and petrol from our rear echelons, I'd throw myself overboard right now.

Brendan introduces us to Willy Townsend. He's a Brigade staff captain who works on the operations ('G' – planning and action) side of things. We will report to him. He is also a captain but he's senior to us; probably due promotion to major at the end of this. He speaks to us with Brendan's authority, Brendan with the Brigadier's authority. Willy is very much in charge of us despite our equivalent ranks.

Willy is line infantry; serious, methodical and thoughtful. A thoroughly decent chap, although I cannot imagine us together on a pub crawl or in a nightclub. Out in his civvies I'm guessing he's all sensible heavy brogues and tweeds. He has a brute of a moustache, not at all like Julian's butch Commando issue, *Viva Zapata* horror. It makes him look positively First World War. I may be doing Willy a deep disservice here. Perhaps, he is a secret *Bat out of Hell*, Harley-Davidson lover who, come the weekend, joins a moustachioed biker gang in ripped jeans and oily T-shirt. But I somehow doubt it.

We are told to wait around as the Brigadier wants to meet us. We wait. And wait. Something we will come to learn is not unusual with the Brigadier, but then again, he's a very, very busy man.

As the morning rolls on we give up the effort to look warry and serious and start to joke and josh amongst ourselves. There's nothing else to do. The radios are being set up or tuned or something – I find radios dull and mysterious and their workings even duller and more mysterious – by the Royal Signals people. We start testing how far we can push it with Willy.

Then, outside the room, people are jumping to attention. Brigadier 'Tony' Wilson is smaller than me, though most are; neat, dapper even. Impeccably dressed, which should not be an observation from a Household Cavalryman like me, used to everyone around him being immaculately turned out, but still is. Everything about him is neat. He looks immensely pleased with himself. But then, why not? He's *el patron* on this ship and clearly knows it. Everyone defers to him, as is his due. Constantly.

Normally, in camp or on exercise, we more junior lot are adept at avoiding the senior lot for fear of being pulled up for something – 'Hair too long'. 'Why are you wearing puttees instead of the latest issue, uncomfortable Para boots?' – or to avoid HQ's latest ball-busting, cunning plan. Back at Windsor, the Regimental HQ building is known as 'Puzzle Palace'. Today we'd call it, to use a euphemism applied to ex-President Trump's daughter Ivanka, 'HABI' – the home of all bad ideas.

But 5th Infantry Brigade HQ looks to be Puzzle Palace/HABI on steroids. And we watchkeepers will be in the eye of the confusion.

His staff may appear to be in near headless-chicken mode, but 'Brigadier Tony' radiates calm and friendliness and smiles. Was it that first morning, or later, that I see him in his red 'Para' beret and thought, '*poseur*'? Because, once on board, we were all literally 'berets off'; we went bareheaded, both inside and out on deck. And yet here is the Brigadier in his red beret, definitely creating a macho impression from the get-go. Not the first general to do so, I know. But still . . .

Moreover, given he was Light Infantry (now The Rifles), convention dictates that he should, surely, be wearing their distinctive green beret? I know little about the Paras, but I do know that they are very protective about who is, and who is not, entitled to wear their red beret. My instincts, I read after the war, are spot on. The Paras don't like him wearing it.

The Brigadier exchanges the usual banalities by way of initial greeting. So far, so normal. What else is he meant to say to us? I hang back to the end as I do have something important to discuss.

I introduce myself, and maybe I rile him from the get-go as, unlike every other person on board, I say, 'Good morning, Brigadier', rather than 'Good morning, Sir'. Although he will not know it, and does not ask, regimental tradition is that The Blues and Royals only call members of the Royal Family 'Sir', even though discretion might suggest I make an exception for him. Once I leave Sandhurst – where I would have happily called an officer's dog 'Sir' to avoid another bollocking followed by fifty press-ups – I only ever call one other person 'Sir': Prince Philip, the day he pops the Falklands Medal on my chest at Buckingham Palace.

I tell the Brigadier that my Colonel wants me to look after The Blues and Royals troops who are on their way south with 3rd Commando Brigade.

He tells me he is fully aware of this. This is why I am here as a watchkeeper, and a 'Forward' watchkeeper at that.

When I went to say goodbye to Colonel James Hamilton-Russell, my Commanding Officer, we discussed what was going on and what he thought would happen to me.

Much of the world is telling us Brits to stop being so macho and 'post-colonial'. They want us to talk nicely to the Argentines, to clear up this unpleasantness over their invasion of the Falkland Islands. If the diplomats have their way matters will be settled long before we get there. But, we both agree, Maggie Thatcher is unlikely to be cowed by international pressure to let the Argentines keep the Islands just because they have grabbed them.

So, fighting it may well be. But most probably not for me as, the Colonel reckons, the Argentines will either be so scared of the approaching Task Force that they will hand the Islands back, or the ferocious Paras and Commandos will drive them into the South Atlantic before we get there. He was almost apologetic as he told me that, chances are, I am in for a long, boring summer (sub-Antarctic winter, that is) of garrison duty. Six months, he reckoned, given the cost of getting us there and then getting us replaced.

Two troops from my regiment, each of two Scorpion and two Scimitar armoured cars, plus a Samson REME support vehicle – Royal Electrical and Mechanical Engineers: beer swilling, foul-mouthed, grease monkeys, Zen masters at keeping our vehicles operational, the army's own AA/RAC breakdown service – are currently sailing south with 3 Commando Brigade. Two more troops and the headquarters element of B Squadron, commanded by a major, were ready to join 5th Infantry Brigade on the second wave. They were then, however, told to stand down. The two forward troops, each commanded by a lieutenant, will now have nobody to fight their corner at Brigade level. Colonel James wanted to send as senior an officer from the regiment as he can get down there. The only available berth on the *QE2* is for a 'watchkeeper', a captain, to monitor radios at 5th Brigade HQ.

So, instead of an extra eight armoured killing machines, each with a main armament that will destroy enemy vehicles and weapons systems at out to 2,000 metres, each with a 7.62mm turret-mounted GPMG (general purpose machine gun) that will monster infantry at out to 1,800 metres, 5th Infantry Brigade is getting me.

I am determined to get on with my 'look after the boys' mission.

'Do you,' I ask the Brigadier, 'anticipate 5 Brigade getting either troop under command?'

He certainly hopes so.

I tell him that as I recently completed a specialist 'long' Gunnery Officer's course I am fully current with the vehicles' weaponry and tactics; their ranges, strengths – including their state of the art night sight – and vulnerabilities; their light aluminium armour. Would he like me to prepare a presentation for him and his staff so they know how best to use the Scorpions and Scimitars when the moment comes?

This is an excellent idea.

'Armoured presentation' is added to Brendan's growing list of 'Action Points'.

Even as I speak I sense that his senior brigade guys – none of them cavalrymen – have little clue or interest in what I'm talking about. I am not surprised. After all, these are perhaps the people who decided not to bring the rest of B Squadron, with the Brigadier's connivance, if not at his command. 'More trouble than they are worth' is what a furious senior regimental officer told me someone at Brigade actually said on giving our Colonel the bad news, pouring scorn into an open wound

I do not question whether the Brigadier and his staff officers should already know the basics about our vehicles and their capabilities, although of course they should. Our Scorpions and Scimitars are not some secret new weapon magicked up for the trip south. They've been in service for almost ten years now. Nor is armoured reconnaissance some new strategic concept. My regiment was free-ranging in their armoured cars across North-West Europe, often well ahead of the main armies, back in 1944/45. Armoured recce is an integral part of any modern battle grouping, certainly in Germany. In fact, and in retrospect, their ignorance is pathetic, their subsequent lack of interest something worse altogether.

I prepare the talk. A day or so later, I tell Brendan, or Willy, I am ready. 'When shall I give it?'

They'll get back to me.

Days later, I ask again.

Same answer.

And again.

I get so exasperated that I contrive to 'bump' into the Brigadier and ask him when he wants to hear it.

He's all ears. Really looking forward to hearing it with his team. 'Brendan will get back to you.'

By then other things are falling apart and any confidence I ever had in the Brigadier is long gone. I suspect I will never be asked. I give up trying.

I never give that presentation. All he needed to do was to spare me 30 measly minutes in the almost three-week voyage south. I hold him totally to blame for the opportunity he squandered. I have little doubt that, had he bothered to listen and learn, a number of his infantry soldiers' lives could have been saved. But he didn't, and so we will never know.

Introductions over on that first meeting, we are told to occupy ourselves for the rest of the day. Like new boys starting a strange new school we explore *QE2*. I've never been on anything grander than a cross-channel ferry, so this is a whole new level of opulence, but once I get used to the trendy chrome and the gleaming walnut, the multiple decks, the fancy chandeliers and what have you, the *QE2* is, I conclude, just a very large, very comfortable, cross-channel ferry. And just as dull.

The battalions are already hard at their intensive 'work-up' training programmes, and we watchkeepers drift around, trying not to get in the way. My battalion mates, when I see them, are usually far too busy to stop and talk. They have also been told they will probably end up doing garrison duty, but they are preparing for war.

There is one moment of pure joy. On the main entrance landing on the main staircase, up on the wall, is a huge wooden map of the world. Each country and ocean is fashioned from a different type and colour of wood. Each country is named. It is a thing of beauty. We lot have finally got it into our heads that the Falkland Islands are not the Faroes or the Shetland Islands – when the invasion took place I knew nobody, including me, who could have pointed out the Falklands or South Georgia on a map – and it is interesting to see where we are going, where the Islands sit in relation to Antarctica and South America in general. There they are, a tiny segment of coloured wood down at the bottom of the map. And there is their name: 'Las Malvinas'.

'*Et tu Cunard* . . .'

Laughing, we wander back to our room. Willy arrives. He wants a watchkeeper roster as one of us needs to be on radio watch 24/7. We tell him that we will arrange this and will give him our list. He's happy. One less thing for him to organize.

He isn't quite sure, he tells us, what we should do right now, but please read the Brigade SOPs (Standard Operating Procedures). There will be plenty to do 'later'.

We look at him and he looks at us. What are we meant to say to that?

He blinks apologetically and leaves.

He's clearly as unsure of us as we are of him and, sensing weakness, we've been mildly taking the piss, seeing what we can get away with. I've obviously been particularly 'out there', for my first day's diary entry tells me: '**I have already announced to him that the Amalgamated Union of Watchkeepers is alive and kicking and ready to start negotiations with the management. He looked perturbed. I feel he will be more so before this is through.**' Willy gone, we write our list. '**A very complicated solution is arrived at. We follow an ancient military** custom: the one who is not present is volunteered for the worst watch.

The next morning we are again informed that 'action' will start. Later.'

We four agree that we are witnessing a headquarters in what looks to be headless-chicken mode; the more they try to do, the less they seem able to. And they have a huge amount they need to do.

We need to look out for ourselves lest we get sucked into the inevitable stupidities, forced to partake in senseless tasks dreamed up for the sake of looking 'active'. However, if we think and plan for ourselves, become '**a self-administering unit within the HQ**' as I put it in my diary, then the staff, personified by Willy, should be delighted to let us get on with it. We'll be one less thing for them to fret about.

By Day Two I am so alarmed by what I am witnessing, sensing, at headquarters that I decide to start writing a diary, something I have never done before. And not done since. If I don't, I suspect I won't believe what is happening, or not happening, later.

First off, we suggest to Willy that, instead of all six of us crowding into the Ops Room at 0830 each morning to be given our daily tasks, as currently instructed, only one person should turn up to receive said instructions. Far more efficient.

Willy agrees.

This is a genius move as it then allows the rest of us to debate who is to do what '**once we have all managed to get up**'.

And, surprise, surprise, HQ are normally so busy chasing their own tails that they rarely dream up any tasks to give us in any event.

However, whilst the subversive in me is keen to avoid being sucked into the inevitable Brigade nonsenses – and even super-efficient Brigades are hotbeds of irritating ideas dreamed up by ever-so-keen-to-impress staff officers – I am genuinely keen to help in any way I can. I want to be the best watchkeeper I can be. After all, the success of this mission – a mission which involves my own life – depends on 5 Brigade being the very best it can possibly be.

Nick and I discuss this and decide to draw up a list of things in the SOPs that clearly need changing, since the current set of 'Orders' are designed for a Brigade fighting a conventional war in Germany, or repelling a Soviet invasion of mainland Britain (in 1982 we are still deep in the Cold War), not a seaborne assault in the South Atlantic.

The list grows. At some point the Brigadier arrives in the Ops Room.

Nick and I discuss the overarching problems in louder voices in the hope that the Brigadier might engage, might formalize what we are trying to do. No such luck, although Willy, while he can clearly see what we are trying to achieve here, is **'perturbed'** by how we are going about it.

Oh well, we'll try again tomorrow.

'Well, the first jug of Harvey Wallbanger [Vodka, Galliano – not too much or it will be too sweet – orange juice and ice] **has been downed; the Captain** [of the *QE2*, Peter Jackson] **welcomed us on our "cruise"; Barbra Streisand is playing on the intercom; we have a film tonight; it is time for a civilised dinner and there are 10,000 cold, hungry but dangerous men waiting for us on an island in the South Atlantic. Looking at my stateroom it is difficult to believe, but they are there. Now it is time for a sense of urgency. We have a long way to go before we are ready to meet them.**

And so to bed. Will the promised "action" happen tomorrow? Secretly I hope not – I am enjoying my cruise.'

Chapter 3

Sailing South

Your radio is dead . . .
You're pinned down by fire . . .
Two of your men are badly wounded
What use is a degree in Medieval History?

This near-existentialist question was asked by the Army in a recruitment advertisement published in *The Times*, probably sometime in the 70s. I file it away as, not only do I have a degree in Medieval History, but I even managed to answer that very question once.

It is 1979. My crew are sitting in the turret of our Chieftain tank, catatonically bored, in an OP line, taking it in two-hour turns to stare out over the North German plains. Lashly, my gunner, puts the question to me, although rather less elegantly: 'Sooo. What fookin' use is your fookin' history degree sitting in this tank 'ere . . . Suur?'

Thinking quickly – because of what possible use is a medieval history degree in an OP line? – I reply: 'This is where Hermann the German slaughtered all those Roman legionnaires two thousand years ago. I'll tell you all about it if you like.'

'Anybody for a brew?' asks Corporal Weightman, my loader, rapidly changing the subject.

For those who are interested in these things, the Army's frankly meaningless answer to that otherwise impossible to answer question read:

A lot of use. You have a trained mind. The capacity to absorb information rapidly and to act on it. It could save the lives of your men . . . Soon, instead of reading history, you might be changing its course.

Oh yeah? I can picture trying to feed that hogwash to my soldiers. They would have taken the piss every time I faced a problem. 'Using your trained mind and capacity to rapidly absorb information . . . Suur . . . '

But back then, that advertisement demonstrated just how badly the generals wanted to start recruiting students. And, as they paid for me to go to university, I was only too happy to oblige.

I need not have worried. There is no action today. Day 3 is much like Day 2 as the ship pushes south-west before turning due south; a dog-leg designed to, hopefully, confuse any Argentine submarines hunting for us this far north. The ship has a top speed of roughly 32 knots, even in heavy seas. This is apparently exceptional; the same as one of our frigates at 'Full Ahead' in reasonably benign conditions. It is also our best chance of avoiding being torpedoed.

Not that we seem to be at war as such. The lights burn at night in the myriad portholes and windows, and we would make a juicy, albeit speedy, target if there is anyone out there waiting to take a shot at us.

What adds a certain grim humour to this war is that the Argentines are mainly supplied by NATO countries. The French sell them warplanes and Exocet missiles (which we also use) as well as Panhard armoured cars, which our Scorpions and Scimitars will be going barrel-to-barrel with.

The Belgians license us to make the FN (*Fabrique Nationale*) 7.62 SLR (Self Loading Rifle), which is the British standard infantry rifle alongside the FN 7.62 GPMG ('gimpy' – general purpose machine gun), our standard infantry-section support weapon. They sell them to the Argentines as well. So, man for man, we are near-identically tooled up.

To add insult to comedy, I discover that we Brits, never ones to miss out on a profitable arms deal with a potential aggressor nation, also do business with them. Their navy boasts two modern Type 42 destroyers, built in Britain and near identical to HMS *Sheffield*, which is deep under the South Atlantic having been comprehensively Exoceted.

We also sell the Argies the bombs they are dropping on us. 'Return to sender', as it were.

Our American Boeing Chinooks are the backbone of our helicopter heavy lift capacity, as they are of theirs. The *Belgrano*, their flagship, also now settling on the seabed, started life in the US Navy.

This is Monty Python gone mad. The real winners here are the arms dealers and manufacturers, who will doubtless be looking forward to a large Christmas bonus as we will all need to restock our already depleting arsenals. While it would be 'unfortunate', to put it mildly, to be scrubbed from the planet by an Argie, it would somehow be even more galling if the weapon doing the scrubbing is something we flogged them. If this wasn't both so serious, and so possible, I'd think it hilarious

Meanwhile, back in our immediate future, the National Union of Watchkeepers-negotiated radio roster requires six watchkeepers to cover 24 hours. We agree, in full union session, that one four-hour stretch per day – as against two 'stags' (radio watches) of two hours each – spent in a comfortable chair is unlikely to unduly knacker anybody. It will be different when we are ashore, but we will face that when we come to it. The main debating point right now is who gets to miss dinner – delicious food prepared by great chefs.

The menu on our first evening at sea is as follows, printed on – what else? – formal, stiff, menu cards:

R.M.S. Queen Elizabeth 2
Wednesday, 12 May 1982
Evening Meal
Smoked Salmon
Oxtail Soup
Fried Fillet of Haddock, Tartare Sauce
Roast Turkey with
Chestnut Stuffing and Cranberry Sauce
Creamed and Roast Potatoes
Sliced Green Beans
Compote of Fruit and Custard [I feel sure I asked for and got cream instead as I don't like custard]
Cheese and Biscuits
Fresh Fruit
Rolls and Butter
Tea or Coffee

This was all washed down with champagne and good red and/or white wine. I keep a couple of those 12 May cards and, a week later, send one home to the Adjutant with a handwritten note designed to wind up the boys in Windsor:

Dear Adjutant,

I want to come home. The caviar has run out, they are making us eat custard with our pud and the ice bucket in our refrigerator has disappeared. I do not think I can survive any longer. What is more they have changed our holiday route. We docked at Freetown (Sierra Leone) yesterday and are missing Ascension altogether. This means we may be splashing around in the jolly S. Atlantic sooner than thought. Please send more Galliano, snorkel and flippers and my orderley [*sic*] as soon as possible.

Roger

I don't think I am 'misremembering' when I recall that I was later told that my driver, Trooper Gibben, got to hear about this *cri de coeur* and immediately volunteered to ship out as requested.

On May 14 it turns out that the Brigadier, or perhaps Willy, was taking note after all, because Willy tells us that we have been officially tasked with redrafting the Brigade SOPs.

SOPs (Standing Operating Procedures) are tedious but necessary instructions as to what everybody in the Brigade is to do and how they are to do it, both as a routine and also in the event of certain predictable things happening.

So, as a routine, SOPs might dictate that battalions send a Sitrep (situation report – stating activity, readiness, admin requirements, to name but a few) at 0630 and 1830 each day. This enables Brigade to check everybody is on the correct radio frequency (you'd be surprised how often this most basic of things goes wrong) as well as get an update of what has happened to each formation during the previous twelve hours. SOPs might further dictate that the Battalions get Sitreps from their companies and platoons at 0600 and 1800 before sending theirs to Brigade 30 minutes later.

Then there are all the 'action ons'; perhaps 'action on' being attacked by the Argie air force; action on finding yourself in a minefield and/or with a casualty. Who to call, what to say and how to say it.

These matters are for the Brigadier to pronounce upon, but someone first needs to list those things he needs to make decisions about.

The Brigade's current SOPs – at least as I remember them now – say nothing about seaborne assaults in the South Atlantic. We watchkeepers have no knowledge of seaborne ops either. That is the area of expertise of the Royal Marines, who train for this sort of thing. Which is why 3rd Commando Brigade is the first wave, hurrying to the islands as fast as the fleet can carry them.

We, however, are experienced enough soldiers to be able to start compiling a basic list. Others can then improve on it. Whatever we end up with has to be better than what we have at the moment.

What's more, our SOP task is good news. Our bosses will see us striding around, notepad and pen in hand – bullshit baffles brains! – and won't get to wondering, with only one watchkeeper in the Ops Room, what the rest of us are doing with our days. If they think for one moment we aren't usefully employed they'll soon find something for us to do. And it's bound to be boring.

Chapter 4

Stiff Upper Lips

'Thanks to St Jude, St Anthony and the Blessed Virgin for favour received. HF.' (Harriet Field)

This announcement, just discovered today as I rootle through my files, was what my mother, a good Catholic Irish girl, either intended to place or actually placed in the Personal Column of *The Times* on discovering I had survived the war.

For some days my family (and my regiment) thought I had been killed on a Landing Craft carrying 5 Brigade personnel and signals kit which was sunk by an Argentine aircraft on 8 June; a perfectly logical conclusion given that I was a signals watchkeeper.

I, however, had done a bit of on-the-hoof volunteering and, somewhat unofficially, slid off and joined 2 Para, who were to end up attacking Wireless Ridge. In the confusion and carnage after the bombing of *Sir Galahad* and *Sir Tristram* on that same day, Brigade managed to lose track of me – fully understandably, by the way! – and ended up posting me as 'missing'. It was only when my parents saw TV news footage of 2 Para, including me, marching to a Service of Thanksgiving in Christ Church Cathedral in Port Stanley on the day after the surrender, 15 June, that they learned for certain that I was alive.

So, perhaps, they were not quite so stiff upper lip as they liked to make out . . .

* * *

It is only a few days since we left Southampton and I am determined to get fit. I am not exactly unfit as I was ski-racing for a couple of months last winter. Back in Windsor, I ran three miles in a maximum of 21 minutes at least three times a week after work, as my own 'extra keeping-in-the-groove' routine since I didn't want it to hurt too much when I restart ski training in the autumn. We have occasional squadron runs, but they are hardly strenuous. Back in the dozy, peacetime days of 1982 nobody could accuse many in an armoured regiment of being fit. Unlike the infantry we drive everywhere, we don't dig trenches, ever, and there's no running around with nasty, heavy webbing, helmets, rifles and rucksacks. So why bother?

We only need to pass our annual BFT (battle fitness test): one and a half miles, run as a squad, in 18 minutes. That's so slow that there's time for fast walking for those who are struggling. Short pause as we line up for phase two – more recovery time – then another mile and a half, run individually, in a maximum of 11½ minutes. No need to carry a rifle or webbing. Hardly taxing for twentysomethings. Unless you are seriously unfit.

In 1980 The Blues and Royals got a roughie-toughie American exchange Major on attachment. He was horrified at his new squadron's fitness levels. What happened next went down in regimental lore. Instead of an 0830 first parade each morning, as for the rest of the Regiment, his is at 0730: PT and a run. He beasts those boys. It gets so bad that a delegation of squadron wives demands to see him.

'Enough is enough,' the spokeswoman tells him. 'Our husbands are knackered come the evening, bad-tempered and good for nothing. Do you understand what we mean by "Nothing"?'

Yes he does . . . and points to the door.

Some months later, he deems the squadron properly fit; time to ease off. The same delegation of wives re-appears. He is to do no such thing. Their husbands are now super-athletes, studs. The wives have never been happier. Please keep them firmly in training. Legend!

I am no 'gladiator', but I am no slouch either. Now I want to get seriously fit.

'These Brigade bozos are going to get us killed,' I tell the others as I get changed for my new twice-daily work out. 'I want to be fit enough to run away as fast as possible and as far as possible when it goes wrong.'

The running is boring. There's nothing to look at but the webbing-covered back of the man in front as we form a continuous, flowing snake. We pound along the decks, up a flight of steps towards the front end of the ship, and back down again. There is nowhere to overtake; one man stepping aside as he completes his run, another stepping in as he starts his.

The sound of hundreds of rubber boot heels striking steel decks thuds through the rooms below. It only stops when night and dinner brings that day's running to a close. We then do it again the next morning. But overnight we have sailed another 400 miles south. It is hotter, the sun sharper, the routine more sweat-inducing as the temperature climbs and the ship powers through calm seas as fast as its now working turbines can push it.

The others agree about the general Brigade inertia but think I'm being overly melodramatic about the consequences and, it follows, my enhanced exercise routine. They, too, are running, but only once a day. They think that, since Brigade HQ will be far behind the lines, we're unlikely to find ourselves in harm's way. If we're going to die of anything, it'll be boredom.

I don't care what they think. I like these guys and respect their opinions, but I've found a new confidence. All my life I've listened to others, perhaps been too influenced by others, all of them forever insisting they know best. Parents, teachers – university lecturers an honourable exception to this list: they wanted me to question and think, anathema to the army – and now the army itself. Everyone always knows better than their juniors. They're the experts, the professionals. Just shut up, listen and do as you're told . . .

Except this is a proper war. And how can anyone possibly know what is going to happen next? I studied medieval history at university, specializing in military history. One lesson keeps recurring, a lesson all too rarely learned: those who insist they know what is going to happen next, or not happen next, are often deluded or just plain wrong.

And it is happening right now. Again. Official thinking is still that it should all be over by the time we get there. However, nobody seems to have told the Argies. They are busy sinking our fleet.

It is 19 May, one week in to our voyage south, and I really don't like what I am seeing. A letter home tells me that Nick and I have been discussing 5 Brigade inertia:

> What scares us is that we might be killed through incompetence. Taking one's life in one's own hands is one thing, being blown to pieces with the Brigade staff in a 24′ x 18′ tent is another . . . I regret not having brought an SLR. I have not even had the opportunity to fire my own SMG [Stirling 9mm sub machine gun]. What a farce. I reckon this little lot could turn into quite a bloodbath . . . Julian [Stanley], normally the most mild, is also quite virulent on the subject.

So while I must obey orders, which may get me killed, I can – like a bulimic trying to control some aspects of his otherwise chaotic life – try and better control certain aspects of mine. A shitty and bloody tour of Northern Ireland back in 1979 has left me with no illusions as to just how haphazard the difference between life and death can be; but be that as it may, I don't intend to find myself bleeding out in a bog because I listened to someone else rather than follow my own instincts. I determine to get as fit as I can. Which, given what happens to me, is one of my better decisions.

Chapter 5

Africa

> 'I'm hot, I'm hot,
> I'm hot, I'm hot,
> I'm hot . . .'

Repeat as often as desired to the 'tune' of *Amazing Grace*; imagine the underlying tune as if delivered with the dull drone of an out-of-tune bagpipe.

Other verses in this funereal dirge sung by we Sandhurst officer cadets at moments of deepest despond include:

'I'm wet, I'm wet . . .'
'I'm tired, I'm tired . . .'
'I'm cold . . .'

This provides endless opportunity to sing about whatever character-building unpleasantness the DS (Directing Staff) are heaping on us at any given moment. Anyone can lead off, and the Greek chorus of fellow sufferers joins in. Our version might not make for a hit record, but such shared vocalizing makes for lasting friendships.

* * *

Today, it's definitely hot.

'The determined and well organised activity below stairs,' my diary tells me (this is where the infantry battalions live and work), **'is in marked contrast to that which we observe in Brigade HQ.'**

The SOPs become yesterday's problem – did we ever write them? I wonder. My diary does not say. It wouldn't surprise me if we did not, and I cannot imagine anybody being organized enough to chase us up on it.

Next up is the saga of the CPX (Command Post Exercise). A CPX is a radio-only exercise designed, in this instance, to test 5 Brigade's ability to communicate by radio 'forward' to its under command battalions' headquarters and they 'back' to us at Brigade. The battalions might also practise communicating 'forward' to their subordinate companies. And, in so doing, practise those SOPs that we may, or may not, have finalized.

A CPX will put us watchkeepers and the senior commanders under pressure and check we all know our drills. Which will be kind of useful, given that we are heading into a war at about 30-plus knots. One core SAS expression is, 'Train hard, fight easy'. From where I am sitting, the HQ element of 5 Brigade is yet to start training.

For a CPX an exercise scenario is first written out – in this case a seaborne landing on the Falklands, of course. Think of a computer game: enter the right hand door and X happens, enter the left door and Y, all of which has to be reported back by those entering the doors and responded to by Brigade, who then tell the 'gamers' what to do next. This requires a fully functioning 'at war' Brigade HQ: maps and people (Intelligence officers usually) to move units and mark up the maps as they do so. All done over the radio, as if we and the battalions are out in the field and unable to speak directly to one another.

As the two sides (one often notional – as will be the case here) probe and fight each other as dictated by the game play, we should discover where the enemy are and in what strength; plan how to destroy him and then do just that. Mistakes will happen and procedures prove inadequate. But that is the whole point of a CPX. Iron out the inevitable glitches; practise our routines; get super-slick now, not when there are shells and bullets in the air.

A well written CPX will make the commanders sweat over fast-developing tactical problems. All in a front of their staff – a horribly public arena.

The British Army revels in this type of gaming; notional exercises that do not require anybody to run or drive around and do things – thus saving scarce taxpayer pounds. We have acronyms (the British Army runs on acronyms) for different varieties of game play exercises, such as:

CPX – as above.

The more arcane NEWD – night exercise without darkness (I kid you not). The exercise is conducted during the day and nobody misses their evening meal. Although I'm being a bit naughty here; it is always best to first practise in daylight before doing something 'for real' in the horribly confusing dark.

JEWT – jungle exercise without trees. Saves flying troops to Belize or Borneo.

The most common, though, is the TEWT – tactical exercise without troops, designed to test more junior officers and NCOs – like a lower level CPX, but conducted on the ground and not in barracks.

For example, you gather on a hill. The DS tell you what forces oppose you and what you have available to attack them, or what you have available to defend this hill. You do a tactical appreciation; decide a plan of attack (or defence) and give your orders; site the trenches if you are defending, explain how the attack will work if attacking. Your analysis and performance, under time pressure, is then judged by your superiors against the 'DS', or 'correct' solution.

These are excellent practice for commanders at all levels, and had 5 Brigade held a CPX prior to Exercise Welsh Falcon – although I fully accept they may not have time to do so – that exercise might have turned into less of the 'cake and arse party' my chums in the battalions are telling me it became.

I, however, instinctively want to test 'the DS Solution'. Maybe it is my university training, more probably it is some perverse and irritating character defect, subsequently hot-housed by said university training. I remember Professor Charles Ross, my Medieval History tutor, once telling me after I had come up with a more than usually outlandish theory – which he then gently knocked down – that when a teacher stops learning from his students it is time for him to retire. This is the polar opposite to the military doctrine of 'the chain of command' and obeying orders – instantly and without complaint.

Instead, on being given a tactical problem to assess, it is usually blindingly obvious which is the 'best' way to attack or defend a position. I then assume that the DS-approved solution will be that blindingly obvious way – at least I've never known it not to be.

I then conclude that, unless the enemy commander is inept – although I accept that the history books are full of khaki-clad numbskulls – he will come to much the same conclusions as I and mass his firepower where the DS will expect me to attack/defend. And defeat me.

Being a natural contrarian I look for another solution. Often the ground gives me no room to be clever and it is 'Into the Valley of Death rode the Six Hundred'. However, if I see an alternative, I try it. Sometimes to the exasperation of my commanders, but occasionally pulling off a blinder.

I only saw my reverse thinking produce unambiguous results twice. Both were spectacular.

First time, I am in Germany. It is my first exercise as a newly minted troop leader in command of three 55-ton Chieftain tanks, c/s (call sign) T13. The T (Tango) means we are 'armour'; '1' means we are A Squadron (2 is B Sqn and so on) and '3' means we are the third troop of A squadron. We are leaguered up (basically hiding) in a wood waiting for the 'Russians' – British regiments from a different brigade, who in turn view us as the Russians – to seize one of a number of nearby bridges. Every troop in the regiment has a bridge. Only one will be attacked.

I drive to 'my' bridge in my Chieftain to plan how to recapture it should it be attacked and taken. It is officer training all over again. The answer is blinking obvious. Running east to west is a river, crossed by our bridge and a 'straight as an arrow' north-to-south road. From due south is the obvious way for tanks to attack: miles of open, flat country, good for rolling tanks across at maximum speed (a lumbering 25mph); good fields of fire for us as we do so. 'Good tank country', as seasoned tank commanders like to proclaim. Although I've never seen what is 'good' about open country where the enemy can see you coming from miles away and pour missiles and artillery and what have you at you as you do so. Then again, those who fought in the tiny fields and roads in the slaughterhouse of the *'bocage'* in Normandy in 1944 would doubtless tell me that I don't know what I'm talking about . . .

North of the river it's something of a dog's dinner. A sprawling farm complex gives us a concealed approach, leaving us with an 800-yard dash to the bridge across open country – very short range for our 120mm guns and, even at 25mph, little time in the open for the enemy to engage us. However, we'll first have to smash, line abreast, through a high farm wall that encloses the complex. Not a problem, I'm told. Most farmers don't mind us causing damage, because they get massive compensation cheques. Also, as the weather has been dry we haven't gouged up the farmers' fields (a major reason for payments) and there's money to spare in the compensation fund.

There's a major potential problem with this attack option, though. Parallel with the east-west river, on this north side, are two deep but narrow drainage ditches. At first sight they are tank-stoppers.

We investigate further. 'Can a Chieftain jump them?' I ask Corporal Andrews, my hugely wise and experienced driver, explaining what I have in mind. 'Jump' is not a word you'd normally associate with these monsters.

He calculates the gaps in the ditches, looks at how steep the banks are and confers with Corporal 'Fishface' Weightman, my radio operator/loader, and Lashly, my gunner, both experienced crewmen.

Yes. We can.

I'm wagering that the bridge commander will look at those ditches and come to the opposite conclusion. Even if he doesn't, anything has to be better than charging across miles of open country. Except getting stuck in those ditches, of course.

We return to our wood and catch up on badly needed sleep and vehicle repairs. And wait. We do a lot of waiting in the army. I'm just reading the final pages of a thriller – it is only later that I discover that a bored Corporal Weightman has decided to show me what he thinks of book-reading officers by eating (literally) the last two pages, including the denouement – when the radio kicks into life.

'Hello 1 3, this is Zero [Squadron HQ]. Mint Tea. I repeat Mint Tea [that's the code word for my bridge]. Over.'

'1 3. Mint Tea. Wilco [will obey orders]. Out.'

And off we trundle.

I gave the troop my orders when I came back from my recce and showed them my plan on a sand table. Corporal Andrews explained the 'jumping'. Questions asked and answered.

We sneak in column through the farmyard and form a line. The infantry will probably know we are around and be listening to the deep rumble of our engines, but as long as we keep our revs low, it is very difficult to work out exactly where we are.

On my command the drivers floor their accelerators and roar, line abreast, straight through the high brick wall, bringing chunks of it down around us. Straight out of a Hollywood film. Very satisfying. Charge! And we jump those damned ditches, just as Corporal Andrews said we could.

Thank God.

Mayhem ensues.

There looks to be a company of infantry and a troop of armoured cars defending the bridge. All are on the far side of the river, facing the wrong way. Their support vehicles are parked up, ready for a quick getaway, on our side of the bridge where we are now notionally blowing them apart as we shoot off Schermuly rockets and Verey pistols to show the umpires we are firing.

The enemy cannot get back to their vehicles without crossing the bridge, which they cannot do as we have three 120mm 'main' guns aimed at it;

three 'ranging' Browning .50 heavy machine guns (perfect for taking out the lighter vehicles) and three GPMGs (perfect for 'hosing down' and killing infantry).

The enemy are right royally fucked because, as Caesar reported when defeating Pompey, we've taken them '*a tergo*' – up the arse.

The Brigadier is there, in a lather of excitement. Huge smiles as we motor past.

On exercise we inevitably have to guess what would have happened after every confrontation. It can revert to the playground.

'I shot you first.'

'No you didn't. My Alpha tank saw you first and shot you before you shot me.'

'Oh, no he didn't.'

'Oh, yes he did . . .'

Boy-scouting with main battle tanks.

Not today though. This is unequivocal. And very public egg-on-face for the defending colonel or major.

I am finally called over. My commanding officer is there, among a gaggle of senior types.

'This is the first example of proper, offensive action I've seen in the past two weeks,' the Brigadier kicks off. 'Real aggression . . . You've all been going through the same old exercise motions. I want to see more of this.'

I feel very chipper and glance at my Colonel, expecting a big smile. He's not looking as happy as I'd have expected.

I've long assumed that his curious reaction is because, a couple of months earlier, I'd had a spectacular falling-out with the adjutant, his main man when it comes to discipline in the regiment, making me rather *persona non grata* with most of the regimental rulers.

An army chum, checking this book for general military accuracy, reckons there is a different answer. My Colonel would have been jaw-boning with the Brigadier and his staff as they waited. This is his regiment being tested after all.

The Brigadier will have asked how I will attack. The Colonel will have looked at that open 'tank country' to the south, discounted the ditches and pointed to where I did not come from.

Cue liberal extra helping of egg on face for my Colonel. No wonder the Brigadier is having such fun. And no wonder my 'triumph' was never alluded to again.

My troop are seriously chuffed, especially my crew who made the recommendation to jump those ditches. It also proves to me – probably a dangerous conclusion to reach so early in one's career – that the obvious DS solution is not necessarily the correct one.

So I'm agog after these days of Brigade inertia to see what our bosses have prepared for us by way of the much talked about CPX. Except that nothing seems to be happening and, surprise, surprise, it's beginning to look as if we will write it. Which is beyond surreal.

How can it test us if we're writing it? But let's not quibble . . . Except let's quibble because, as my diary tells me, '**I was right. We watchkeepers have ended up writing the damned CPX. What sort of organisation is this? It really is pathetic . . .**'

Instead, something intervenes that breaks the growing monotony and growing infighting: 18 May, Freetown, Sierra Leone – Africa! I'm not sure quite what we're doing here although we are getting re-supplied with fresh food and we receive our first load of mail, including the inevitable whingeing one from the bank manager; the one letter that will always get through: 'You're overdrawn. How do you plan on paying it?'

We gaze over the railing at the scenes of near-pandemonium below as stuff is loaded on to pallets by teams of dockers and then winched aboard. The head man is easily distinguished as, unlike his men in flip flops and trainers, he sports a massive pair of black wellington boots and carries a stick. We discuss the sheer horror of the moment he takes those wellies off after a day on the docks in this sauna-like heat. Is he married, we wonder?

The soldiers, being soldiers, amuse themselves by throwing coins to the dock workers far below – up on our decks it is as if we are on the sixth or seventh floor of a tower block – instigating instant punch-ups as the workers fight each other for them. This sport is quickly stamped out by the officers.

I later learn that the real action was elsewhere. I saw dugout wooden canoes on the seaward side with locals waving fruit and Lord alone knows what for sale. I've soon seen enough and go dockside. Fiendish soldier minds have other ideas. At the stern there is an open lower deck the troops use to fire their weapons from out to sea, rubbish bags their targets. Much sign language, and a rope is lowered to a waiting canoe. A basket is attached and up it goes; a bottle of sprits is put inside (turns out that Nick and I were not the only ones to make sure we have adequate supplies aboard) and lowered back down. What follows is a wacky Central West African 'lucky dip'.

The soldiers have no idea what will come back up in the basket; fresh fruit and tribal artefacts, some 'good', others not. However, the *pièce de resistance* shocks even the guardsman who gets it. Down goes a bottle of whisky. Back up comes a shrunken human head. Welcome to Joseph Conrad's dark, steaming, sweaty, hot *Heart of Darkness*.

There is no question of us being allowed ashore. Anyway, the humidity is like the proverbial wet blanket and we would be dripping in seconds. Before long, with nothing new to look at, we drift back to our air-conditioned cabins.

That night, the ship's crew board over the windows. When we sail tomorrow the ship will be 'blacked-out' and ready for war, although you would hardly know it from what is and isn't happening at HQ, as my diary for 22 May tells me: **'Brigade knifing each other in back. It is mindboggling. We just do own thing. Farce.'**

Chapter 6

Tropical Torpor

'Last Harvey Wallbangers – tragedy. Now onto Screwdrivers.'
[Vodka and orange juice, but without the all-important Galliano, which has run out].

We go to sleep tied alongside Africa and awake the next day far out to sea, powering south towards Ascension Island. There we will do more re-supplying and pick up General Jeremy Moore (Royal Marines) and his LFFI (Landing Forces Falkland Islands) Headquarters. He will command all land forces on the Islands: 3 Commando Brigade and 5 Infantry Brigade. What this will mean for things on the ship I have no idea, although Brigadier Wilson will clearly no longer be top dog. At least there is no mention of us losing our amazing stateroom to any of the incoming staff officers. Yet.

First, some fun when on 19 May we cross the Equator.

The ship's crew rig up a stand-up swimming pool on the foredeck, normally out of bounds to us soldiers. In time-honoured tradition, a gruesome 'King Neptune', regal on his throne with a bog brush (or some awful such) in hand, orders his retainers, outlandishly dressed in all sorts of costume (a couple in drag, of course – what is it with sailors and getting into drag at any opportunity?) orders them to go and find 'virgins' crossing the equator for the first time. He will then sentence them to a forfeit. A helicopter pilot is hauled before King Neptune, and a nurse from hell announces what the victim does. 'Off with his chopper!' the king yells, to the delight of the huge crowd gathered around, many hundreds more leaning over the upper decks; everybody on board ship not doing some essential job must be here enjoying the moment. The pilot is then pelted with gunk and flour bombs and Lord alone knows what else, then hurled into the 'swimming pool' to be baptised, before being allowed to clean himself off. And then it is the turn of the next unfortunate.

After a time I make my way to the bow and, in a scene reminiscent of the film *Titanic* – no Kate Winslet sadly, I could really have done with a pretty girl to put her arms around me – gaze out at the deep blue nothingness before me, then back at the jostle of soldiers crowding the superstructure, tier above tier, as they strain to see the fun and games below. Perhaps I am being overly morbid, I think to myself as I look at them cheering and laughing as another Equator virgin splashes into the gunk-filled deep, but how many of them won't be coming back? Quite a few as it turns out.

That night, the party mood continues, and my diary tells me we watched *Escape to Victory*, a good-natured film of British prisoners of war playing their German guards at football. There is even an Argie on the prisoners' team, and the soldiers hiss and boo him every time he appears, laughing as they do so. I happily join in. However, the newly blacked-out ship – Ascension Island is approaching fast and the next stop after that is the Falklands – introduces a mood of introspection – and concern about what is not going on.

I've been to a few Brigade headquarters in my time, but I avoid them whenever possible because they tend to be full of keen-eyed staff officers issuing orders designed to make our lives difficult. In stark contrast, 5 Brigade HQ is almost a dead zone. Nothing happens here. There is often only one of us and a signaller in there. To be fair, we watchkeepers hope there are hugely important and deeply cunning planning sessions going on somewhere else in the ship. But where, and what is decided at these sessions, we have no idea. This demoralizes me, and I find it increasingly difficult to get inspired. When Willy mentions the dread word '**CPX, we now just grin and he goes away**'. Even he seems to have given up.

Our minds have now turned full-time to women and the absence thereof. At Ascension one of those many helicopters flies out a load of 'Electric Blue' Playboy videos, kindly donated by the *Sun* to 'Our brave boys heading down south', or some such. Needing to stretch my legs after a very late-night radio watch, I wander into an all-ranks reception lounge. The lights are off, a screen has been set up and an Electric Blue video is in full erotic swing. This is seriously soft porn by today's gynaecological internet standards – a long-ago world where naked women had hair – but pretty full-on for the fusty early 80s. There are lots of viewers, and I sit down to watch. It soon becomes clear, from the deep breathing around me, that some are already over-involved.

Beside me is a fellow Guards officer I vaguely know. He, like me, is struggling not to giggle at this rather bizarre scene. We set one another off, and soon my shoulders are shaking. Finally it is too much, even for us, and we retreat to find a late-night drink. We are still the greatest of friends, and still giggling all these years later about what the *Sun* did for the troops.

Elsewhere, and I only discover this after the fighting is over, another officer decides to make a profit out of this growing need. He hires hardcore porn and a projector from the crew – apparently the crews of these cruise ships, at least in pre-internet days, are purveyors of the finest international porn; no perversion unthought of or uncatered for, the world their shop window when it comes to selection and variety.

Needing somewhere private for his soirées – Brigade would have been less than amused – the crew suggests the synagogue, a room unlikely to be visited late at night on a decidedly Gentile ship.

When I later discover who the pornographer in chief is I remonstrate with him for not inviting me.

'But you were Brigade,' he tells me. 'We didn't know if we could trust you.'

Even the Brigadier seems to be feeling the lack of female company. We officers occasionally see him at dinner in the Queens Grill and, sometimes – even often – he is tête-à-tête with Linda Kitson (known behind her back, with no hint of malice, as Linda Kitbag – the obvious military nickname for anybody with her name). She is the official war artist the Imperial War Museum has sent on the trip. Why he chooses her to chat to we can only speculate. And so speculate we do.

One of the more innocent theories is that, given his clear obsession with image, he is persuading her to draw his portrait. He obviously makes an impression, because when she publishes her book of drawings, *The Falklands War: A Visual Diary*, it is dedicated to; 'The "x2 Tony's" – remember the laughter', one 'laughing Tony' being Brigadier Wilson. Suffice it to say, we scurvy juniors are not overly impressed.

On page 33 of her book there is a sketch of Brigade HQ on *QE2* – all she ever drew, it seems, were sketches. Who the people in them are it is almost impossible to tell. She is not much given to 'faces'.

Her 'note' on that drawing reads: 'HQ Ops was fairly quiet at the start of the session I was recording . . . By the end of this particular evening the pace had dramatically changed, and Brigadier Wilson, who had arrived yawning hugely, and most of Brigade Staff had been through.'

An entirely atypical evening as I recall evenings aboard *QE2*. I would not have put it past 'the laughing Brigadier' to have ordered a full flow-through of Brigade staff to give an impression of dynamic activity while she was in there drawing. He might well have calculated that the more normal scene – 'Captain Rog', feet up, on watchkeeping duty, face buried in a thriller for four straight hours in a near-empty room – would not make for a dynamic depiction of 5 Brigade HQ to hang in the Imperial War Museum. I may of course be plumb wrong. Then again, I may not be . . .

Did we watchkeepers ever while away an hour or two in discussing how it was, or why, each of us got here? If we did, I have no memory of it. I know why I am here: to try and help our boys in any way I can. The others, I guess, are representing their UK-based regiments who will remain at home. Whatever the reasons, we are all acutely aware that this is probably a once in a lifetime chance in an otherwise mainly – Special Forces the sometimes warry exceptions! – dull peacetime army career to get into a proper shooting war. This is an opportunity not to be missed and, as we also know, anyone with a pulse, and certainly with any dreams of higher rank, called in every favour, tried every trick, to get on to *QE2*. And we six are the lucky few; although we also know – never mentioned of course – that there are certain, possibly terminal, downsides to our apparent good fortune.

My stance is simple: if I was not 'up for a fight' why did I join the army in the first place? Why did I go through that endless, sometimes dehumanizing training if it was not to be capable of doing just this? That said, it's not as if I want to start killing anybody or, every bit as much to the point, getting killed or wounded. A neat scar on my cheek along the lines of a Heidelberg University duelling mark, something to impress the girls, would do nicely. But that, I also know, is rarely how it works. I never bought into the concept of the 'Glorious Dead' as preached to us at Sandhurst; soldiers gently expiring with a wry smile on their lips and a pithy word for their comrades as depicted in a certain type of Hollywood war film. This, remember, is 1982 – Quentin Tarantino is only nineteen and hasn't yet started trying to show us the realities of death on the big screen.

I am under no illusions. A tour of Northern Ireland taught me what a bullet does to a body. I've heard high velocity rounds ripping past. They don't discriminate.

I'm also aware that what I witnessed in Northern Ireland is as nothing compared to what my father's generation went through in the last war, or the Americans in Vietnam; that whilst I've already experienced more bloody nastiness than most of my generation, I've doubtless seen nothing yet. Not that this puts me off. I'm being given an opportunity to see if I am up to it.

To prove myself to myself. I have little doubt that most on board, each in his own way, feel much the same.

'I am not ordering you to go,' the Colonel told me when he summoned me to his office a few days after the Argentines had so unexpectedly invaded on 2 April. It was my view then and remains so to this day that if the British Government had had even half an eye open they'd have seen what was developing and put a stop to it before it ever came to this. After all, even the defence-lite, hopeless, previous Labour government had spotted something similar developing in 1977 and stopped it before it turned nasty by sending a small task force of frigates and a submarine in the general direction of South America. But Maggie's Conservative Party – the party, I had always assumed, who were the ones to be trusted with Britain's defence – had comprehensively fucked up. Not only did they fail to spot the Argentines planning and then mounting an invasion – a pretty massive failure of intelligence by any standards – but they were so keen to save money that they were busy selling off the Fleet; sending all the wrong signals to the Argentines which they duly misinterpreted as a green light to invade.

And here is the result. A couple of days later, the Colonel is asking me if I would be happy to join the Task Force.

As the initial shock wears off and I start to process what he is saying, he is already explaining that he has managed to secure a slot for a watchkeeper from The Blues and Royals to join HQ 3 Commando Brigade on the *Canberra*. Two troops from B Squadron are going in the first wave. The rest of the Squadron, with their major, will follow in the second wave. It'll be my job – as well as being a watchkeeper, of course – to represent their interests as best I can at Brigade HQ until he arrives and takes over.

'It's your choice.'

Of course I'll go, although what he cannot know is that I could never look myself in the proverbial mirror again had I taken his get-out option because for me it's already become somewhat personal.

My diary tells me: **'Like most Englishmen it was with a sense of outrage and insult that I read of the Argentinean invasion of the Falklands.'**

On Saturday, 3 April, the day after the invasion, my friend Anna, who works in the House of Commons, gets me a ticket to the Strangers' Gallery to watch the emergency debate about the invasion. The last time the House sat on a Saturday was 3 November 1956, when they debated the Suez Crisis.

Those few Saturday morning 'Visitor' tickets – the Strangers' Gallery is only a few rows of tiered seats – must be like gold dust. How she got me one I should have asked, but never did.

I had never been to a Parliamentary debate before (or since), but what a one to witness. There is a palpable sense of drama and barely contained fury both up in the gallery where I am sitting with the other 'Strangers' (members of the public – doubtless mostly close family of the MPs) and down below in the chamber, which is packed, everyone wanting to add their voice.

Maggie T is imperious and impressive. The House, except for the usual whingers and hand-wringers, rally four-square around the Task Force, whose departure she announces. It is not all plain sailing for the government, though. John Nott, the Secretary of State for Defence is defensive and flat-footed. He gets heckled. Hansard records:

> Mr. Nott: I conclude by saying – [HON. MEMBERS: 'Resign'.] – that the Government do not pretend that the situation is anything but extremely grave . . .
>
> [More whiffling and foot shuffling by Nott]
>
> . . . The military problems are formidable, but they are certainly not insoluble because of the professionalism, the preparedness and the quality of our defences, which for our nation's size are unique in the free world. I do not believe the claim that the new Labour Party, with its well-known and well-advertised anti-defence bias and lack of commitment to defence spending, would have done any better. The Government will accept criticism – [HON. MEMBERS: 'Resign'.] But I believe . . .
>
> Hon. Members: 'Go.'

Cracking good stuff. A Parliament to be proud of.

Silly plonker, he tried to get in an anti-Labour swipe, but today even Michael Foot is being patriotic and supportive, and Nott hits a sour, petulant note.

The government was caught with its pants tangled around its ankles, and both sides of the Commons are giving Nott, a principal architect of the foul-up, a well-deserved kicking. Writing this, I remember his lacklustre performance the next time I see him, saying goodbye to us lot on *QE2* on 12 May. From my diary again:

'He waves.
Silence.
A wife or girlfriend waggles her boobs at the boat. Huge cheers.
The British Army has just voted and found Nott wanting.'

From that moment – Day Two of the crisis and the Emergency Debate — I feel morally bound, compelled by the emotions I experience during the debate. Like the politicians on the green benches below me, I want to go to war, to demand war. I have to control myself and not jump up and tell them so. So, when the call actually comes, I know I have to put my body where my mouth would have been had I not succeeded in keeping it shut.

Cynics might easily object and say that I am grabbing far more of a *belle rôle* for myself than I deserve. But this is how I feel. The Royal Marines who fought the Argentines at Grytviken and Port Stanley will doubtless give me the finger and a chorus of 'Crap Hat! We were the only ones there at the start', and they are right. They were. But so was I, in a way, if only to witness the very start of the fightback. History . . . And who else, says I, was there in the House of Commons on that momentous day and also charged into Port Stanley on Victory Day, 14 June? If anyone else was, I'd love to meet them. I can taste the hangover already!

Agreement given and accepted, the Colonel gets down to details. He doubts whether the Marines and Paras who make up 3 Commando Brigade will have much idea about our vehicles' capabilities and weaknesses, as they will probably not have worked alongside them before, let alone had them under command – unlike the regular army, which should have. In the hierarchical military world I will, as a captain, be that bit better able to fight their corner at Brigade HQ than Mark Coreth and Robin Innes-Ker, the two troop leaders, who are 'mere' lieutenants. In this, however, the Colonel completely under-estimated the imperious abilities of the two of them to fight their corner, regardless of their very junior rank. But all this lies in the future . . .

This will be my mission from him, he tells me, until the rest of B Squadron arrives on the second wave with 5th Infantry Brigade. That Brigade is currently being reconstituted, having lost their two Para battalions to 3 Commando Brigade. Once B Squadron Leader arrives on the Islands he will be the one briefing both the Brigadiers.

Then, within hours, it is 'Berets on. Berets off,' and I am told to 'stand down'. A message has come from 3 Brigade HQ saying I'm not needed after all.

I'm guessing here as to why 3 Brigade don't want me, but logic dictates that any Commando and Para officers not already assigned a berth on a boat heading south – and there will be plenty of them – will be clamouring and politicking and pulling every string they can think of to somehow join the trip. Missing out on this gig will doubtless have major detrimental consequences for the career keenos, and nobody, I guess, is much minded to hand a 'Crap Hat' like me a coveted watchkeeper slot in place of a tried and trusted friend.

And they probably have something of a point, beyond their natural disdain for all Crap Hats. They doubtless have their own singular and extremely well practised way of doing things in Commando Brigade HQ, and now might not be the best time to take on and teach a newbie Household Cavalryman like me. Although in this, as you will read, they perhaps made a very grave mistake . . .

Also, I suspect, they might well wonder whether a Blue and Royal would be fit enough to keep up with them if the going got extreme. And they might well have a point. I am fit, but not Para/Commando fit. Although I did end up keeping up with them . . .

As for me, I do what most soldiers would do after receiving a severe shock to their system and get extremely drunk with friends – **'A form of reaction I suppose'**, my diary tells me.

Hangover over, I get back to enjoying my relatively uneventful, semi-sybaritic life. My diary for April is a list of 'dates' and drinks and suppers with various girls; some friends, others girlfriends. My love life is in a state of fairly shambolic, unfocused but enjoyable drift. My military career is not much better. My compulsory five years' service after university and Sandhurst is soon up, and I have to decide whether I want to get serious about things military and make a career of it, or leave. My problems are twin: I have no idea what else I would like to do instead – the thought of 'becoming something in the city', like so many of my chums, fills me with dread, compounded by the fact that I am having such a fun time at Windsor that I don't want it to end. I really am drifting.

'Then, on Tuesday 4 May, I was warned that I really was most probably going. Having had the shock once I was not unduly worried on the second occasion. One must define shock. It was not worry,

at least not in particular. I was quite happy to go. It was just that dreaming had suddenly become reality. It was a gut reaction to the fact that I was off.'

But only me. 5 Brigade has said a formal 'no thank you' to any more armoured vehicles. 'More trouble than they are worth,' B Squadron Leader tells me is the astonishing and ignorant unofficial message. Meaning it is 'Berets off' for B Squadron, much to their disgust. My mission remains the same, the Colonel tells me as he re-drops the bombshell: look after the boys as best I can, at both Brigade HQs, if possible.

However, the second half of this second briefing is not so cheery. The Colonel apologizes. The prospects have changed now that I will be going with the second wave. Current wisdom is that the Argentines will either have surrendered or been booted off the Islands by the time we get there. All I probably have to look forward to is a long, boring summer of garrison duties. Six months maximum, he hopes. But no guarantees as to when he will be able to get me home.

That at least is how I got on to the *QE2* because, as my next diary entry makes clear, military thinking on 'What next?' is changing by the day. Dramatically . . .

21 May: '**Spent the afternoon packing kit and listening to news of the landings.**' Right up until this moment we have wondered, half-believed even, that talks might lead to a diplomatic solution. That changes today. 3 Command Brigade are ashore. Nothing short of an unconditional Argentine surrender will, I believe, now stop this war. And that means that we will soon be fighting.

Packing my kit, finding the best balance between bringing what I need and not carrying too much weight becomes an obsession for all of us. Essentials go in the pouches on my 'belt order' webbing, which I will keep with me at all times: water canteen, mug, mess tins (cooking pans that double as eating bowls), knife/fork/spoon, food, spare socks and shreddies (underpants). My front two pouches are pretty much reserved for ammunition. A rolled-up waterproof poncho hangs off the back of my belt. Clip it together with a second one and it makes a sort of two-man tent.

Next up is my Bergen. I was given a good quality 'civvie' Berghaus mountaineering rucksack when I as good as forced 5 Brigade to issue me my so-called 'Arctic' kit instead of being sent back to Windsor empty-handed. This has my spare clothes and all sorts in it, stored inside a thick plastic bin liner to keep it dry, with my green Maggot (army issue sleeping bag – because we look like green maggots when we are zipped up inside them, only our noses showing) on the very top in another bin liner.

I will go ashore with only my webbing and my Bergen. I have to assume that I will not see anything I leave in my army sausage bag and suitcase until after the war. I'm right, I don't.

First efforts are hopeless. Even after weeding out stuff I thought was essential and now decide is not. It's so heavy I cannot lift it on to my back myself. Someone has to do it for me.

Julian and Adam, as infanteers, are much more clued-up than Nick and I, but even they are struggling. We are going into the teeth of the South Atlantic midwinter and we are going to need every bit of warm clothing we can carry. Dry spares as well. We weed and we weed. I only stop when I can swing it on to my back unaided and know I can march with it. But march any distance? I'm not so sure. I decide that, should that happen, I'll do more weeding – followed by throwing. I'll face that hurdle should I hit it.

In cabins all over the ship kit is being checked and double-checked, packed and repacked, as 3,000 men realize they really are going to war.

Chapter 7

Active Service

INFANTRY BRIGADE

Routine Orders

By

BRIGADIER M J A WILSON OBE MC 23 May

1. **DECLARATION OF ACTIVE SERVICE**
   Active Service conditions have been declared by MOD for all personnel serving on 'Op Corporate' south of Ascension Island. The QE2 entered the Active Service zone with effect from 1000 hrs Sat 22 May 82.

So there we have it. We are finally on 'Active Service'; at war, although I had rather assumed we were on active service from the moment we set sail. Shows how little I know.

What if that Argie sub had sunk us before 1000hrs yesterday? Would that not have counted? I suppose it is something legal or 'civil servicy' to do with larger payments if we are killed or wounded whilst 'at war'. Not that such technical niceties will matter much to me. I made my first will – we all had to – when I did a tour of Northern Ireland. My brother Rory would get the lot. This amounted to a bank overdraft, my shotgun and a sometimes broken-down car. In a good month, selling the gun and the car might clear the overdraft; in other months he'd be out of pocket. Before heading off on this jaunt I signed a codicil to that will. Rory still inherits my overdraft, but I've brought the shotgun with me and my car has broken down – again. The codicil is a list of chums who are to get a fine bottle of malt whisky in the event of my premature departure from the planet. Rory will be seriously pissed off if I get killed; that whisky codicil will cost him a fortune. This amuses me immensely. As we like to say in my regiment, 'If you can't take the joke, you shouldn't have joined.'

By 24 May life on board has become a dull and easy routine. There are occasional small jobs to do and then, hey presto, it is evening and cocktail time, the most exciting part of the day. Small incidents assume huge proportions. Brendan Lambe, the Brigade Major, stomps into the Ops Room. He's normally a nice enough chap but this morning he's not a happy bunny. Perhaps it is all the flak he's taking because of the Brigadier's failure to command. Maybe he's just having a bad day. Anyway, he proceeds to rip into us about rumour control – in the army's inimitable strangulation of the English language, 'rumour control' means not spreading rumours, and the dangers of doing so.

'People are saying that the *Canberra* has been sunk,' he tells us. Where the rumour started he does not know, but he's looking hard at us.

I do.

'**Outside the Ops Room is a huge board showing Argentine weapons and their casualties. This normally draws a lot of interested people. Top of the "aircraft destroyed" list it reads: "*Canberra* destroyed – one".**

Outside, two Cunard stewards are saying, "Oh my God, they have destroyed the *Canberra*."'

In fact, we have shot down a Canberra aircraft that the Argentines were using to spy on the fleet.

Just a smidgeon of common sense from Brendan, a question asked and easily answered, and he could have avoided giving us this unnecessary grief. We are grown-up boys, keen to do our jobs as best we can, and we are not into spreading rumours. This pisses us off, but then so do a lot of things.

Major General Moore (Royal Marines) and his Royal Marine headquarters came on board at Ascension Island, and Brigadier Wilson will report to him. Given the ongoing vacuum in Brigade HQ I'm guessing that the Brigadier and his staff are now being run ragged pleasing their new master.

Apart from ensuring we watchkeepers do not trip over or offend these new bosses, life continues much as before. We wake up one morning to see two Browning .50 machine guns and some GPMGs have been mounted on the flying bridge of *QE2*. Blowpipe hand-held surface-to-air missiles have been positioned along the top deck.

At lunch we get a briefing. We are now officially in a 'threat zone'. There is still at least one Argentine sub out there, undetected. We are the perfect target. Sink us, and it is probably invasion over.

Plans have changed. With some of our war supplies, including our all-important ammo, on the wrong ships, the original plan had been to cross-load at sea with the ferries which are being used as store ships. We will now sail straight to South Georgia and cross-load there.

ETA (estimated time of arrival) is 27 May, in three days' time. Although, on the 'berets on, berets off' principle, we suspect this is subject to limitless change. And we'll be leaving the luxury of the *QE2*, as she is deemed 'Not ready for war'. Whatever that means. It probably means that she'll cost the MoD more than the *Canberra* if she ends up on the seabed. Anyway, that's my theory.

That timeline and those anti-aircraft weapons silhouetted against the cloudless blue sky every time we look upwards energize us to complete our final re-re-re-pack. We still have no real idea what we will be up against. The Falklands are deep down in the South Atlantic, perhaps in the sub-Antarctic, although I am not too sure about this and nobody really seems to know.[1] Does this mean lots of snow and ice? Probably not, we learn. The Islands are going to be more like a turbo-charged Dartmoor: blasting winds so fierce that trees cannot grow, new weather systems constantly powering in, pissing rain changing to snow, even to sun. 'One day; four seasons', as I later discover.

What is blindingly obvious is that we are not properly equipped for this. We note from photos in the newspapers that most Royal Marines wear special mountaineering boots and gaiters. They don't wear the standard issue DMS boots, which is all the rest of us have. All except the Brigadier, that is. When I do occasionally see him on land, neat as a pin as ever, he sports a natty pair of green Hunter wellies. He clearly doesn't expect to run anywhere . . .

Staying dry is a big issue in these pre-Gore-Tex and 'wicking' micro-fibre days. We discuss this endlessly. Our training has drummed into us the importance of staying as dry as possible. When we are warm, dry and well

---

1. Wiki maps tell me that the Falklands are roughly the same distance north of the South Pole as South Georgia, which is in the 'polar' region – the world of permanent ice and snow. However, the Falklands, doubtless for reasons of currents and weather and proximity to the South American land mass (just as certain islands off North-West Scotland have micro-climates as they catch the Gulf Stream) are deemed to be just north of the 'polar region'.

fed, we can address most of our focus to the tactical problem we are facing; to fighting. The more we degrade – and cold and wet are prime degraders – the more of our mental bandwidth is required just to function, and the less is available for thinking and fighting.

On exercise, misery is time-finite. A two-week exercise is just that: two weeks. Not where we're going, though. Get wet and go down with hypothermia and will anyone get us out? Can they get us out? Even the poor bloody infantry in the death zone of the trenches in the Great War knew that there was a vast support network a mile or three behind them: hospitals, hot food, showers, replacement kit.

During training our DS minced around in slimline waterproof jackets, which we covet, not least because we are not allowed waterproofs during training as (obviously) they will prevent us getting wet, and getting us wet and watching how we cope as we degrade is all part of our training. However, and it is a huge however, run in one – and our DS mainly stand around drinking coffee and rarely run anywhere, so presumably never face this dilemma – and we sweat inside them since, unlike Gore-Tex, they do not 'wick' moisture out.

As a captain I now have my own slinky waterproof jacket. But it does not fit over my webbing. It has to be worn under the webbing, making moisture escape impossible – which risks turning me into a mobile sauna.

Become slowly sodden with warm sweat from the inside out, or drenched with cold rain from the outside in? An easy choice, but not a good one. Waterproofs on, or waterproofs off? It is a constant military conundrum.

And how long will we be ashore fighting this war? Weeks? Months? We have no idea. I need to get my packing as right as I possibly can.

Another treasured regimental adage is, 'Any fool can be uncomfortable', and I want some 'comforts'. We are the first generation to go to war with boogie packs blasting music into our individual ears. However, much as I like the idea of 'doing' the Falklands to Meatloaf, David Bowie and Hazel O'Connor – the haunting, melancholic saxophone solo from *Will You* plays in my mind on semi-permanent loop as I pound the decks of *QE2* – it'll probably get soaked and broken. Into my suitcase it goes. I just hope I see it again. I've heard stories about what today's soldiers call REMFs (Rear Echelon Motherfuckers – great expression, younger generation, thank you!) 'checking' the suitcases of the forward troops and 'liberating' anything desirable.

The same goes for my 12-bore shotgun. There's said to be good goose and duck shooting on the Islands, and I'll wager we lot stuck on garrison duty will end up on a near-solid diet of army compo rations. I'll be desperate for fresh, delicious meat. And for some sport. However, I can't lug it around, and it joins my boogie pack.

A bottle of 12-year-old Laphroaig malt whisky, the last survivor from that lifetime-ago Oddbins raid, makes it into my Bergen; my hipflask into my jacket. This will give sustenance at dark moments. As I write this I can picture Frodo, in the film of *The Lord of the Rings*, being given the 'Light of Eärendil' by the Lady Galadriel (Cate Blanchett at her most fetching); a phial to 'be a light for you in dark places', she says as she hands it to him. I'll take a shot of 12-year-old 'Leapfrog' to light me in the darkness any day of the week . . .

That bottle ends up getting an honourable mention in Major General Frost's book, *2 Para Falklands: The Battalion at War*. I'm tabbing with 2 Para (Royal Marines 'yomp'; Paras 'tab'; everyone else marches) towards Wireless Ridge. I make the mistake of confiding my Laphroaig-related thoughts to Captain David Benest, the Battalion Signals Officer, who I am teamed up with. He passes them on to the General, and this appears in the book: 'Roger Field of The Blues and Royals plodded on . . . although his thoughts wandered to a large bottle of whisky left behind in his rucksack in the LUP (lying up position).'

My thoughts certainly did, although I was much looking forward to telling David – only now I discover, sadly dead – that things weren't as bad as I made out. My hip flask, full of Laphroaig, was in my camouflage jacket. But I wasn't telling an ever-thirsty Para that.

My final indulgence is my Pentax SLR camera, which I load into my large NBC (Nuclear Biological and Chemical) pouch, along with spare films and bars of chocolate, although, as I was to discover on the Islands, when the opportunities to take really interesting 'war' photos came along, any soldier doing his job is far too busy being a soldier to be a photographer. It was only when the shooting or whatever stopped and the danger/drama over that I ever thought to take out my camera, by which time the award-winning photo opportunity was gone. That is doubtless why – thinking about it now – there are so few really good 'action' shots ever taken, even in modern wars.

We were ordered to bring our gas masks and 'Noddy' suits as the high-ups are worried that the Argies, if they are losing, may resort to gassing us.

I disagree and leave them on the boat. Firstly, I doubt they are that criminally insane, and secondly, what idiot would release gas on an island where the wind blows so hard and so consistently that trees cannot grow?

I hope I am calling this right as it could, literally, be the death of me. 'Gassed' is not the epitaph I want on my gravestone.

Chapter 8

Towards Grytviken, South Georgia

Daily Routine Orders, 23 May, issued by Major Mike Forge (Royal Signals), Brigade Signals Officer. A 'Notice' at the bottom of that day's Orders:
   Notices
   Warning Order
   Defence and Employment Platoon – Entrance Exams [they protect Brigade HQ in the field and are part of Mike's command].
   With a view to improving the defences of Bde HQ, future members of D & E will be required to take an entrance exam. Two questions will be listed each day for the next eight days. Budding scholars would do well to note them down and start researching now.

1. History. Describe the history of the Papacy from its origins to the present day, concentrating especially, but not exclusively, on its social, political, economic, religious and philosophical impacts on Asia, America, Europe and Africa. Be brief, concise and specific.
2. Public Speaking. Two thousand five hundred riot-crazed aborigines are storming the classroom. Calm them. You may use any ancient language except Latin and Greek.

The Defence and Employment Platoon, splendid soldiers though they undoubtedly are, tend to be chosen more for their ability to dig a trench and hump radios than their intellectual dexterity and command of ancient languages.

What a wonderfully Monty Pythonian thing to put on Brigade Daily Orders. Which is why I kept it.

Mike is a lovely chap. I enjoy his wayward approach to matters as much as he seems to enjoy mine. In the vacuum that is HQ he is a rare kindred spirit.

* * *

On 24 May my diary tells me this is meant to be CPX day: **'What is going to happen? Bugger all, we suspect.'**

I suspect 'bugger all' did happen, otherwise I am fairly certain I would have recorded the great event. Instead, my second entry for that day describes another luxurious, indolent day of brigade idleness: sitting in deckchairs on our balcony in the blazing sun, reading books and listening to our boogie packs, the lifeboats on the sunny south side of the ship full of Brigade Staff doing the same.

And then the Ops Room is being taken apart; the radios readied for transhipping to *Canberra*, the maps and log books stored away. We really do now have no job to do.

I have to call a puzzled 'time-out' here. I am reading a book, *5th Infantry Brigade in the Falklands,* which tells me I am completely wrong. It describes a state of constant headquarters activity on *QE2* – which was certainly the case with the battalions who were training super-hard all the way down. According to the authors, who were not there and who interviewed participants afterwards – the book was first published in 2003, so quite possibly almost 20 years afterwards – 'Headquarters and command posts carried out endless appreciations.'

And again, after we left Sierra Leone, a time of maximum torpor according to my diary, the book says: 'The time was not wasted and in the nine days it took the liner to hammer its way through the South Atlantic to South Georgia, the headquarters on board exercised and carried out tactical appreciations for landings, including landing at Teal Inlet.'

I've always wondered whether there were high-level planning meetings and what have you going on elsewhere, perhaps in the Brigadier's even more super-luxury, duplex stateroom. I would like to think there were. But wherever they were happening, it was not in Brigade HQ – at least when I was present.

This puzzles me. Headquarters training exercises are CPXs, and CPXs require radios, and we watchkeepers operate those radio nets – which means that someone has got it wrong, and I don't think it's me.

Then again, the cynic I long ago became tells me that 5 Brigade staffers are hardly going to tell the authors that they could not even organize a CPX in a headquarters when interviewed for a book; especially a book that finally seeks to give 5 Brigade HQ a far more *belle rôle* than it has previously been accorded.

But what do I know? Maybe I was gonking (asleep), or mixing Harvey Wallbangers or watching Electric Blue porn videos and missed out on all this 'endless' HQ activity. Lucky me if I did . . .

And then, all too quickly, it is 26 May and our last night aboard the wonderful *Queen*. Tomorrow we arrive at Grytviken in South Georgia, where we will tranship to *Canberra*. OK, it is not yet 'war' as such, but it is beginning to feel very much more like it.

On our first night aboard we watchkeepers had gone to the dining room for dinner as a group and found a table, as presumably did everyone else. It then became 'our' table, and a table comes with its own steward.

Ron (not his real name, which I have sadly forgotten), our steward, is splendidly but toughly gay. I wouldn't want to get into a dock bar brawl with him. Homosexuality, however, is absolutely *verboten* in the army back in those buttoned-down days, and he is very different to anyone else I have got to know. We think he is the best, and he seems to care for us.

Using the homosexuality card, a chum of mine did manage to escape the army soon after we finished Sandhurst. Times were hard, pay was bad and recruitment poor. Those who asked to leave were told 'No'. We'd signed up for three or five years, and they were keeping us.

'How did you manage it?' I asked him over a beer.

'Simple,' he told me. 'I was the regimental rugby officer. The Colonel was very keen on rugby. I asked to see him. I was ushered straight in.'

'Enjoying things?' asked the Colonel, keen to talk team tactics. 'It's great how well the team is doing.'

'Well, that's what I want to see you about, Sir.' says my chum. 'I'm worried that I'm beginning to enjoy it too much. It's the showers after the game that are the problem. I can't help getting excited when I see the boys naked and I'm not sure how long it will be before someone notices.'

Paperwork for his premature withdrawal, if that is the right expression, arrives the next day. Oh, and by the by, my chum is heterosexual. He just could not face the prospect of spending the next five years going quietly mad with boredom in Germany. He's a cunning boy and, having made his decision, worked out which homophobic button to press.

Another chum trumped that story. He was the regimental adjutant in the late 1980s. The RMP (Royal Military Police – the army's police force) demanded to speak to him. They are following up a complaint from Mrs

Snooks. Corporal Snooks, her husband, apparently tried to have anal sex with her. No violence was involved, but she is still complaining.

'And what business is that of yours? Or mine for that matter?' my chum asked the furious-looking MPs. 'What Corporal and Mrs Snooks get up to in their bedroom is their own business, surely?'

'Well, yes,' says senior Monkey (as soldiers call MPs; profound apologies here to all fans of Major Jack Reacher, US Military Police). 'But if he tried to have anal sex with his wife he might try to have anal sex with a soldier.'

'You've got to be joking?'

They weren't. They interviewed the anally thwarted corporal but, thankfully, wiser heads intervened and it went no further. So, and to put it mildly, our experience of proud gays back then is somewhat limited. Ron looks after our watchkeeper table beautifully. This from a letter home:

> I am now fully ammo'd up and victualled right down to the obligatory bottle of malt. Menu for day 1 [on land] is Breakfast – Baconburgers. Lunch – Beef spread, hard tack biscuits and lots of choccies. Main meal, Oxtail Soup, Snake and Pigmy (steak and kidney), Spaghetti, +apple and apricot flakes. The Cunard stewards [That's Ron] have given me silver plated cutlery so I shall be in fine style – the original Boy Scout. It all weighs so much I can hardly move!!

We all become chums, albeit in that class-conscious, let's all remember our place in the grand dance of life way that we Brits are so good at. However, we are trans-shipping tomorrow and we have just been hit with the ghastly news that *Canberra* has been drunk dry.

Tonight is our 'last supper'. The food has been getting less 'luxy' of late, but the *QE2* is determined to see us off in style:

R.M.S. *QUEEN ELIZABETH 2*
Wednesday 26th May 1982
<u>Evening Meal</u>
Apple Juice
Cream of Mushroom Soup
Grilled Fillet of Haddock, Parsley Butter
Sirloin Steak, Marchand De Vins
Green Peas

Trifle with Cream
Cheese and Biscuits
Fresh Fruits
Rolls and Butter
Tea or Coffee

Ron, bless him – although I'd wager this conversation is being repeated on other tables – asks whether we would like a bottle of champagne that he has kept for this last evening and, his *pièce de resistance*, he's also hidden away 'the last of the camembert'.

Does the Pope use Viagra? Do bears crap in the woods? Of course we would like it. And it is a wonderful, albeit slightly melancholy, last dinner. What will tomorrow bring?

Chapter 9

Grytviken to Bomb Alley

QE2, 5th Infantry Brigade HQ, Ops [Operations] Order, dated 23 May 1982: 'Never use enemy slit trenches – these are often found to contain explosive devices or AP [anti-personnel] mines.'

A typical edict from a keen-to-impress, busy-bee desk warrior, whose trench will doubtless be dug for him. I always look for a 'nice' pre-dug trench, first checking it for turds and then explosives before making it home. Just surviving on those islands in the deep South Atlantic midwinter is quite testing enough without wasting precious, exhausting hours digging a new hole beside a perfectly serviceable old one. A somewhat cavalier attitude perhaps, but then I am Household Cavalry.

I keep this Ops Order because it not only makes me smile – it still does – but it encapsulates the ageless 'us-and-them' divide between HQ staff and the fighting troops.

* * *

Grytviken, South Georgia. Out on deck it is cold, but utterly still.

Beating along at 28-plus knots, the *QE2* creates its own wind system and it has been so bitter outside these last few days that, even with my cold weather kit on, I can only bear to stand there for a short time gazing out at the ocean. It is now far too cold to run, and I feel for the sentries manning those machine guns all along the rails. I suspect they are 'only' doing one hour on duty instead of the normal two, but even that would soon be painful.

However, with the ship now at anchor, we stand outside in our sweaters, overawed by the bleak grandeur of the massive harbour, the mountains dropping near sheer into the sea, cut in half by a thick layer of cloud which hides the summits. Off to the left of the bows a glacier reaches down into the water, the ice glowing white and blue in the distance. The majesty, the sheer immensity and rawness of the scene, shrinks and humbles me.

We have been unbelievably lucky with the weather so far; not one storm, although it is somehow much darker down here. Sudden mists roll in and just as quickly roll out again.

On either side of the bridge those .50 Brownings are skylined against the mountains, and a wrecked Argentine submarine lies half-sunk beside a pier. This is the real face of the aftermath of war. It is a sobering sight and, after the inertia of the past days, a timely reminder of what we are really here for.

The SS *Canberra* is anchored up inshore of us, waiting. She looks tired and rust-streaked, as does MV *Norland*, the roll on/roll off ferry that The Blues and Royals and 2 Para travelled down on. These two are real warriors; survivors of the air battles in San Carlos Water when the Argentine air force tried to sink the fleet and stop the invasion before it started. We really are the new boys in our shiny new ship. Looking at them I feel not a little frightened. Our turn next.

We tranship in a smallish boat. With the sea flat calm it is uneventful, but exhilarating to be doing something at last, even if I don't want to leave the comfort and familiarity of *QE2*. But I also know that the long road home leads via the *Canberra* to whatever waits beyond. I am a tiny part of a huge, camouflage-jacketed ant colony, and I move as instructed.

We board *Canberra* and, horror of all horrors, instead of heading up the stairs towards first class, we watchkeepers are directed down into the bowels of the ship, to a cramped two-bunk, four-bed cabin on the inside of the ship. When I later work in publishing I learn to judge a person's importance from the size and position of their office. We have been consigned to Dante's seventh circle of insignificance. Not only is it a bummer – we were looking forward to comparing Cunard luxury with its P&O competitor – but it looks to me like a clearly signposted Brigade riposte to our hitherto somewhat smartarse approach. The Blues and Royals is a veritable library of wise and unwise, but nearly always amusing sayings, and 'Nobody likes a smartarse' is another regimental favourite. Someone at HQ has clearly decided we are. Smartarses, that is.

'This really is a bit more like it as full of survivors and wounded when we arrived. Masses of war stories being told. They have now been put on to *QE2*. All in excellent heart.'

We raise anchor and our meteorological luck turns. We sail straight into the teeth of a Force 10 (plus) storm. It is so violent that the Captain announces he is reducing speed as the waves are causing superstructure damage.

I stand on the Promenade Deck some 80-plus feet above the water line as the waves foam past me at head height. As the storm worsens, most retreat to their beds and the stench of vomit fills the corridors. I'm a yachtie and believe I'll be fine. I climb to the Crow's Nest observation lounge, right at the very top of the ship, one floor above the Captain's bridge, to better watch the drama. *Canberra* shoots down the back of a wave before burying her nose deep into the trough of the next giant green roller heading towards us, spume flying off the crest. There is a long shudder as she digs deep into the water. Then up comes her bow, and up the next wave we climb, before going through it all again. I'm up there for well over an hour, enjoying the solitude and the spectacle and feeling rather pleased with myself. I'm no landlubber.

But Poseidon has little time for smartarses either. The higher up the ship one is, the more extreme the motion. In fact, the best place to be is in our cabin in the bowels of the ship; far less movement down there. The Crow's Nest is at the very pinnacle. One moment I'm enjoying myself, the next I am gagging. I rush to the heads (naval parlance for loos). The stink of whoever puked in there before me makes my sudden nausea far worse. I take to my bed and suffer with the others.

I re-surface, sea-sickness gone, some 24 hours later. The sea has calmed somewhat, and when I venture out, the grey of sleek warships is all around me. We have joined the fleet. GPMGs are mounted on pivots all along the wooden rails on the decks, loaded and ready in case of low-level fighter/bomber attack. Whilst I've been ill, the ship has been readied to re-enter San Carlos Water – Bomb Alley – or possibly a different landing spot. San Carlos is on the far west of East Falkland, Port Stanley on the east. Perhaps they will land us somewhere half way. Because, with all but one of our heavy-lift Chinook helicopters sunk by the Exocet missile that destroyed the SS *Atlantic Conveyor*, how will we cross the island otherwise?

Brigade, I learn, has a new worry which originated in London. They are fretting that those who have 'done' Northern Ireland, and that's most of us – Gurkhas excepted; they do not 'do' Northern Ireland as it is deemed too incendiary to use soldiers who will be certain to be denounced as 'mercenaries' – might lack aggression, might hesitate to shoot.

I can sort of see where our worried generals are coming from. Most of the pre-Ireland training I did before my tour of West Belfast in 1979 was about not shooting people; about theoretically giving the IRA so many bloody warnings that they almost have time to stroll off. We have a 'Yellow Card' that we study and must carry on us at all times. It tells us when we can open fire. Fail to follow the Card to the very letter and we risk criminal sanctions, as is happening to some veterans at this very moment, decades later – although, that said, they may well have followed the Yellow Card to the letter; on that I have no idea.

YELLOW CARD: INSTRUCTIONS FOR OPENING FIRE IN NORTHERN IRELAND. 'Wherever possible a warning should be given before opening fire . . .'

Let's examine this hypothetically, as we did endlessly in our pre-tour training. I see someone with what looks like a rifle. That person is probably at least 100 metres away and probably set up to shoot at us – any closer and he/she (mustn't be sexist here) could use a bow and arrow, and latterly at least, the chances of coming across IRA gunmen (gun persons?) wandering around with rifles is extremely unlikely. This, after all, is Belfast 1979 and not the OK Corral 1881.

They'll probably be well hidden behind a wall, or a window. The IRA are not stupid, regardless of the endless 'thick Paddy' stereotypes. In fact, they are highly professional and usually deadly. The early days of barely aimed Thompson sub-machine gun fire are long over. These days it is one-round one-kill snipes.

So, what to do?

If they have already fired, it is legitimate to return fire. But by then it's probably already too late; I will have a soldier on the floor and the shooter will be legging it along a pre-planned escape route and probably have already handed over their weapon to A N Other who, if caught, will have no explosive residue on their hands, therefore facing a lesser criminal charge. In fact, short of surprising a gunman carrying a rifle which he/she points at you – unlikely – we pretty much always must shout a warning, or be certain – courtroom certain – that the baddie is about to fire at us before we can shoot.

It is a near-impossible situation to be put into.

In May 1982, on our way to the Falklands, the spectre of the Yellow Card hangs heavy on our commanders' minds. After all that indoctrination, will we hesitate to open fire when we first make contact with the Argies? Want to shout a warning? Lose those vital first seconds when firefights can be won and lost? Our bosses have been driving desks far too long and need not have worried. I for one have seen the bodies of my soldiers with bullet holes in them; have been shot at and, if not bombed, been threatened with bombing. Most of us on that boat have experienced similar. We know the victims of the IRA and would love nothing more than to get even with them. We Northern Ireland veterans, fed up to the bottoms of our souls with being walking targets in Ulster, cannot wait to go weapons-free in the Falklands. And if our targets are Argentines instead of IRA? Well, bring it on.

In the Pacific Grill (the First Class dining room) we listen in awed respect as *Canberra*'s equivalent of Ron serves us soup – they long ago ran out of fine food and smart, stiff, menu cards – whilst regaling us with stories of low-flying Mirages and bombs and machine guns and missiles. It sounds terrifying. And he's about to go back in for, perhaps, a second helping of air attacks. I begin to understand why Britain once ruled the waves and how the likes of Ron and his forebears kept the shipping lanes open through the carnage of two world wars. If this is what the dining room stewards are made of, then our navy really is possessed of 'hearts of oak'.

> Heart of oak are our ships, jolly tars are our men, We always are ready; Steady, boys, steady. We'll fight and we'll conquer again and again.
> (The chorus of *Heart of Oak*, the official march of the Royal Navy).

Brigade does not set up an Ops Room on *Canberra* as we will not be on board long enough. Anyway, even as we were transhipping in Grytviken, General Moore, the Brigadier and key staff flew off to join Admiral Woodward on his flagship. They have cunning plans to hatch and they need to do so face-to-face.

We watchkeepers are now out of the information loop. We have no idea where the ship is going, or what Brigade wants us to do when we get there. Will we land, perhaps in the north, to attack Port Stanley in a pincer movement? Or follow into San Carlos Water and reinforce 3 Brigade from there? There are spirited debates in our poky little cabin. Julian is adamant that it would be madness to risk the *Canberra* and the whole Brigade by landing anywhere but San Carlos. It may be on the western end of the island and the furthest point from Port Stanley, our ultimate objective, but it alone has those all-important, land-based missile defences.

I am not so sure what my answer to Julian tells you about my abilities as a high level strategist...

I look at my map and the 65 miles distance from San Carlos to Port Stanley; no roads, a couple of tracks and only one heavy-lift Chinook helicopter. The rest of the Chinooks were sunk on the *Atlantic Conveyor* along with God alone seems to know what else by way of mission-critical war fighting kit. How, I ask the others, is 5 Brigade going to get itself from San Carlos to Port Stanley?

Whilst conceding that Julian is probably right – where else can *Canberra* land us where she will, first, not run aground and, second, not get sunk? – I can't see how the high-ups are going to make it work. The more sensible solution to my mind is to leapfrog forward so we have less far to go, which means landing us nearer Stanley. The others disagree, and I concede defeat. Anyway, who cares what we watchkeepers think?

As things turn out I am not as 'wrong' as I thought I was with my poohhoo'ed map appreciation. How to move 5 Brigade with enough material to perhaps fight a number of battles, overland, without vehicles, is a logistical nightmare that is bedevilling more experienced brains than mine. The answer is by smaller landing ships. An eminently sensible-sounding solution that will lead to the disaster at Fitzroy. But that lies in the future.

Instead, as we listen to the BBC News on the radio in our cabin, we now have something else to fulminate about:

'**We reckon the silence about what is going on is because if 3 Cmdo Brigade sends any secret info back it seems to be announced on BBC within hours – so they seem to be refusing to say anything, even to us. The suppositions given on the radio must be quite invaluable to the Argies.**'

On 31 May we four listen aghast as the BBC announce over the radio that Julian is calling it right and we will be landing at San Carlos tomorrow. If we are listening to this, then so are the Argies.

Did the BBC perhaps fail to mention what time we will land tomorrow? Maybe. But, had we had our fists within striking range of that BBC reporter at that moment, well . . .

Chapter 10

Ashore

'There are no atheists in trenches.'

It is probably safest to attribute this saying to 'Anonymous', although the web throws up various possibilities, from 1914 in England to 1942 in Bataan, during the blood-soaked battle for the Philippines.

Revd David Cooper, front-line padre of 2 Para, tells me that his congregations increase greatly in the Falklands before, and especially after, the Battle of Goose Green.

In my various trenches I long to bump into a deity of whatever faith or denomination. I'd love to know that He (or She) is preparing a celestial welcome party if things go tits-up and I find myself 'Upstairs' far earlier than planned

The Almighty, however, persists in remaining AWOL (absent without leave).

* * *

'It's the Glorious First of June', one of the modern history-minded watchkeepers points out to the rest of us; otherwise known as the Third Battle of Ushant, a great victory for the Royal Navy over the French in 1794. 'A lucky day to be anchoring in San Carlos Water,' he assures us.

And luck *is* with us. The fog is down. We can hardly see the surrounding hills through the murk. The Argie jets are unlikely to be able to attack us. Nevertheless, they want us off *Canberra* and her back out to sea as quickly as possible, before the fog lifts and these waters become a target-rich environment for the bombers.

We troops also want off this huge white 'X-marks-the-spot' ship. They may have missed her first time around. That doesn't mean they'll miss her this time. We've seen the TV footage of what that Exocet did to HMS *Sheffield*.

In 2007, the 25th anniversary of the war, I am on an MoD-sponsored media trip to the Islands. I visit Elephant Island, where the memorial to HMS *Sheffield* stands. It is a large steel cross on a south-facing cliff. Next stop south is Antarctica, nothing but spume-tossed seas in between. I've walked the high Himalayas and soldiered in strange places; but this is without doubt the loneliest, most desolate, ghost-haunted place I have ever stood in. The thought of those boys out there, on their own, standing guard duty in those vast icy wastes makes my heart want to break for them. That spot and that simple cross beat me into insignificance.

In no time, landing craft – the ones from old war films with front ramps that lower down for beach assaults – are pulling alongside. The battalions go first. We stand on deck and watch. They're moving like greased weasel-shit, I'm told, but it still takes hours. And then I too am standing in a queue in a corridor. It's darkish. In front is a square of bright light, the 'pilot' door I think it is called, much lower down and very much smaller than the grand entrance.

That is the opening through which I'll walk before turning and climbing down a scramble net to the landing craft below. I've built up no affection for *Canberra*, but all of a sudden it feels like being in the dark safety of the womb compared to a bright, hostile world awaiting me through that square of light.

I suppress that wimpish thought. We are landing on a well-protected beachhead. If I'm feeling this level of trepidation, how must the Commandos and Paras have felt as they stood in this same corridor a few weeks ago, about to step on to a genuinely hostile beach, into the complete unknown? Or the men on those landing craft, almost identical to ours, about to hit the beaches in Normandy in 1944? I have no right to feel trepidation. But I do.

Scramble down in belt order. Bergen is then passed down. Then wait. Take photos. It is cold, but not 'Antarctic' cold. We chat and joke and stamp our feet. Now we have left the warmth of *Canberra* we want to be ashore. We're helpless out here if we're attacked. Finally the boat is full. Short transit to a wooden pier. Scramble up. Thank God we don't have to get our feet wet; we'd never get them dry again.

The battalions have moved slightly inland, defending the high ground that rings San Carlos. The Commandos and Paras have moved forward and on. Other than 2 Para, which is now at Goose Green, I have no idea where the others are. 2 Para captured it a couple of days ago, although with heavy loss of life including, of course, their colonel.

We hang around waiting for a helicopter to take us to Darwin, near Goose Green, where the Brigadier wants to set up his Forward HQ, of which I am a part. It's beret on, beret off; get ready, there's a helicopter coming. False alarm. No it's not. Stand down. Will we, won't we? Get a ride that is.

I'm not surprised, just fatalistic, which a soldier needs to be if he is to retain his sanity. I have no idea who is on the radios requesting helicopters, because it is not Nick, Adam, Julian or I. Not that I am complaining at getting this 'breather' before it all kicks off. The relentless, dull work of a watchkeeper will start all too soon.

It sounds as if it is going to be pretty brutal. With two of us to each of the three nets it will mean one on, one off. Eight hours on, eight hours off. Except that it is not really eight hours 'off'. We need to be at HQ half an hour early to learn what has happened during the last eight hours; what orders and plans we need to know about. In the remaining seven and a half hours 'off' I will need to shit, shave, wash and eat. And only then try and get some sleep. Before starting it all again. Relentless. And essentially boring. But I will do it as best I can. Both for myself and because I represent The Blues and Royals. It is down to me to enhance, not tarnish, their name. Seriously pompous-sounding – 'keeno' even – I grant you. But also true.

And so we wait, wondering what to do next.

Duty rumour is that the RAF helicopters are refusing to fly if there's any risk of them being shot at, and Brigade, it appears, are very worried about Argentine 'stay behind' parties shooting at our helicopters. Which is why we are still here.

Rumour hardens into reality. The RAF refuses to fly us forwards. This is a huge green (army) versus blue (RAF) bugbear. The RAF sees its helicopters – and aircraft for that matter – as 'strategic' assets. They will not risk them for small tactical gains. We soldiers see them as glorified taxis, there to help us. This difference in outlook can lead – and has in past wars – to genuine anger.

The Navy (Fleet Air Arm) sit somewhere in the middle – 'debate' puts too polite a spin on it. Yes, they'll risk their helicopters and planes for tactical advantage, but pretty much only if they are helping out ships or Marines. The RAF and Royal Navy have, of course, got a point, but it infuriates us nonetheless.

Hallelujah! A Navy Wessex (I'm guessing) finally hovers and then settles in front of us. It takes about sixteen men. The first bunch of us from

5 Brigade – no Brigadier mind you; I have not seen him since Grytviken – climb aboard and off we go, flying low and fast across the Dartmoor-like, marsh-green landscape. We've probably not been flying for more than two or three minutes before the pilot pulls a sharp U-turn. The load master gives us the bad news. Another helicopter flying the same route ahead of us thinks they may have been fired at. They're not taking unnecessary risks. We are returning to base.

We are seriously unimpressed.

We land back where we started. It is now getting on for evening and it will soon be dark. It's midwinter, we are a very long way south, and the days are short. We only see eight hours of daylight, and the days will continue to shorten.

We are ordered to dig in for the night. Someone – Willie probably – tells us that the Brigadier has given specific orders that we must dig new trenches. He is really worried about booby traps in old ones.

Hmmm. The same brigadier who is doubtless currently warm and comfortable on a navy warship? Perhaps even now chewing at a nice whisky and soda before dinner. 'Fuck that for a game of soldiers', as my troop used to say.

'Will do,' I say, looking (presumably) Willie in the eye.

Nobody tells us where to dig. No suggestion that we join some sort of defensive Brigade position. This looks to me to be a 'come as you please' hole-digging party. None of which surprises us watchkeepers.

Once out of earshot, I tell the others my plan. They like it.

We move uphill and away from the rest of Brigade HQ. Nobody seems to notice or, if they do they don't object. Perhaps they don't even consider us part of HQ and couldn't care less where we doss down for the night.

Anyway, they are already very busy, getting down, dirty and sweaty with their entrenching tools.

While the others look after our Bergens and pretend to be busy, Nick and I go searching. Further up the hill we find a 'nice', clearly British four-man trench, neatly dug to 'Stage 2' (with overhead cover).

Turd check.

'Clean.'

IED check.

'Clear.'

The others move up with our kit. Whilst we heat up our supper before night falls, we debate the pros and cons of sleeping in the trench or outside it. I believe that the chance of the Argies attacking and then penetrating the outer cordon of Scots and Welsh Guards and Gurkhas is so laughably small as to be inconsequential. I want my beauty sleep. I lay out my sleeping bag along the top of the trench and make a semi-waterproof outer cover with my poncho. I can roll into the trench if the unexpected happens.

The others elect to hunker up and sleep safely in the bottom of the trench. *Chacun à son goût.*

As I write in my 1982 *Guards Magazine* article that Prince Philip so enjoyed, '. . . and with the rain gently falling we were lulled to sleep by the sound of the rest of Brigade Headquarters digging in around us.'

So, after all these years of training, I am finally at war – although it doesn't look as if it will start until tomorrow.

Chapter 11

Tractors at Darwin

Scene: Early autumn 1982, an Army lecture hall, 100-plus officers present. I am briefing them on the war generally and the role of Scorpion and Scimitar armoured cars in particular, to be followed by a Q and A session.

Q. (From fearsomely keen-sounding young Royal Artillery officer who subsequently became a chum and turned out not to be as keen as he was pretending to be in front of his flinty-eyed bosses). 'Reference fire discipline with aircraft. How did you know which were theirs and which were ours?'

A. 'Simple. If they were distant specks they were ours. If they were low and dropping things they were theirs.'

Cue general 'manly' laughter. I could get into this . . . Except that this is no joke. I only ever see our planes once. Day Two at San Carlos I point out two far-off contrails in the high stratosphere of a bright blue sky.

'Harriers flying CAP [combat air patrol]', says a sharp-eyed fellow watchkeeper.

While I know that the Navy and RAF are doing their job, far out to sea, stopping enemy aircraft before they can get to us and do us damage, like every soldier in every war before me I'd far prefer it if our boys were roaring around overhead, giving me personal protection.

* * *

The others are long up when I awake. They had an uncomfortable night scrunched together in the bottom of a narrow trench. I feel like a well-rested smartarse.

I brew up coffee, scoff my baconburgers with my silver-plated *QE2* cutlery and revert to the 'rush to wait, wait to rush' mode that represents so much of army life.

Finally, with nothing looking as if it is going to happen any time soon, I pull out my notebook and pencil (pencils write on damp paper when pens will not) and start a new diary – I left the first one in my suitcase on board *Canberra* as I reckoned it stood a far better chance of survival that way – and start writing. I apologize for the fact that this reads as unformed and rambling, but this is what I wrote (exactly as I wrote it) as I sat on my Bergen, all the better to keep my arse off the sodden ground, waiting for something to happen:

June 2
Ashore – 1st Morning. The Time has come to launch into the dairy again, having got bored earlier on. The reason for my first 'surrender' [stopping writing] is the feeling that I was not important enough to write an interesting diary. Then having been buggered about I realised I did have a message – of military incompetence on a large scale. It seems that an efficient person can only effect a cock up in a very localised area. This is as long of course as there not 2 eff [efficient] people in the same cock up. They will create an even worse mess, order – counter order.

I will describe events on land so far and then a brief resume of the week . . .

Whop! Whop! Whop! A Navy Wessex roars in.
'Move now!' someone shouts at us, pointing.
It is 'berets on' again. Thank God.
Notebook away.
I never did get around to crafting whatever profound and damning – although deeply convoluted as drafted – sentiment I started trying to express that sunny June morning, and sadly I can no longer remember what exactly I was trying to say – although whatever it was, it was clearly not complimentary to my bosses.
Webbing on. Belt clipped to. Quick look around, nothing left on the ground. Grab shooter and, holding my Bergen in the other hand, jog to the helicopter, where a load master gesticulating, 'Hurry it up!' is indicating his absolute disgust that we aren't already lined up ready to board. Clamber in, find somewhere on the floor to sit; engine roars and off we go; low; south to

Darwin, about 21 miles away as the helicopter flies. No problems with 'stay behinds' this morning, it seems.

The tiny settlement lies at the northern end of the isthmus that leads to Goose Green and from where 2 Para began their attack. This is where we will set up Brigade 'Forward' HQ.

We land and, having rushed, it's back to wait until the radios are set up and the antennae are erected. We've been given – requisitioned would be too strong a word for it, since the islanders (although I never meet any till long after the war) are doing everything they can to help us – a nice warm farmhouse to use, complete with a peat-fired Raeburn in the kitchen. So, with time to kill, I walk over to the battlefield.

I get to a gorse-covered gulley which, someone tells me, is where A Company were pinned down and from where Colonel H launched his final assault. To all of us Colonel H is an out-and-out hero. Although, even as I listen to the stories, I reflect that I have never, in all the training I have received, heard of a scenario or read a tactics 'memoir' in which the DS solution is for the Colonel, with his small 'Tac 1' forward HQ group, to lead the manpower equivalent of a section attack. Colonels going 'over the top', the whole regiment line abreast alongside him as in the First World War, is one thing. Mel Gibson's Colonel Hal Moore in the film *We Were Soldiers*, fighting to survive as his position is overrun, is another. Punchy Colonels, even Generals, have always got themselves killed. Just not quite like this.

The gorse is still smouldering. I look back down the hill towards Darwin, bathed in sunlight. It is difficult to imagine that this was a scene of carnage and death only a few days ago.

We walk up to the Argie trenches on the lip of the hill. There are still human giblets in the bottom of some of them; the bits left over when the bodies were presumably removed for burial. The trenches have been ransacked, stuff lying everywhere.

I assume the Paras wanted the Argies' ammo and weapons – there are none lying around – as the enemy use variants of ours. I'm guessing our guys would have been very short of ammo. But it is more systematic than that. It is only later that I discover that the Argies have miniatures of whisky – 'The Breeder's Choice' (I still have a bottle with three handsome-looking bulls' heads on the label) – in their ration packs. Doubtless the Paras wanted the ration packs themselves.

2 Para attacked in 'belt order' (webbing only – no Bergens) and – I admit I'm guessing here – they probably needed everything they could grab just to keep themselves and their prisoners fed until they were re-supplied from San Carlos.

It is while inspecting the trenches that I decide – 2 Para heroics aside – that we will win this war. In some trenches I see plastic flip flops. *Flip flops?* At Goose Green? In midwinter? What sort of soldier would even think to remove his boots and wear flip flops in a trench in this cold and wet. What sort of officer would allow him to do so? It just doesn't make sense. At least not to me. These guys cannot be that well trained, or led.

It is only when I am back in England that I learn that many of the Argies were recruits who had no idea where they were being sent, or the conditions they would face. Hence, presumably, those weird, sad-looking, discarded flip flops.

'Two 1000 lbs UXB's (unexploded bombs), one "friendly", the other "enemy", both apparently made in Britain, and the sight of cartloads of Argentine dead still being brought for burial, indicated that we were at last catching up with the war. Any worries about the unexploded bombs were dispelled when a gargantuan pig tried to eat one; both bomb and pig survived.'

The bodies are in a hay trailer, pulled by a tractor. If it were not for the uniforms, weapons and bodies, the scene would all look so, well, normal and agricultural. The bodies have been chucked on board anyhow, and occasional arms and legs flop over the sides. Not disrespected in any way, but the exhausted soldiers detailed off to do this rotten job will not have the time or energy for any finesse.

Fortunately, I am too far away to see the dead faces and I have no desire to go further. That's enough 'sightseeing' for today.

I return to Darwin and the start of my life as a watchkeeper. It is night, and Adam and I are manning the nets. I am on 'G' (Operations) listening in on the 'forward' net to the battalions and the rear net to HQ LFFI (Land Forces Falklands Islands).

There is a Brigade HQ officer – I'll spare him the ignominy of being named all these years later – in charge. They also have a rota. He is senior to us. All the Brigade officers are.

Nothing is happening. The battalions have reported in for the night as per SOPs. We have their positions and those of their rifle companies, including inter-battalion boundaries marked on our map – very important for preventing any 'blue-on-blue' (friendly fire) incidents.

There is no Brigadier. Have I even seen him since we landed? I cannot remember now, but I am not sure I have. All is at peace and nothing moves, not even a mouse . . . You can picture the scene in that nice warm, dozy farmhouse; the cold, dangerous Falklands night kept firmly outside the closed front door.

Up on the radio come the Welsh Guards (I am 95 per cent sure it is them). There is a major problem. They are either in a minefield or being shelled. Perhaps both – I know that did happen to them at one point; they didn't know whether to stand and take the incoming 155mm shells 'like men', or dive to the ground and risk blowing themselves up on a mine. Not their most cheerful of evenings.

They need to move 'now!' They give me the grid reference of where they want to move to.

The inevitable 'Wait out' from me. I just listen to the nets and pass on anything important. I am not there to make decisions. End of.

Nothing unusual so far.

The brigade officer overseeing us and the net, who is *in loco* the Brigadier, rushes off to find someone senior to authorize the move. There are, it appears, when he returns, no senior people immediately to hand.

In the meantime, Adam and I have been discussing this situation and studying the map. We both agree that the suggested move looks thoroughly sensible. No risk of 'blue-on-blues', and it is not as if they are actually facing the Argies, who are nowhere near. They are simply hunkered down in the wrong spot and need to move.

However, knowing 5 Brigade, we two can predict where this might be going. Adam supports what I reckon will need to happen.

Sure enough, Brigade is not going to allow them to move without the say-so of the Brigadier.

The shelling or whatever has not stopped, and Welsh Guards are getting increasingly pissed off – frantic would be the wrong word, but they are sounding seriously unimpressed.

Time moves on. Did a colonel appear and just as quickly disappear, saying he was trying to get the Brigadier to authorize the move and to hold them there in the meantime? I think so, but I would not swear to it.

I have had enough. I turn to the staff officer and tell him that he has to allow them to move, on his own authority if need be.

'I can't do that. It's more than my job's worth.'

Do I say, 'Then fuck you . . .'? Probably not.

But I do tell him that I don't care about my job. I will give the order and I will take any adverse consequences that might flow from it. I might even have added that I have no desire to belong to an army where officers appear to care more about their next Annual Report than the lives of the men under their command, but I very much doubt it. One bit of gross insubordination is quite enough for the evening.

I order the battalion to move.

When I check this story out, no one I am still in contact with these days now seems to remember it. One does, however, say (is this confirmation I ask myself?), 'Well, we had moved by then in any event.' They're not stupid, the Welsh Guards.

Nothing more is ever said about the incident. By anyone. Although I wonder if what happened that night is not reflected in the 'Insert Slip' to my personal records that Brigadier Wilson writes about me after the war, and which Colonel James subsequently slides me a copy of. Lots of praise for my 'tact and confidence' and my 'reliable and responsible manner, although . . .' and here comes the stiletto to the future-career ribs, the word 'although' being a near-guaranteed precursor to any 'damning with faint praise': 'although he is clearly a man who finds it difficult to come to terms with dull and routine tasks . . .'

I would not argue with that. In fact I have always been rather proud of the Brigadier's criticism of me.

Will Townsend writes me a rather nice letter after we get back to England. 'Personal', not one for my Army file: 'Your constructive criticism certainly gave me no grounds for complacency.' What an irritant I must have been to everyone. Sorry Willie, but . . .

On 4 June the Brigadier finally puts in an appearance and addresses us. 'A chat', he calls it. **'Called at 15 minutes notice – in the wrong place,'** says my notebook.

I have grown wise to the Brigadier's predilection for grandstanding. I must be on my eight hours off when I am told to attend this 'chat', otherwise I'd be on the radios and not present. As he whiffles on, I take notes to demonstrate that I am paying attention. He's in his ever-impeccable uniform and inevitable shiny green Hunter wellies. 'Sharp as a carrot', as we say in The Blues and Royals. The rest of us are, however, looking mankier by the day.

For any ex-military these jottings will demonstrate how inherently chaotic this 'chat' is. This is not how it was meant to be done. And I – even sitting there on 4 June 1982 – made a couple of side/snide annotations about how rackety this was. He was effectively grandstanding to a captive audience – us. General Situation – our situation and that of the enemy. These notes are verbatim:

1. **OP still at Mount Usborne, FGA** (fighter ground attack) **and high level bombs.**
   Counter-offensive expected tomorrow and paras (attacking)
   a) Naval attack on (our) **capital ships**
   b) Attack on San Carlos – FGA etc (Fighter ground attack)
   c) Prestige attack on Darwin (a counter-attack by the Argies)

Friendly Forces
We are in great strength in Bluff Cove. Unloading chaotic – no local naval and air support. Only one Chinook left.
He [the Brigadier] then discussed the weather at length.

Enemy
There are many stay behind parties – Commandos etc.
Long chat about vagaries of loading/unloading. Bad luck etc
1/7th GR (Gurkha Rifles) in Darwin – one company. They marching here. Brigadier doesn't know where they are.
Problem: how do we use Snowcats (Royal Marine cross country vehicles) when we get them?
We can buy/ask for anything on Falklands, but sign receipts.
2 Para – 29 Battery forward but no ammo.
Brigade priorities:
Brigade HQ – establish properly

1. 29 Battery must be established properly. 500 rounds minimum.
2. Must get helicopters flying; fuel drama looming.
3. Welsh Guards marching forward to Hill House. Possibly tonight. 2 Para in very bad way – over 20 frostbite cases. They and Welsh Guards do not have their bergens.
4. 2 Scots Guards possibly LSL'ing (landing ship logistic – Galahad and Tristan) to Bluff Cove.
5. Wants Gurkhas forward for patrols and psychological value.

76 *Scimitar into Stanley*

    6. **Brigade has commandeered Monsoon – a Falkland Islands Company boat.** Hopefully sailing 1600 (Zulu) tomorrow with all 2 Para and 1 Company, 1/7 Gurkha Rifles kit. **This is now a 5 Brigade ship!!!**
    7. Also looking for a beached fast patrol boat.
    8. 2 x UXB's (unexploded bombs), **1000 lbs, need defusing.**
    9. Get telephones working.
  10. 1/7 Gurkhas plus mortar section in Land Rovers after (hunting down) **three (Argentine) stay behind parties**.

      a) A guide will take us over (by) track to Bluff Cove in 4–8 hours. Check all commandeerable vehicles. See what we can motor forward.
      b) Batch of journalists arriving: Brigadier – 'very keen they arrive' [My contemporary, cynical, emphasis on the Brigadier's enthusiasm for the media].
      c) 450 prisoners in sheep pens in Goose Green – rations running out. **Prisoners terrified of Gurkhas.**
      d) Use all captured weapons.
      e) The Blues and Royals to Bluff Cove.
      f) Fight for Stanley from Bluff.

Researching this book to make sure I have not got something 'wrong', or have misunderstood things, a chum directs me to the 'Phoenix Think Tank Report' given at the Australian Chief of Army History Conference, 2 October 2013. The author, Professor Eric Groves, describes what really happened amongst our High Command both in the Falklands, at sea, and back in London. It is eye-opening stuff to a mere participant like me.

Grove quotes Brigadier Ian Gardiner, who wrote a very highly regarded book about his experiences as a rifle company commander and what he subsequently discovered went on behind the scenes: *The Yompers: With 45 Commando in the Falklands War* (I have underlined certain key – nay, gobsmacking – words.)

> The methods applied [in the 5 Brigade advance] were controversial. It started (on 2 June) with 2 Para discovering by telephone that there were no Argentines in either Fitzroy or Bluff Cove. Now back under the command of 5 Infantry Brigade, <u>and with the agreement of their brigade commander Brigadier Wilson, 2 Para hijacked the</u>

precious single Chinook on 2 June and packing men in as if on a London tube they flew 50km forward and took possession of Fitzroy and Bluff Cove. They were now sitting on ground of great potential value, but they were also very isolated and vulnerable. They needed to be reinforced very quickly indeed. But an inherent problem was that the brigade was hobbled by poor communications and no transport of their own. They had no means to back this view up and had not consulted those upon whom they would have to depend to do so.

When he heard about it by accident, this bold but unilateral initiative placed the commander of land forces, Major General Moore, in a very difficult position. He either had to tell 5 Infantry Brigade to back them up. A withdrawal would have been humiliating for Wilson and the Paras and would have been difficult to explain to Northwood, forever looking for good news to give to the politicians. And yet to back them up would put even more strain on a fragile logistic chain which was already struggling to sustain 3 Commando Brigade in the north.

Moore chose to back them up. The advance along the southern route finished with the capture of Sapper Hill, twelve days later. In between these events, the Chinook and its strap-hanging Paras were very nearly destroyed by British artillery; 600 Scots Guardsmen were almost sunk at sea by British warships; four soldiers were killed by HMS *Cardiff* which shot down their helicopter; a landing craft from *Fearless* was bombed in Choiseul Sound, killing six men: and fifty men, mainly Welsh Guards, died when the Argentine Air force damaged *Sir Tristram* and destroyed *Sir Galahad*. Many more were injured. These disasters and near-disasters were individually the results of many and various factors, but they were all a part of a struggle to balance 5 Infantry Brigade after its initial, precipitate, ill thought-out move.

Further, Gardiner tells us that Wilson was causing so much concern that he was almost sacked, but 'In the event the problems of replacing a commander in the heat of battle outweighed those of any problems of personal leadership.'

Wow! I knew none of this.

But, even if I had known all this – not first agreeing this major change of strategy with General Moore excepted, that of course being astonishing behaviour by a subordinate commander on almost any analysis – I am not so sure I don't sympathize with Wilson's strategy of attacking on a broad front. Some of Gardiner's criticisms look to me to be a somewhat Commando-centric view of the war. It was as good as a given, especially after Goose Green, that the Commandos and Paras were going to defeat the enemy on their own. 5 Brigade were envisaged as little more than post-war 'Garrison Troops'. Remember the 'expert' predictions of it all being over by the time we arrived on the Islands, back when we left for the war? Now, however, given that the Argies were not yet defeated, the Commandos and Paras, it seems, had upgraded our role to that of a strategic reserve. Trudge behind them – I gather it was estimated to be a five-day march from San Carlos – and support them if required. I am rather with Brigadier Wilson on this. He, I now learn, thought that putting his Brigade on a war footing and travelling 8,000 miles just to be a strategic reserve, probably not see action, and let the Marines and Paras take all the laurels, was taking the piss somewhat. He wanted an 'equal' role for 5 Brigade, but wasn't getting it.

Also, I think he may have been more right on the overall strategy than he is credited with – since he is given the credit for nothing in the history books. I heard that on Tumbledown, and probably at Goose Green, it only took a few 'professionals' spread amongst the Argie conscripts to dig in and make a proper fight of it, for our troops to get into real difficulties and the attack to stall.

Bang! A sniper with a night sight takes down a soldier. Two of his comrades go to his assistance.

Bang! One of the two rescuers goes down.

Now there are two men on the ground and four men trying to help. That's most of the section of eight fully occupied and as good as out of action. It wouldn't have taken many more such men, not least as there were no direct fire weapons like our Scorpions and Scimitars to hand at either of those battles to blast out those snipers and machine-gun nests, for our attacks to have been slowed right down. Perhaps even stopped. Modern weapons, properly handled by well trained and determined soldiers, are fearfully efficient in defence.

So, what if we had attacked on a much narrower front, which was General Moore's original plan? What if more of the professionals in their army had been grouped together? Would they have been better able to confound or halt our attacks? Would we, with almost no heavy-lift helicopters, have run out of ammunition and steam? Who knows? What we do know, however, is that Wilson's broad-front strategy did work once General Moore chose to adopt it rather than sack him. The proof is that we won the war. And I for one am grateful not to have travelled all that way to the South Atlantic just to trudge along behind the Commandos and Paras. Yes, it would have been far safer but also dull; both conducive to a longer and healthier life. But 'safer' and 'dull' are two words that are never used in Army recruitment advertisements. And they certainly weren't in the lexicon of any cavalrymen I ever knew. For all of which, I now learn, I have Brigadier Wilson to thank.

In retrospect, the Brigadier must have flown to Darwin to give us our 'chat' fresh from playing high-level chess, having first got his way over there now being a 5 Brigade 'southern front', and second, having survived defenestration. No wonder he wants to tell us how clever he is.

And no wonder the Brigadier is so brutally cold-shouldered by the military establishment when he returns to England after the war. He receives no honour in recognition of his services and leaves the army seven months later, in January 1983. He is only forty-seven. Most who force their way that far up the greasy pole of high command retire at fifty-five.

As I listen, I have no idea of any of this. I doubt any of us do. Whilst I am pleased to be told what is going on, I wish the Brigadier would hurry it along as I am desperate to get back into my sleeping bag. My next eight-hour stag starts in a couple of hours. I need some sleep.

Chapter 12

The Power of Command

Sunday, 6 June. Gazelle of 656 AAC Sqdn accidentally shot down west of Fitzroy by Sea Dart SAM fired by HMS Cardiff (1.10 am). Pilot, Staff Sgt Griffin, crewman L/Cpl Cockton and two Royal Signals passengers killed. (www.naval-history.net/F63-Falklands-British_aircraft_lost.htm)

Life has turned into a rather dreary slog. We watchkeepers help update the maps and respond to stuff on the radio. We keep a log, an A4 page designed for this purpose, with lines of horizontal boxes. This from memory: 'Time of transmission. From/To [call signs]'. Then a brief précis of message. There is, perhaps, an 'action taken' box. I can no longer remember.

Each page has carbon under it so a copy transfers to the page below. Below that we place an A4 piece of cardboard which stops the writing going through to the third and subsequent pages. Get to bottom of page; tear off; put in pile; hand in at end of watch. What happens to them thereafter I have no idea. They are doubtless still being kept 'safe' and 'secret' somewhere.

We watchkeepers share a tent. The Gurkhas are defending Darwin. This is fine by day; they smile and salute us, and we reciprocate in kind. I feel super-safe with them here. Not, however, come nightfall. Few Gurkhas speak English, and I speak no Gurkhali. I have no desire to discuss tonight's password, in the pitch black, with a kukri-wielding fiend who is wondering whether I am a Brit or an Argie. I avoid all Gurkha positions come dark.

Adam is prepared for most eventualities. He not only brought his SLR but also a 9mm pistol. He has taken to sleeping with it 'to hand'.

Watch over one night, I move as quietly as possible back into the tent and my sleeping bag. Snick, snick – the unmistakable sound of the well-oiled top cover of a pistol being pulled back and then released. A 9mm round feeds into the chamber.

'Put it away, Adam.'

'Okay.' The multiple snicks of a pistol being unloaded and then half loaded.

'Good night.'

'Good night.'

It is the 'wee', hours of 6 June. My memory is that it is black and windy. Raining even, but I have no diary entry to confirm this. Google tells me the moon is full, and *5th Infantry Brigade in the Falklands* says that it is a 'fine' night. I am not so sure about that, not least as, out on the water a few miles to our south, the books record that the Scots Guards are being pounded by heavy seas as they make their way in four open LSLs (landing craft) towards Bluff Cove, a few miles further along the coast from Fitzroy. I doubt that many of them would describe the weather that night as 'fine'. Then again, a 'fine' night in the Falklands in winter would probably be categorized as a 'grotty' night almost anywhere else in the world.

I'm on watch and it's super-tense in the Ops Room.

The Brigadier is here and he's in a mood. The whole of 2 Para, now back under command of 5 Brigade, is in Fitzroy, over 30 miles away, on the east side of the Island. They are about to be reinforced by the Scots Guards in those wave-lashed LSLs. I have no idea about the pressure the Brigadier must be under, having 'hijacked' the whole land campaign and 'opened' a southern front. He needs to make this reinforcing movement work or, I realize writing this now, he'll be out on his ear.

On the surface there's little going on; certainly, little actual fighting.

In the north, 3rd Commando Brigade – and again, it is the Phoenix Report which only now reveals the extent of our Brigadier's evident need to, if not beat, then certainly match Brigadier Thompson's achievements – are yomping (Marines) and tabbing (Paras) towards Teal Inlet, a small settlement on the direct San Carlos to Port Stanley track.

Meanwhile, 5 Brigade are looping up from the south. But first, like a lion preparing to spring at its prey, we have to position our forces and gather supplies of ammo, food, water and petrol where we need them. Only when they are in place and in sufficient quantities can the Brigadier give the order 'Attack!'

The Brigadier demands to speak to 2 Para. Today we can chat on our mobiles, or satellite phones, to someone on top of a Himalaya or in a distant jungle. Back then, 'poor comms' are a frequent and massive problem. The Brigade has very recently been issued with state-of-the-art (at least compared to the previous generation of 'Larkspur' equipment) Clansman radios. Sometimes they work very well, albeit over shortish distances. At other times they can be pretty punk. Sometimes we struggle to speak to someone a few miles away.

Compounding matters is a range of high hills between us at Darwin and 2 Para at Fitzroy. Radio waves want to travel in straight lines, and high hills can cause havoc with that. Havoc is, in fact, putting it mildly; chances are that the hills mean that we will probably be unable to communicate direct with 2 Para.

Then add to that the fact that radio comms always get far worse at night, and we have a double comms problem. I can tell you that the 'ionosphere' is to blame for poor radio reception at night. I remember this much from my Signals lectures at Bovington, without ever understanding a) what part of the ionosphere is actually to blame, or b) what the ionosphere is, or does. But I can look anyone military, apart from the Royal Signals, in the eye and know I speak with authority when I tell them the ionosphere *is* to blame.

Major Mike Forge (Royal Signals), the Brigade Signals Officer, has predicted this and established a 'Rebro' (rebroadcast) station on top of Pleasant Peak, the intervening highest point between Darwin and Fitzroy, 750ft up. The Rebro Station comprises a couple of specialist signallers with two radios and a 'magic' connector box freezing their nuts off in a tent. When we in Brigade want to talk to 2 Para we talk to radio 'One' in the Rebro Station on top of that peak on our Brigade frequency. This means that our radio waves go up to the Peak in a straight line. The magic box receives our signal from radio 'One' and gives it to radio 'Two', which automatically rebroadcasts it forward – now downhill in a straight line – to 2 Para on their different Para frequency. And it's vice versa when they speak to us. It is as if we are talking to them direct.

Unless something goes wrong.

Tonight something has gone wrong.

The Brigadier is in the Ops Room demanding and failing to speak to 2 Para 'now!'

Not least because there's nothing on the other nets for me to record, I have been told to surrender my usual chair in front of the map. I sit by the door and listen to the spiralling argument.

Mike's view – given that the Rebro station has not been taken out by the Argies, which seems unlikely as Pleasant Peak is now technically in 'friendly' territory, although who knows what is really up there as nobody has 'cleared' the ground – is that there are five possibilities.

First, some sort of mechanical problem. Unlikely, as comms were working earlier, but possible.

Second, the radio batteries have gone flat. Quite possible. This cold, damp weather degrades batteries very quickly.

Third and fourth are a sort of either/or or both combo. It is now after midnight. The frequencies have to be manually changed at midnight (we do this to confuse the enemy). Have the two operators been issued with the correct new frequencies? It is not unknown for mistakes to happen. One number out and that is goodbye comms. If they have, have they dialled them in correctly? 'Finger trouble' is not unknown, especially on a cold South Antarctic night on top of a 'peak'.

Or fifth, are the two men on that exposed hilltop hunkered down in their green maggots, just trying to stay warm, and have they slept through the midnight frequency switch-over? Possible.

Who knows? Because neither Mike nor the Brigadier do.

And, given the Paras did their midnight frequency switch correctly – or did they? A new set of variables – they will probably not be concerned by the silence from our end; they will assume there is nothing we want to say to them. It is a golden rule of signals that the less you say on your radio the better. First, this minimizes the chances of the enemy finding your frequency and listening in; and second, it minimizes the chances of the enemy vectoring in on your radio and dropping a salvo of shells on you.

The Paras may not even know there's a problem. They will doubtless be only too delighted not to have Brigade bending their ear about whatever bee is currently buzzing around under the Brigadier's red beret.

Doubtless there are all sorts of signals SOPs for this very scenario, but if there are, they are not working.

The Brigadier is not interested in Mike's explanations. He needs to speak to Fitzroy. Mike is his Brigade Signals Officer. Mike, he says, needs to get up on that peak and make the Rebro work. Now.

Mike says that it is not for him to go.

The Brigadier as good as demands he does. I won't swear he orders him to go – although he may have – but he makes it very clear that he considers it Mike's job to do so.

This to my mind is bonkers. Mike is a major. He runs the whole Brigade signals net, and much more beside. He is not a 'sparkie' with a screwdriver who fixes radios, or checks the frequency settings, or delivers fresh batteries. He's got guys under command who do just that.

Nor is he the person who administers a size 10 boot to the bum of sleeping soldiers. A sergeant does that.

But the Brigadier wants Mike.

Someone from 657 Squadron AAC is summoned. This is an emergency. Can they task a Gazelle to fly two signallers up to Pleasant Peak to sort out the problem?

Those Army Air Corps pilots have balls of steel; indeed, I think theirs are twice the size of most males of the human species. During UK-based training exercises those 656 Squadron jokers have flown me under electricity power lines just to see if I threw up. They failed.

But as we 'passengers' clamber into their tiny recce helicopters, they issue us with a brown paper bag in case they succeed. Nobody who has flown with those loons ever needs to get on a fairground ride again. Ever. What could possibly be scary about the world's largest rollercoaster after you've been 'contour flying' with 656 Squadron?

Nor do Gazelles have radars or anything sophisticated. The pilots like to say they use IFR ('I Follow Roads'). But there are no roads in the Falklands. The pilots use primitive night sights. They won't be able to see much, if anything.

I'm going with my dark, rotten night memory. I wouldn't have sent a helicopter out there. But what do I know?

Of course they'll do it.

An ex-656 Squadron chum, reading this chapter for general accuracy, tells me that the pilot always has the last word on whether to fly. Although he adds: 'It was said in the AAC (Army Air Corps) that Brigadiers were the most "at risk" passengers. They were too senior for pilots to easily overrule about flying and too junior not to be worried if it was seen they were being overruled by a pilot.'

Mike has become something of a chum on the trip south. He's got a zany sense of humour – he's the one who issued Brigade Orders for 23 May with the existentialist exam questions for his infantry platoon. He is also highly efficient. He makes things work and, above all, has the good taste to appear to enjoy our equally irreverent sense of humour – in stark contrast to some of the ever more careworn-looking brigade officers.

Mike gathers his kit. He's a tough guy, and now he's tried and been overruled he shows no emotion.

The Brigadier studies the map, doubtless pleased to have so publicly exercised his will. As Mike passes me on his way out he rolls his eyes and gives me a rueful half-smile.

I shake my head slightly in response, careful not to be seen doing so. He and I both think that this is little more than a fit of petulance. Does the Brigadier need to speak to 2 Para so badly that he has to send somebody that night? With all the risks? Maybe. Maybe not. That decision is way above my pay grade, although as I sit there watching this I think not.

Turns out I am wrong. He did need to. Badly.

Next morning, the Phoenix Report now tells me, four Scots Guards LSLs arrive in Bluff Cove Inlet. Sergeant Morgan, Royal Artillery, is startled to see what could be an Argie invasion force. With no comms back to Brigade, nobody has told him about the imminent arrival of reinforcements. Going to 'action stations' (or whatever they do in the Gunners), he orders his gun team 'A' to prepare to engage over 'open sights' – meaning the target ships are so close that his gun will fire flat and 'direct' instead of lobbing their shells up into the air and then down on to the target. The two other guns in the battery 'stand to'. A couple of salvos at that range and there will be four LSLs and 600 Scots Guards at the bottom of Bluff Cove Inlet.

Nor do 2 Para know about the imminent arrival of the Scots Guards. This is the 'fog of war' with knobs on – which the Brigadier tried to 'clear' by sending the Gazelle to get the comms working.

Only now, almost 40 years later, do I understand why. Somebody needed to go. But, should he have as good as forced Mike to go? Absolutely not.

Mike and I grin at each other and he is gone.

In *5th Infantry Brigade in the Falklands* the authors state that Brendan Lambe (the Brigade Major, whom they interviewed) ordered Staff Sergeant Baker of the Signals squadron to be i/c the task – which makes sense to me. This frequency-changing, arse-kicking job is one for a (staff) sergeant. However, the book says, 'Major Forge then unexpectedly arrived and insisted on accompanying Baker.'

Hmm . . .

I hear the helicopter take off. About ten minutes later, someone from 656 comes into the Ops Room. They've lost contact with the Gazelle. They have a bad feeling that's it's been lost. It could be radio failure, but they suspect not. The radios were working fine only moments before. Engine failure? Crash? A stay-behind patrol? Nobody knows. Pretty soon we learn that it has been shot down.

It is only years later that I read that, unknown to 5 Brigade, the Navy has instituted a 'shoot to kill box' that covers Pleasant Peak. HMS *Cardiff* sees a radar bleep heading towards Port Stanley within said 'box' and, assuming it is enemy, gives it two Sea Dart missiles. The second one hits. Everyone aboard is killed.

Nothing is said in the Ops Room that I can remember. There's nothing to be said. The Brigadier exits stage left before too long. There is no more talk about needing to speak to 2 Para until the morning.[1]

---

1. The Marines, I later read, who work with the Navy all the time, have a naval liaison officer at 3 Brigade HQ to stop something like this happening. 5 Brigade, however, is Army, and has no experience of working with the Navy, and vice versa. Hence...

Chapter 13

'Bloodied but unbowed'. Wazzock!

Cryptic diary note: '**8 June: Galahad and Tristram bombed. Terrifying afternoon in cattle sheds.**'

On 6 June I crawl into my sleeping bag at some stage but only get a few hours' sleep. With very limited access to helicopters, a very trimmed-down Brigade 'step-up' HQ will fly to Fitzroy. Adam gets the nod, and since I am (as my diary says) '**to advise Brigade on the correct deployment and use of the two troops of The Blues and Royals armoured recce who have come under command of 5 Brigade**', I go as well.

There's no time to mourn Mike. We have little idea what happened except that there was an explosion. The Rebro team, I later learn, were trying to move to a better position to re-establish comms and saw the fireball. We assume it is either an Argie missile or a 'stay-behind' patrol. It is only persistence from the families in demanding an inquiry that finally forces the MoD to admit it was an 'own goal'. What is it about our British governing class's knee-jerk instinct to cover up mistakes and declare them a 'secret'? It was a mistake. An awful mistake. But such things happen in war. Always have, always will. It is an insult to the families to try to cover it up. It's enough to make anybody wonder what else they might be hiding.

I expect to be more upset than I am about the waste of such a good officer, a man I like. I put this coldness down to my experiences in Northern Ireland, a hardening of my sensibilities.

Anyway, there's going to be a lot more death before this luxury cruise 'down south' is over. That said, I cannot shake the memory of Mike's half-smile to me as he walked out of the Ops Room, and I am deeply pissed off with the Brigadier

I may be a captain working in Brigade HQ, relatively senior in the rank structure on the islands, but I am still something of a mushroom, 'kept in the dark and fed on shit'. I do not know what is going on much of the time. Or, put another way, I don't know why things are happening. That 4 June 'chat' that I was so scathing about in my notebook turns out to be a one-off. Mostly I just listen, record, say 'Wait out' as I pass on messages where necessary, and start over again eight hours later. Right now, I wouldn't mind a few more 'chats'.

However, this deadly foul-up does play directly to my 'These bozos are going to get me killed' theory of existence. So, fellow watchkeepers, we are reasonably safe back at HQ, are we? Tell that to Mike and the three others in that Gazelle. Next time, it could be one of us ordered on to a helicopter to do whatever, for no better reason than the Brigadier wants an officer there. And nobody can argue with the Brigadier. Even when he's getting you killed.

I cannot be totally out of the information loop as I am hearing good things about the performance of The Blues and Royals, as my *Guards Magazine* article tells me:

> The two troops had driven over the mountains from Teal Inlet on their own. Brigade reckoned it might take two days. They made it in about six hours. The exceptional cross country performances of CVR(T) [Combat Vehicle Reconnaissance Tracked] in the hands of experienced drivers had scored its first major success.

My memory is that I hear that the Commando Snow Cats are coping with the conditions, but only just. They may be the dog's *cojones* on the snow and ice of Norway, but this is sodden bog and rocky scrabble. Our Scorpions and Scimitars, with amazingly low ground pressure per square inch on their wide tracks (I remember being told that the imprint is lower than the pressure of a human's boot) roar over this terrain. The grunts are amazed. And they have guns. Big guns. And machine guns. And they can give lifts. And help carry kit. No mention now of their being 'more trouble than they are worth'.

This explains a cryptic list of headings I have in my notebook for my still to be delivered 'Scorpions and Scimitars' talk for the Brigadier. If you remember, the busy Brigadier spent so much time on *QE2* 'laughing with Linda' Kitson that he never had time to listen to my briefing. Maybe he'll find time now?

I'm not holding my breath. In what follows, my verbatim briefing notes are in **bold**. The rest I have added to make better sense of them and add context.

1. Must not use for barrages

The infantry love the idea of using the small 76mm gun on the Scorpion as an artillery piece – turning them into a highly mobile gun platform. The artillery has 105mm guns towed by Land Rover and (I think) Snow-cats. Or the 105s need to be underslung from helicopters and flown forwards as there are no proper roads, only the occasional track.

This idea is totally inappropriate. The 76mm shell (forget the 30mm on the Scimitar) is far too small and has too little explosive in it to be an effective area artillery weapon, although they will turn out to be highly effective when fired at sangars (semi-trenches/semi-strong points) built into the rocks on Wireless Ridge; lots of shrapnel and stone splinters zinging around.

Just as important, the Scorpions will need their limited supply of main armament 76mm shells to fight the 90mm French-built Argie Panhards when the time comes.

The best weapon on the island for knocking out an armoured car is another armoured car. Run out of ammo, or wear out our guns – so killing their accuracy – and it will be the Panhards chewing us up, instead of us mullering them.

On the Top Trumps of a Western European battlefield – for example against the Russians; these are still Cold War days after all – our vehicles are deemed pretty puny weapons systems. Our skill is very much in sneaking around, remaining undetected and reporting back. Our cannons and machine guns, we are taught, are a last resort, not least as they won't penetrate tank armour.

However, in the kingdom of the blind the one-eyed man truly is king, and down here in a world of infanteers we look like the armaments equivalent of a Chieftain main battle tank. Which means that the infantry will doubtless want to misuse us as both tanks – which we are not – and artillery. Hence my urgent need to brief the Brigadier.

Failing him, someone . . . anyone . . .

2. 2 Para said that RHG/D [The Blues and Royals] would have been key to stand off at approx. 1000 – 1500 [yards] and take out strong points which Paras had to use Milan and 84mm [anti-tank missiles] on. They ran out of these at

Darwin [Goose Green] **as a result Col. [H] killed because no one could take out S.P.** [strong point].

Which is exactly what I want them to do in any set piece battle, and is what we train for.

3. **Could carry 5 men tactically max. Commander opened up. Driver difficult to see.**

This refers to doubling them up as troop carriers, an amazing added extra on an island where it is pretty much helicopter or walk. We will happily oblige.

4. **POL** [petrol, oil, lubricants] **problem urgent with 34** [meaning 3 and 4 troops].

5. **Can take out Panhard at 1500 +** [yards-plus].

Exactly! And what else can take on their Panhards apart from anti-tank missiles, which will have to be carried into battle, and the infantry will need for strong points as well?

Apologies. I'll go with a spoiler here. I never get to give even this shortened five/ten-minute version to the Brigadier, or any of his staff. *Quelle surprise* . . .

We helicopter to Fitzroy, where some tactical genius has put Brigade HQ in a large, enclosed, wiggly tin sheep-shearing shed. Just in case any Argie fighter pilots fail to spot exactly where we are, there are tall antennae outside and trenches dug around it. X marks the spot, Jorge and Pablo, should you find it difficult to spot us.

I'm not complaining about this staggering lack of tactical nous, however, although I should be. This sheep shed may not be a fraction as warm and comfy as that farmhouse in Darwin, but HQ is at least out of the wind and rain, although the floor is concrete. Not recommended, though, should things that go bang land and explode on it. Shrapnel and chunks of concrete will fly everywhere. Concrete, however, is excellent for keeping feet, if not warm, then dry. Unlike mud.

Hands up here. Sitting for eight-hour stretches at a time, I am content to be as tactically unprofessional as my 5 Brigade bosses if it means remaining dry. Because, let's face it, I never thought we'd be attacked either.

Adam and I 'liberate' a flimsy wood table and a couple of school chairs. The radios are beside us on more tables. As G 'Forward' net I have an extra radio which I will use to talk to the RFA (Royal Fleet Auxiliary) landing ships *Sir Galahad* and *Sir Tristram*. They are bringing up the Welsh Guards and other elements of 5 Brigade, along with massive quantities of stores; everything we need for the big leap forward to Stanley.

I went on board *Sir Galahad* when she docked in Belfast with The Royal Green Jackets aboard in February 1979. We drove to the docks; quite some distance in our stripped-down – no roof or doors – Land Rovers, driving Irish rain doing its miserable normal. Our job was to escort them to their barracks. By the time we got to the docks we were wet through and frozen. I can still remember the Hong Kong Chinese crew welcoming us with huge smiles, cups of steaming hot coffee and heaped plates of chips. I could murder a plate of *Galahad* chips and lashings of ketchup right now.

The two ships arrive tomorrow, and I will be the contact man between them and HQ as they disembark and unload. In the meantime, we are protected by 2 Para, who are dug in around us. Scots Guards are a few miles up the coast at Bluff Cove. Welsh Guards will be joining them. Another 24 hours in watchkeeping paradise beckons, although this time with no shift relief, as Adam and I are the only two watchkeepers here.

The morning of 8 June is crisp and clear. Someone, I know not who, is really worried about a suspected enemy OP on top of Mount Harriet to our east, in the direction of Port Stanley. If we can see the top of the mountain in the clear morning air, then anyone up there with a pair of binoculars can study us, and the two huge ships now sitting just off Fitzroy. None of us in 5 Brigade has experienced the terrors of San Carlos Water – 'Bomb Alley' – and we've seen no enemy aircraft since landing. That doubtless makes us far too cavalier in our attitude to the air threat. I let all this slide over me. I am not too worried, although I am not over-impressed to be sitting on a concrete floor in a large shed, with lots of antennae and surrounded by trenches, in sight of that Argie OP. How would my Sandhurst instructors have scored me for such a tactical decision?

Nul points. 'Move! Now!'

But did I think we would be attacked? No. Those who had survived the air battles over San Carlos knew otherwise. Brigadier Thompson was later quoted as saying, 'I can tell you, if I'd have been on board that ship I would have swum ashore rather than stay there.'

Someone else, I know not who, is very worried about the fact the Welsh Guards are still on those ships. I thought it was the commanding officer of the Welsh Guards – two companies were landed yesterday and are also now dug in around Bluff Cove – but I subsequently discover it cannot be him as he is up there with his men. This guy is kneeling on the floor beside me, desperate to get the men off first. Pleading, almost. He asks to use my dedicated shore-to-ship radio, and of course I oblige. I fully agree with his sentiments, although nobody cares what I think.

The trouble as I see it is the usual one. There's no Brigadier. I have not seen him since leaving Darwin yesterday. There appears to be an agreed unloading plan, and the only way it gets changed is if someone senior – the Brigadier, for instance – orders it. And as I now know after the near-hissy fit about me unilaterally moving the Welsh Guards a few days ago, no Brigadier, no change. Nobody dares.

One of the landing craft ferrying troops and supplies from boat to shore develops ramp problems, slowing things down even more.

I remember someone's fury that the plan dictates that the Rapier anti-aircraft missile battery is unloaded as a priority. What I don't know – my ignorance of Rapier is as complete as the infantry's about our Scorpions and Scimitars – is that it takes time to get them set up and working. They are brilliant, I gather, when they work. But they won't. Not for hours.

But what do I know? This all seems like a fairly standard army SNAFU or 'Clusterfuck', to use the American expression. But not a humungous, lethal Clusterfuck.

Did I expect 5 Brigade to be super-efficient? As you will have realized by now, no.

But they don't seem to be doing too badly today, all things considered. Stuff is being unloaded, albeit slower than anybody would like. The sun is shining at last, and if my bum was not getting numb from endless hours sitting beside this radio, I might even be smiling.

I have been on watch for 18 hours straight when someone finally tells me to take some time out and get some food down me. My eyes are hanging out and I am starving. When you are cold, your body burns more calories trying to stay warm and you get hungrier. I am a tall guy and I am hungry. Time for food.

'**Sitting in barn chatting to journalists** [Michael Nicholson, ITV] **cooking up frankfurters for lunch.**' Where I get the 'frankfurters' from is a puzzle. They are definitely not standard army issue.

I like the journalists. They are irreverent and fun and talk about stuff other than the army. They are the proverbial breath of fresh air. They seem to like me too, although – I am not completely naïve about this and I later write for newspapers and magazines so learn how it really works – they are doubtless 'grooming' me as a possible source. Be nice to everyone if you are a journalist, you have no idea when they might come in useful. Especially in a war . . .

Maybe it is today, more likely tomorrow when the press descend on Fitzroy en masse, that a well-fed Colonel who looks as if he has been camping out beside a warship cookhouse takes me aside and warns me off. It has been noted, he tells me, looking suitably colonelish, that I have been 'fraternizing' with the press.

I hope I tell him that they seem to know more about what is going on than I do at Brigade HQ (they do – although whether their information is accurate is an entirely different matter) and that they have a far better line in jokes. But whatever I do say makes him very cross. He gives me an 'Official warning'. He sounds like a junior school master, all talk and no power. What's he going to do about it? Do me a huge favour and take me off my endless radio watch? Pillock!

Anyway, although I do not justify my actions by telling him this, I am all too aware of our anger as we sat on *Canberra* listening to the BBC announce, to us, the Argentines and the world, exactly where to find us the next day – landing at San Carlos. Does he take me for an idiot? I would not dream of telling the journos anything. I enjoy their company and I am not going to stop talking to them just because this clean, shiny, self-important prat tells me to.

My next memory is sitting in a small workroom off a barn cooking those franks with Mike Nicholson and having a laugh with him. It is not impossible that they are his and he is sharing them with me. I've got a mess tin, hexi blocks (vicious little firelighter things that are used to boil water and heat food) and a mini cooker. That would be a fair swap – he provides the food, I cook it.

'**Air Alert Red – ignored**'. What form the alarm took I no longer remember – whistle blasts, I think, and much yelling of 'Air Raid' – but the alarm definitely 'went'. Mike, war reporter, veteran of Vietnam and other wars, looks at me for guidance. Old soldier that I am, never having been under air attack, I am making a nice cup of coffee, using the boiling water I used to heat the tin of frankfurters.

'Ignore it,' I say. 'Bound to be a false alarm.' I look for a sachet of sugar.

Then – are those aircraft?

CRACK! BOOM! The sharp and then deep sounds blast across the settlement. Boom! Boom!

Even as the first of the bombs hits I am hurling myself under a large, solid, carpenter's table. A nanosecond later, Mike lands on top of me. Perfect. I now have two layers of overhead protection.

We wait. Silence. No more bombs.

Then action. Mike is straight off, he has a job to do. So do I.

Gather cooking kit and store in pouches. If Rule One of the army is 'Never volunteer', Rule Two is 'Hold tight to your things or you will never see them again.'

Cooking kit stowed in seconds, I head back to the sheep shed. No running – it achieves nothing and only panics the troops. The time for running is when someone is shooting at you.

Over the hill I can see a thickening pall of black smoke. This looks bad. The Argies must have hit one or both of the ships.

Headphones back on, I am once again in control of my radios. I start noting the messages in and out on the official pad. I write furiously, and the sheets of paper pile up beside me. Everyone is demanding to know exactly what is going on but we, only a few hundred yards away, have little idea beyond the absolute basics. Apart from the fact that we are in a windowless sheep shed, there is a long, low hill between us and the burning ships. I might have been 'there' but it is only when I get home and watch the TV footage that I see for myself what happened.

For a moment the historian in me wonders whether to slip that A4 piece of cardboard down an extra layer and keep a page for myself. Something to show my children, if I survive to have any, that is. I dismiss the thought. Keeping a sneaky copy of who is saying what to whom doesn't sit right, not with those ships fiercely ablaze a few hundred yards away and reports of the scale of the human tragedy unfolding getting ever worse. Anyway, no point, they'll be little more than sodden throwaways in no time on this godforsaken, rain-lashed island.

Nothing from the forward link to the ships. I don't try to speak to them. They have enough going on without someone safe on shore asking questions.

The books on the subject tell me that about 50 minutes of this elapse as the troops on shore wade into the icy waters to pull the survivors in their lifeboats and rafts on to land, and the helicopter boys fly into the smoke and flames and exploding ammunition to winch the guys out.

'I was only scared twice during the campaign. The first was the day *Sir Galahad* was hit and I was on duty, on the radio, in a shed, on a concrete floor; nowhere to take cover; unable to see what was going on, with airplanes howling overhead; waiting for a bomb. Since I was on the radio we heard the reports from the forward troops.'

Scots and Welsh Guards radio in: 'Four aircraft'. The sound of gunfire clear in the background. Machine guns, rifles. Our boys are giving them everything. 'Over our position, NOW! With you in two minutes.'

All we could do was lie on the concrete floor. It was a very unnerving first experience of battle.'

'Zero' – that's me. 'Roger. Out.'

Now I'm shouting. I never shout. Like running, it causes panic. But now *is* the time to shout. 'Air Raid Red! Everyone OUT!'

That sheep shed empties in seconds. But someone has to man the radios, forwards and back. And those someones are Adam and I. We are the only two left.

Nice concrete floor to take cover on. Under the flimsy school table we go. Adam warns 'rear' on his radio about what will soon be heading their way. There follows one of the more surreal conversations I have ever had.

'How does a Rolo sound, Adam?' I ask, super-polite.

Our 'Arctic' ration packs include many more varieties of chocolates and sweets than the 'standard' Western Europe pack, Rolos among them. I like Rolos. As do most of us. In fact, they are considered a bit of a delicacy. They not only taste delicious but the toffee interiors jam between your teeth. It can take many contented minutes to prise the sticky goo from between your molars with the tip of your tongue. All of which wastes more minutes of tedium and discomfort in a thoroughly pleasant, lip-smacking way.

I proffer my packet.

'Oh, I couldn't possibly take one of yours,' says Adam. 'You must have one of mine.' He digs into a pocket, takes out his Rolos and offers them to me. 'I insist.'

'Oh, no. I couldn't possibly accept that. I offered mine first . . .'

I am about as scared as I have ever been. Four Argie jets with us in moments. Adam and I and Brigade HQ – he and I are at that moment Brigade HQ – have to be a top target.

So the pair of us continue to debate whose Rolos we should eat. Anything to take our minds off what is coming next.[1]

We are still discussing this important issue when Fitzroy erupts. Gunfire everywhere. Machine guns – .50s and GPMGs – SLRs, even Stirling sub machine guns, I learn later.

I lie there waiting for the worst. Muscles tensed. Sounds of planes roaring beside and overhead. Low. Then silence.

Back on the radio to the Welsh Guards. 'Confirm four planes'. Yes, they confirm, four planes.

And yes, shouts from the trenches outside, four planes went past.

'Air raid over'.

Everyone wanders back in. Some look very chipper to have loosed off their weapons 'in anger', chatting about it. No suggestions of first reading the Argies the Yellow Card before they squeezed the trigger, I note . . .

The Welsh and Scots Guards are claiming hits from their .50 machine gun sections. Chunks were seen coming off the aircraft. It is later (after the war) confirmed that all four were damaged by small-arms ground fire. None knocked down, though, and they 'just' make it back to the mainland.

We go back into our routine.

Welsh Guards: 'Four more Skyhawks'. I again hear gunfire from their end as they talk to me. 'Heading towards you'.

'Air Raid Red!' This from me.

'Here we go again,' I think, gut knotting, as the shed empties and Adam and I get back under our table. We both reach for our packets of Rolos, ready to resume our time- and fear-deadening debate.

Major Barney Rolfe-Smith, a Para who is on the Brigade staff, a good guy who talks sense – and may well have been talking on the rear radio at the time – tells us to go outside and grab a trench. It doesn't need all three of us to get killed. This time he will man the radios alone.

He's right. It only needs one in here for the next few minutes, although I would have no more left Adam alone than he would have left me.

---

1. Anyone who nonchalantly watches TV news footage of civilians being shelled or bombed in Syria, or wherever, ought to sit on a concrete floor with the sound of approaching bombers low overhead. Man's cruelty to his fellow man. In fact, I prefer not to watch it. It can become overwhelming.

I am pretty certain I said, 'Are you sure?' Good military manners dictate that one should sound suitably coy at these rather tense moments, but I am delirious with agreement. Nor can I remember Adam arguing.

We run outside. Hotfooting it hard and fast with four Skyhawks screaming towards you is entirely legitimate in my 'not panicking the troops' lexicon. The trenches are full. We run up a hillside and find an empty hole.

Aircraft noise. I may have caught a glimpse of a high-speed, low-flying speck for a split second, but that is it. No chance to fire our weapons. Which pisses Adam and me off, for two reasons.

First, we would have loved to. Some payback, however small and doubtless ineffectual, for what the Argies have just done to us.

Second, on some long-ago, Harvey Wallbanger-fuelled, tropical night on *QE2*, we six watchkeepers made a quasi-bet-cum-pact. If any of us fire our weapon 'in anger/for real' – we know what we mean – then the non-firers will buy the shooters a bottle of champagne. This would have been a champagne moment, no ifs, no buts, and a definite 'one up' for Adam and me.

Yes, I know. Soldiers can be overgrown children when it comes to guns. But we join up to play with guns.

What does happen, though, is something I still wonder if I have dreamt, for I can find no reference to it elsewhere, not even in General Frost's 2 Para book, which is where it naturally belongs. And it is such a good story that its omission from the histories worries me; makes me wonder if I have been imagining it these past decades. The human brain can play some strange tricks, I know. But I don't think so.

Up above our trench, on the top of a low hill, is one of those Rapier missiles. It is a big bugger. It looks menacing and dangerous on its launcher, all set up and ready to rock and roll. One account I do find on the internet about events at Fitzroy on 8 June is from a Rapier corporal. He recounts pressing the trigger as the Skyhawks fly by and nothing happening.

Maybe that 'no-fire' occurs during one of the two earlier waves. Because this Rapier fires.

It immediately starts corkscrewing. Goes perhaps a couple of hundred feet, almost straight up, in an ever more erratic way and then breaks apart.

The tail section falls straight back down and lands right beside a trench just down the hill from us. A Para gets out. Picks up the tail section. Hefts it over his shoulder. Marches back up the hill to where the Rapier crew are now cowering in their trench.

'If you ever . . . bleep, bleep, bleep . . . you useless wankers . . . bleep, bleep, bleep.' I cannot remember his exact words. But they are choice. And he throws the tail at them.

My first reaction is to laugh. This is so very 'army'. But I then see that the Para is really, really, really unamused; furious at seeing the waves of attacks going in; the smoke billowing from the burning ships over the opposite ridge; the Rapier misfire and then being nearly killed by the tail fin falling on his head. He doesn't see anything funny about this.

I keep my face straight as he storms back down the hill to his trench. I hope I have not imagined it, and I can only apologise if I have . . .

I later learn that two of our Harriers chase that last wave of four Skyhawks back towards Argentina and knock down three with their Sidewinder missiles.

Back to the sheep-shearing shed we go, and back on to the radios. At some stage Brigade 'Main' arrives and the other watchkeepers relieve us. Adam and I have pushed about 24 hours straight by now, and what with Mike two days ago and this today, I am feeling a trifle stretched. Time for bed.

But no. The Brigadier has sent instructions that he wants to talk to us. Nobody is to go to bed. We are to remain in the shed and wait for him.

When will he arrive?

Not sure, but soon, they hope.

We wait. And wait. How long I cannot remember. I do recall getting cold and slightly shivery just waiting there with nothing now to occupy me. There's nothing to say. There are fifty dead and upwards of a hundred and fifty wounded; numbers still approximate. Every conceivable conversation is too depressing; other possible conversations inappropriate. Dark army humour will usually find a way. But not tonight. Now, there is quite simply nothing to say.

It is pitch black when the Brigadier does finally appear, fresh-faced, natty green Hunters, warry red beret. He gathers us around, much as Montgomery used to in those posed newsreels with his troops just before the Battle of El Alamein.

'We're bloodied but unbowed . . .', he starts by saying.

I'm pretty sure those were his words, or something very similar. I've never read these words anywhere else and so cannot confirm this. Nor did I diary it. I was too damned tired and despondent to do so.

Up to the moment the Brigadier starts speaking I consider what has happened as nothing more than terrible luck. That it is 5 Brigade that has managed to engineer this monumental balls-up does not surprise me. But I do not blame 5 Brigade, or the Brigadier, as such, although, as ever, a little worm at the back of my brain is telling me that, had he been in the shed and controlling operations today, he could have changed the unloading plan and ordered the Welsh Guards off the ship double-quick-sticks. And the worst of this would have been avoided. Ifs, however, are all too easy in hindsight.

But hearing his ill-considered opening words, I feel something far stronger than disdain.

We lost almost half a Guards battalion today; dead and wounded, the survivors without their kit, rendering them *hors de combat*. We lost two major ships. Not, it is already beginning to seem, as part of the vicious cut and thrust of warfare – casualties the inevitable consequence when people set to killing one another – but because something went awry. Had we inflicted something this massive on the Argies we would now be trumpeting a glorious victory. What's more, I have chums in the Welsh Guards. I have no idea if they are alive or dead. Odds must be that some are casualties.

And this self-regarding wazzock, whose most singular achievement today has been his absence until right now, who has kept us waiting in this freezing cold shed for ages, waltzes in all squeaky-clean and gimlet-eyed and tells us that we're 'bloodied but unbowed'. He clearly expects us to be inspired by this meaningless bollocks. In the history of ill-judged military 'pep talks' this has to be up there in the top ten all-time fuck-ups.

Psyching myself up to write this section I wonder, as I have for years, if I have imagined it. Could any half-sentient senior British commander have come up with something so crass just hours after such a disaster? Deliver such drivel to a bunch of soldiers who lived through the attacks when he wasn't even there? Have I dreamt it?

Having already written the section above, I double-check with *5th Infantry Brigade in the Falklands*. It may have my answer: 'One officer's lasting memory of Brigadier Wilson was at an Orders group at Fitzroy, which was being filmed, standing up and beginning, 'Well, we have suffered some setbacks...'

Half a battalion, two major ships – 'Some setbacks'? Different words, identical drivel. Published in 2003, that officer was interviewed almost twenty years ago. I have not been dreaming this.

AND (my capitals – I am getting angry all over again as I write this) the book goes on to report this officer saying this was a 'staged Orders Group' for journalists. The overly pink-tinted spectacled authors believe, however, that 'this particular criticism is a little unfair' as Wilson is 'always seeking an opportunity to promote his Brigade.'

Bollocks. Wilson *is* 5 Brigade. He is grandstanding. Promoting Brigadier Wilson. Again.

Here's another possibility, given the near identical reports of his opening statement. This is the same occasion – although I cannot remember the journalists being there; I was half asleep as I waited and could easily have missed their arrival. I thought it was a 'pep' talk. That other officer remembers it as an Orders Group – in which case, where are my notes of this O Group? But I see little difference between the two, not least when the last time he spoke to us it was deemed by him to be a 'chat'.

Perhaps that officer 'reined back' on Wilson's opening words. But he too was obviously aghast. He was interviewed less than twenty years after the event, when it was even more raw. Many Falklands veterans were still serving back then. None are today. I too might have 'reined back' twenty years ago, might not even have told the story. But that was then and this is now.

Maybe I have over-dramatized those opening words. But I don't think so. But the more I ponder this, the more convinced I am that we must both be describing the same occasion.

I do recall this talk feeling 'staged' – see my 'El Alamein' parallel above, written before I now discover this briefing was as much for the journalists who have descended on Fitzroy as for his soldiers.

If so, he kept us guys, his troops, some of whom have not slept for 24–30 hours, hanging about for hours as he needed us as an audience for the cameras. Little different conceptually to crowding telegenic gyrating teenage girls in front of the cameras on *Top of The Pops* so the viewing public is conned into thinking everyone in the studio is having a blast.

Whichever way it happened – keeping us waiting to spout rubbish at us, or using us as a backdrop to impress the journalists – it tells you much of what you need to know about Brigadier Wilson.

A fellow soldier, reading this passage, tells me I am perhaps using overly harsh language about the Brigadier; my chum's natural good manners and dislike of criticizing fellow soldiers instinctively kicks in. 'Let the readers draw their own conclusions,' he advises.

No. I want you to know exactly how I felt then, and still feel now: shocked at what I have learned today in my researches; all those brave, dead young faces suddenly clamouring to be heard.

I tell my wife what I have just written.

'It's enough to make you weep,' she says.

At her words a great sob rips through me from I know not where. A rent in the dam wall I started building in Belfast and was busily reinforcing as Mike died and the jets screamed overhead, a wall I have been cementing up ever since. This war is obviously closer to the surface than I care to acknowledge.

I never eat another Rolo. Ever. I can hardly bear to look at them. If I smelt one I'd probably gag. That said, I still have that unopened Fitzroy packet in my sock drawer. Just to remind me.

Chapter 14

Playing with the Paras

'Yea though I walk through the Valley of the shadow of Death, I shall fear no evil . . . because I am the meanest motherfucker in the Valley.' (Bruce H. Norton, *Force Recon Diary, 1969: The Riveting, True-to-Life Account of Survival and Death in One of the Most Highly Skilled Units in Vietnam.*)

I'm not sure I feel much like a 'mean motherfucker' when I join 2 Para. But *they* certainly are . . .

Note: *From here on, my verbatim entries in* **'bold'** *below are a mixture of my jottings in my 'battlefield notebook', 'diary' recollections written on 16/17 June, and my* Guards Magazine *article written in early/mid July. In places, because my different source materials tell the same story in a slightly different way, or mention different things, I have taken the liberty of 'mixing' the sentences together so that they read not only better but in sequence.*

On 8/9 June, the self-serving load of entirely forgettable hogwash – I don't even bother to note his *spiel* – from the Brigadier over, I am allowed to go and get some sleep. Someone directs me to another sheep shed where, I learn, most in Fitzroy have been dossing down while I sat on those radios. This one is rather dirty, has no walls and is draughty. But it has a metal roof to keep off the rain which is what matters most.

It is light when I wake. Someone has let me sleep on. Well, that or they couldn't find me to tell me that I was back on watch.

Breakfast. Then back to work.

It has been all change overnight. Fearing more air attacks, someone in possession of a couple of tactical brain cells has moved Brigade HQ to a hedge line outside the settlement. HQ is now a square command tent. Two Land Rovers have been backed up to either end of it – to supply power to the radios and the interior lights. The whole lot is covered in camouflage nets so it will look like more hedge to high-speed fighter jockeys.

When I arrive, someone seniorish is fretting mightily about the radio antennae being too vertical, too high and therefore possibly visible to attacking Argie aircraft. They should have been here yesterday, in that blasted X-marks-the-huge-spot shed. What a difference in tactical outlook one day doth make . . .

The tables and chairs are now on the sodden earth. Damp feet, here we come. A kerosene-fired portable stove provides the only heat. Yesterday is not mentioned. There's nothing worth saying. Recrimination will come later, and it certainly does, although I can see from the Brigadier's rather tight smile that even he realizes there must be downstream consequences. We do what trained soldiers should do and get on with our jobs: eight dull and cold hours on, eight off.

There's one flash of excitement when 'Air Raid Red' is called. Much rushing for dug-overnight trenches and hopeful cocking of weapons, but nothing happens. Although we do not know it, 8 June was the last 'big' day for the Argentine air force, even if they are not finished with us yet. Of the thirteen Skyhawks that attacked Fitzroy yesterday, three were shot down and four had so many lumps taken out of them by ground fire that, I read later, at least one of the pilots thought he would never make it home. Other waves of aircraft, of different attack varieties, hit the fleet. Our Harriers and Sea Dart ship-launched missiles knocked a number down. However, we will only discover this when the books come to be written. Right now, we worry about what they are planning for us next.

First stag in our new home in the hedge completed, I go looking for a Blues and Royals Scimitar which, I am told, is broken down at Fitzroy. This, for the record books, is the only major automotive failure any of our vehicles suffer throughout the whole campaign – a testament to both the vehicles themselves and the professionalism of our crews in looking after them. It is one thing to have a great vehicle, quite another to keep it working under these super-hostile conditions.

'More trouble than they are worth', eh? That idiotic rejection by some 5 Brigade ignoramus keeps echoing in my head. Sorry, but . . .

Directed to a hay barn, I find T23B, commanded by Lance Corporal of Horse Dunkeley, with Gunner Trooper Ford and Driver Trooper Round. I vaguely know L/CoH Dunkeley, but not the other two, although Ford, I will discover, knows me. I move in with them. **'They saw me and took me in as they would an orphan – fed me and gave me somewhere warm and comfortable to sleep. Thank God to be back with the Regiment.'**

This is the first time I have seen any of the boys Colonel James sent me 8,000 miles to look after them, and they have some great tales to tell. It turns out that both troops arrived in Fitzroy yesterday – when I was pulling that long radio stag – and then moved out again, leaving 23B's gearbox to be fixed by the REME, who are somewhere near in their armoured Samson repair vehicle. Best of all, they were here for yesterday's attacks.

The civilian inhabitants of Fitzroy were gathered around, admiring the Scimitar and asking the sort of questions that civvies always ask at Village Open Days when our boys go recruiting. When the first wave of fighter bombers hit the ships, the boys jumped into the vehicle and prepared for incoming. Undaunted, the spectators moved behind the vehicle, no thought of hiding or ducking, to watch what happened next – 23B engaging a Skyhawk.

Fully loaded, the 30mm Rarden cannon – the main armament – carries six rounds. When the gun is empty, the rounds are first laid horizontally by the commander, who doubles up as the loader, across the top of the open breech. Close the breech and then turn the cocking handle clockwise, fast. This slowly winds the barrel back until it releases a sear (part of the trigger mechanism) and flies forward, ramming the first round into the chamber. The cannon is now loaded and ready to fire.

The Rarden usually fires single shots. It takes less than a second for the recoil to load the next round. After every three rounds fired, a new clip of three is loaded into the gun. The Rarden can fire as fast as the commander can keep loading and the gunner pressing the Fire button. However, *in extremis*, it can let off all six in rapid succession if fired on 'Automatic'. Only problem, the gun will then be empty, and it takes time to do a full reload. Hence, only select Automatic when in a complete pickle.

As I said, the cannon is loaded/reloaded with clips of three rounds that are slotted into place; a rear 'holder' automatically releases the shells, and the commander drops the holder on to the turret floor. The commander needs to constantly count the number of rounds fired. Three rounds fired; reload with a fresh three-round 'clip'. Keep reloading every three rounds and you can shoot all day. In battle the commander is giving orders to the crew; manoeuvring the vehicle; giving and receiving orders on the radio; perhaps map reading; loading the main armament; using his left hand to feed belts of 7.62 ammo into the GPMG; making sure the belts do not snag and the gun does not misfire as the gunner lets rip; while keeping count of the number of main armament shells fired. All at the same time – who said men cannot multi-task?

Of course, the gunner is going to get a bollocking of truly Titanic proportions if he is not counting the three-round clips with you.

Miscount in the heat of the moment – easily done – and fire four, and there is now a gap. Fail to notice and 'fill it' by extracting a single round from its clip – not easy if you are in a fight – and there will be an ominous empty click instead of a reassuring bang when the gunner presses the button to fire round four.

Now you are in trouble, as the breech will not recoil and load the next round. And the commander now has a new problem. He doesn't know why the gun hasn't fired. So he has to go through his 'misfire' drills in case something has gone wrong internally with the gun or there is a problem with the round. Again it happens. Short circuit your misfire drills and you can blow yourself up.

Only when the gun is 'Clear!' can we go through the whole long, boring drill all over again, winding the gun back to load the next round.

Stressful when there are folk firing at you.

The Rarden is a brilliant gun, just as long as you remember to keep counting those rounds. 'Count Your Rounds!' as our Gunnery Instructors never stop drilling into us, all the while choosing your optimum ammunition type for the next target.

I'd guess HE (High Explosive) for aircraft. But if you don't have HE loaded, and don't have time to unload and then reload (unlikely!), we are taught to fire whatever is in the breech. The very least 30mm of high velocity steel is going to do to a soft-skinned aircraft is punch a 30mm hole right through it. In one side, out the other, eviscerating anything metal or human it meets on the way.

The theory is to make to make low-flying Pablo or Jorge 'pucker up' and wince as he sees tracer rounds race towards him. Perhaps spoil his aim – a twitch of the joystick at the speed they fly could be enough to turn a hit with a bomb into a miss. Which is what 23B did when they saw that Skyhawk swoop low over Fitzroy yesterday: switched to Automatic and gave it welly.

The locals were ecstatic. **'It seems that whilst British soldiers dived into trenches the interested inhabitants of Fitzroy watched 3 Troop firing back. A group of excited civilians all agree that a 30mm shell knocked a chunk out of an attacking aircraft.'**

Although, the boys whisper to me later, smiling, either the locals are brave beyond measure, or they are one sandwich short of the proverbial picnic. Because it was a scary moment, and they would not otherwise have stood there, as if on a pheasant shoot, giving the guns marks out of ten. This particular high-speed pheasant carried three 500lb bombs and cannons and would have made mincemeat of them had the pilot had time to zero in.

It really is good to be back with my regiment.

Two more days at Fitzroy and we are almost ready for 'the big push'. There's a ring of high hills between us and Port Stanley – our goal. The Argies are well dug in on all of them. To take the capital and win the war we first have to storm those peaks, so 3rd Commando Brigade is punching straight from the north, while 5 Brigade will 'hook' up from the south.

It is 11 June, three days after the debacle with *Galahad* and *Tristram*, and I have had enough. I wake early as I have moved from disappointment to anger. I somehow need to find and collar the elusive, uninterested Brigadier and force him to listen to what he needs to hear about the capabilities and limitations of our armoured vehicles. I need to do that before I start my next stag, as once I am back behind my radio I'll be stuck there. Leaving my radio, even if it is to try and find the Brigadier, would be tantamount to deserting my post. And I have to do it right now. The various formations are moving into pre-battle positions. This is my last chance to try and influence what the high-ups are planning for The Blues and Royals. 3 Troop has been re-attached to 3 Brigade, and I have already said goodbye to 23B, which is now heading back north to rejoin the rest of their troop. That means it is already too late for me to speak to somebody in authority about them.

However, 4 Troop remains under command of 5 Brigade. I no longer care if I cause offence by demanding to speak to the Brigadier. I became a lawyer when I left the army, and it is my view now, although I did not know how to articulate it back then, that the Brigadier's almost wilful refusal to ask me about our vehicles is tantamount to negligence.

I have no similar issue with HQ 3 Brigade. I never get to meet any of them during the war, and they have no idea I am here to advise and help. I met Major General Thompson (Brigadier i/c HQ 3 Commando Brigade during the war) at a lunch at Bonhams, the auctioneers, a couple of years ago. He was sitting at the far end of the table, and we only spoke briefly as we were all leaving. However, our host had mentioned to him who I was and which regiment I had been in. He knew what I got up to on

Wireless Ridge. He told me that it was one of his regrets that he had had no idea just how good our vehicles were. Had he realized, he told me, he would have sent a troop to Goose Green and, had he done so, he had little doubt that they would have been as devastating there as they were to be on Wireless Ridge.

Even while I smiled and agreed with him that they would have been game-changers, battle-winners, I also wondered what the consequences might have been. In daylight, on those wide open slopes with nowhere to hide where the battle took place, every Argentine heavy weapon would have zeroed in on them, including their aircraft. Their slow-flying Pucaras, natural tank-killers with their 20mm cannons, would have chewed them up for breakfast. Their .50 machine guns could have knocked them out. I wondered what the butcher's bill might have been for The Blues and Royals.

Who knows?

My entire upbringing – school, Brigade Squad (squaddie training), Sandhurst (officer training), Bovington (specialist armoured training), my regiment (university an honourable exception) – has been predicated on one simple premise: my 'olders and betters' know better than me. That is why we are expected to obey them and punished when we do not. That is why they are my superiors.

I very soon discarded that notion about my schoolteachers – encouraged by my university tutors, who wanted me to question everything – but all my military training is underscored by one persistent drumbeat: 'We are the British Army. We are the professionals. We know best. We *are* the best.'

To join the army as an officer and pass officer training meant buying into that ethos. And, even if I do not necessarily respect my seniors per se, I am fully cognisant that it is one thing for me to privately question and criticize, quite another to be able to do better myself.

But this thing with the Brigadier goes above and beyond any such considerations. He appears totally uninterested. That makes him ignorant. If he listens and subsequently ignores me, then that is his prerogative, and at least I will have tried. This morning, I decide, I might have tried to get him to listen, but evidently not hard enough. I've got a couple of hours before I'm back on stag again. This time I won't take 'Excellent, but later' for an answer.

As I head towards Brigade HQ, someone tells me that 3 Troop is being attached to 2 Para, which is still at Fitzroy. I thank him and head on my way.

Seconds later, as if in a poorly plotted film, a Para major walks towards me along the path. I see him clock my cap badge. He stops as I do and he introduces himself as Major Chris Keeble, second in command of 2 Para.

'Are you the troop leader?'

'No,' I reply. 'But as they're under your command, I've got a few words of advice on how best to use them.' I then hit him with some key facts and figures.

Chris Keeble is already legendary. He took command at Goose Green when Colonel H was killed, winning the battle from there (for which he wins a DSO). We lot are rather surprised that he was not allowed to continue to lead the battalion, having done so very well, but that was not to be. Instead, Colonel David Chaundler parachuted into the South Atlantic to take over command of 2 Para.

'Rather him than me,' is the near-universal verdict on that particular parachute jump.

'Come and see Colonel David,' says Keeble, 'and repeat this to him.'

He's in a shed brewing up a cup of coffee.

Introductions made, I give him the ranges at which we can fire, by day and night. I warn him about the weakness of our light aluminium armour. We can probably be knocked out by .50 machine guns, certainly if they are firing armour-piercing ammo. Missiles and bazookas will kill us for certain. Sustained bursts of GPMG could theoretically chip through our far thinner side and back armour.

The secret is to stand our vehicles well out of range of the enemy's lighter weapons and let our super-accurate main armament knock out enemy positions without putting them in unnecessary danger for no obvious gain. An enemy position knocked out from 1,800 yards is as dead as if we had hit it from 500, and with far less risk to our vehicles. It's that simple. He's only got four armoured cars. Each casualty is a 25 per cent loss of a battle-winning, life-saving weapons system.

As I talk with them, keeping it as tight as I can, I can hardly believe I am having this conversation. After a month of trying, and failing, to get someone, anyone, to listen to me, I now have two of the hardest men on the island listening very intently indeed.

'What,' I ask, changing tack, 'are your plans for them, Colonel?'

He had planned to use them 'blitzkrieg'- style, he tells me: running his soldiers in alongside them as our vehicles fire direct on to the enemy strong points, overwhelming them.

However, he says, he is now reconsidering this in the light of my briefing.

This is the age-old problem with the infantry. They see tracks, turrets, armour and biggish guns – far bigger guns than anything they can carry – and they think, tank.

'They aren't tanks,' I tell him. 'They're armoured cars. They aren't designed for blitzkrieg.'

This, I explain again, is a near-guaranteed way of losing some, perhaps all of the vehicles. How to reinforce the point? He's still thinking tanks, I suspect. Time for some cunning.

'Don't forget, Colonel. You'll end up facing those 90mm Panhards at some point. If they're up there on the mountains waiting for you, we will be easy targets if we're blitzkrieging it. We need to stand off and outshoot them.'

'Go on.'

'And, even if they're not waiting for you up on the mountains, then they'll definitely be waiting for you in Port Stanley. If you've lost some or all of your armour, those Panhards will eat you alive when you get down there.'

Chris Keeble interrupts. They are super-busy and don't have time to go into this right now. The battalion will shortly be helicoptering north to Mount Kent.

'Do you want to come along?'

'Why not?'

Even as I say it I sort of know that I am delivering the required, deadpan, Hollywood-scripted, Sandhurst-approved answer. Furthermore, I also realize that I'm swapping a life of irritation and frustration and relative safety for one of danger. My brief wander around the giblets of Goose Green has left me with no illusions about what being 'in/with' 2 Para will probably involve. As the old adage goes, be careful what you wish for . . .

We decide that I will be 2 Para's 'Armoured L.O.' (Liaison Officer) – everyone in the army has a designation. **'Get your kit together, we fly out at 1600hrs.'**

I look at my watch: 1400hrs.

Quick thinking from Keeble has me replaced as a watchkeeper by the 2 Para Education Officer. They brought him along to help on the radios at Battalion HQ, and that means he's relatively 'spare'.

'5 Brigade panicked. "What about the stag rosters...? Oh, this is all very irregular . . ."'

I ignore the inevitable carping and focus on getting my kit sorted. Anything unnecessary really does get jettisoned. I'm going to be carrying my webbing and Bergen 'for real'.

Next priority: high-speed scrounging. Thinking I would not need it, and keen to offload weight, I stupidly left my steel helmet in my suitcase on *Canberra*. The Quartermaster finds me another. I borrow an entrenching spade; I suspect I am going to have to reacquire that long-ignored skill.

Most important consideration of all is my shooter. I really, really do not want to face the Argies carrying my SMG (Stirling sub-machine gun). We are issued with them in tanks and armoured cars as there is nowhere in the turret to stow a 'long gun' (rifle). Whilst they look dead warry in Hollywood films – much favoured by Para/spy types and just the thing for a shoot-out in an inner city drugs den – in reality, out in the mountains where I am going, they will be pretty useless. It is a short-range weapon, with little stopping power. **'If you shoot at a man the idea is to knock him over, not play with him.'** Although, I later read, Colonel H launched his VC-winning attack carrying an SMG. Apparently, he never got a chance to fire it.

Adam is very decent. He swaps me his SLR and five loaded magazines, 100 rounds. I am now rigged for battle.

Even as I try to act as nonchalant as possible with my fellow watchkeepers and try to come across all 'Lucky me, I'm off with the Paras . . .', I feel rather nervous and, perhaps, ever so slightly silly. I just hope I am up to this.

Nervous? Well, I am not suicidal. My fellow watchkeepers say nothing negative, but I can guess what they are thinking. I am swapping a near-guaranteed voyage home at the end of this trip for what has, up until now, been the most dangerous gig on the islands: running around with 2 Para. What's more, Adam would not lend me his SLR unless he thinks I might need it.

And as for feeling 'slightly silly'? I am armoured-car fit. Thank God for all that extra running I did on *QE2*, not forgetting the two months of near constant leg exercising that was ski-racing last winter. But am I anywhere near Airborne fit? I very much doubt it. I have lived a very different army life to these guys since I left Sandhurst five years ago; motoring whilst they marched and ran – with packs. They have been building muscle and endurance to become ever better airborne soldiers. I have pretty much been exercising to maintain Sandhurst levels of fitness. I'd go up against

Above: Crossing the Equator Ceremony, 19 May. My view from the bow looking back. 'Perhaps I am being overly morbid, I think to myself as I look at them, cheering and laughing as another Equator virgin splashes into the gunk-ridden deep, but how many of them won't be coming back? Quite a few as it turns out.'

Below: 21 May. Diary: **'Spent the afternoon packing kit.'** The author in his cabin trying and failing to pack his over-full Bergen. That cold-weather cap – known as a cap VSI – cap Very Silly Indeed – was binned. Yes, those ear flaps would keep your head warm, but you cannot then hear what you may badly need to . . .

QE2 anchored in Grytviken. Browning .50s on the bridge. SS *Canberra*, our destination, awaiting us.

The watchkeeper group on the tug trans-shipping us to *Canberra*. Julian Stanley, rather bizarrely, seems to have a briefcase.

Approaching *Canberra*, which will take us to 'the war', those impossibly cold-looking mountains behind.

Above: HMS *Broadsword* in the setting sun. Very artistic! *Broadsword* ('Pork Sword' to mariners) was my Regiment's 'sister ship', hence my taking this shot. In autumn 1982 I engineered a trip up the eastern American seaboard on her – a truly memorable trip for non-military reasons: I only spent one night at sea! I presented them with a blow-up of this photo. In that blow-up you can see the hole in her stern caused by an Argentine bomb.

Right: San Carlos Bay, 1 June. Welsh Guards on board the landing craft about to go ashore. A scene perhaps not unlike that of a D-Day landing craft.

Above: My view from our landing craft back towards *Canberra* and the illusion of safety she represented. That murk kept the Argentine Air Force away.

Below: Ashore at San Carlos. Why those soldiers are lying down and getting wet in the process – perhaps to avoid non-existent enemy fire? – is a mystery to me.

Above left: Against Brigade HQ orders, Nick Schrayne and I went into the 'recce' role and found a nice pre-dug trench. As my subsequent article for *The Guards Magazine* said, 'The other four watchkeepers joined us and with the rain gently falling we were lulled to sleep by the sound of Brigade Headquarters digging in around us.'

Above right: 2 June. Approach to Goose Green. An abandoned Argentine trench, ransacked by the Paras.

Goose Green; close-up of the gorse gulley, still smouldering four days later. The Argies had no lack of heavy weapons . . .

Left: 9 June, the day after Fitzroy was bombed and HQ 5 Brigade – from having sited itself in a large, concrete-floored, shed – has suddenly decided it might be an idea to 'go tactical'. We moved to a hedge line above the settlement. It's 'Air Raid Warning Red' again, and all eyes are on the sky. You can just see the Land Rover beneath the camouflage.

Below: 11 June. Having offered my services to 2 Para as 'Armoured Adviser', two hours later I am off with them by Wessex helicopter to Mount Kent and from there to Wireless Ridge.

12 June. Furze Bush Pass, digging in behind Wireless Ridge under an artillery barrage. General Frost (of Arnhem fame) in his 1983 book *2 Para, Falklands* wrote: 'But to some, digging was a novel experience. Captain Roger Field was introduced to the art, with moderate success. He later confessed to the CO, "When I left Sandhurst, I swore I would never again march, dig a trench, or blacken my face, but within twenty-four hours you have managed to get me doing all three."'

Captain David Benest, Battalion Signals Officer (David went on to command 2 Para) digging in with me, and doubtless making a far better job of it.

The rest of 2 Para digging in. Up under the rocks, only mortars or airburst artillery was going to hit us direct.

Above: In the foreground is my Scimitar – note the slim 30mm Rarden cannon. Behind is 23A, a Scorpion with its short, stubby 76mm gun. Note the 7.62mm ammo replen boxes already laid onto the front 'decks' – so many that my driver could hardly see where he was going. Not as taught at Gunnery School.

Below: 23A Scorpion and my Scimitar crew: Tpr Ford, my gunner, Tpr Pilchowski (gunner), CoH Thompson in the turret, L/Cpl Birch (driver), and Tpr Round, my driver.

Moving back across Wireless Ridge, the scene of the previous night's fighting. Lieutenant Robin Innes Ker, 3 Troop leader, wearing his distinctive helicopter flying helmet.

Driving back across Wireless Ridge, last night's battlefield, to continue the attack; the ground still frozen.

The desperately lonely 'grave' of a British Para – like a scene from the First World War. I didn't want to over-think it as it was our turn next; our four vehicles up against any number of Panhard armoured cars with their much larger 90mm guns.

Above: The actual moment of victory – note Round giving a Churchillian V-sign – delight on everyone's faces. We are up on the final ridgeline of Wireless Ridge, looking down on Port Stanley. We can see the Argies running and we are awaiting orders to pursue. We will give 2 Para Milan Platoon – note those massive-to-carry rockets on the front decks – a 'cabby' until we hit resistance. And then up over the radio comes the news that the Argies have surrendered. I jumped out of the turret to grab the photo.

Below: A moment later. Ford is determined to look even more warry and is posing with my SLR, which won't fit inside the turret.

Looking back as we advance though Moody Brook, the Royal Marine barracks captured by the Argies on 2 April. The ridgeline in the background is Wireless Ridge itself, where we were waiting to continue the attack when the surrender was announced.

Right: Motoring towards Port Stanley, Milan Platoon enjoying the lift.

Below: Looking back. The 'C' Scimitar behind me also giving the Paras a lift. Others Paras tabbing alongside, some in helmets, others already proudly wearing their red berets.

The crew of my Scimitar, 23B: Tpr Ford, self, Tpr Round.

The author sitting on 23B parked outside the troop house in Stanley

The filthy, not exactly inspiring entrance to Government House: 'REMOVE MUDDY BOOTS'

Above: After his Scorpion was blown up by an Argentine mine on Tumbledown, Lt Mark Coreth (sitting on the right), 4 Troop Leader, was determined to drive on to HMS *Fearless*, which was taking the two troops home. He commandeered this Panhard (and one other) which were towed aboard – they kept breaking down. One is outside the Regimental Museum in Windsor, the other at the Tank Museum in Bovington.

As I took this picture I was officially 'CRACFI' (Commander Royal Armoured Corps Falkland Islands). The moment the two troops boarded *Fearless* I reverted to being a bored watchkeeper with only one thought in mind: getting home.

Below: 1 December 1982, Buckingham Palace Gardens. The author being presented with the South Atlantic Medal. Prince Philip is smiling as we discuss my just published article in *The Guards Magazine*

Left: 1 Dec 1982. The author, as 'Senior Detachment Commander of The Blues and Royals' (the senior Regiment on parade), leading the final march past.

Below: Spring 2007. Twenty-five years on, the author having a 'cabby' on the latest weaponry at Onion Range in the Falklands.

Above: Spring 2007. Twenty-five years on, the author beside the blown-up remains of the 20mm AA gun that almost took his turret off. The Falkland Island Battle Tour didn't even know it was there. But it was, just where I said it would be . . .

Below: Spring 2007. The British (probably 105mm) shell hole that 'killed' the gun is plainly visible.

Spring 2007. Twenty-five years on, the author standing on his long-filled-in trench under Furze Bush Pass

most in the normal army and reckon to match them. This lot play in an altogether different league.

At that moment I make a commitment to myself, a promise. No Para is ever going to say that a Blue and Royal could not keep up with them, could not hack the pace. I will have cause to remember this in the days to come.

Two hours later, I line up to board a helicopter. The TV crews are there filming us.

'What on earth are you doing?' asks a surprised Michael Nicholson.

I explain.

He looks duly shocked. 'You look very tall compared to this lot,' he tells me. 'Keep your head down or you'll get it shot off.'

And he's right. Most of them are square-built, medium to short arses, not lanky, 6 feet 2 and a bit inches cavalry types. Thanks, Mike . . .

'**1800hrs saw us on Mount Kent; "O" Group in the setting sun. Estancia House burning in the distance, hit by aircraft earlier.**'

3 Para are attacking Mount Longdon tonight. We will follow them, the Colonel tells us. We are their reserve if need be.

We are to leave our Bergens here. He has no idea when we will next see them. We will march with light scales only. We should carry as much food, water and ammo as we can. Any non-essentials must be binned. Sleeping bags are not allowed.

At the last moment I am given a spare backpack radio and five batteries so I can communicate with the armoured vehicles directly. This is extra weight I had not planned on carrying. Nevertheless, with the ban on sleeping bags, I tie my 1950s Korean War-era parka on to my radio. My kit weighs a ton.

The Blues and Royals have not joined us yet, which means I am currently surplus to requirements. I will tab with HQ 'Main'. The Colonel as good as hands me over to Captain David Benest, the battalion Signals Officer. He's a delightful, friendly chap – refreshingly normal and un-Para like.

'**Then to sleep in our bags.**

Woken 2230. "Move out 15 minutes."

It was so cold that the outside of the sleeping bags were frozen. God what cold. What must it have been like on the Eastern Front [in the Second World War]? Unbelievable I should think.

We marched a few minutes to a green [torch] light and dropped off our Bergens – very efficient.

We marched to an orange light – our Release Point.

We marched.'

The Paras form a double 'Airborne Snake', two long lines about 20–30 yards apart, one man usually behind the other, although at various times I walk beside David and chat, as do others. This is not a tactical 'fighting' formation as such, it is just the Airborne way of getting from A to B as quickly as possible.

One or other, or both, snakes stop or they concertina. At other times we rush to catch up as a gap appears for no apparent reason – not unlike rush hour on the M25. There are occasional much longer pauses and, just as at Sandhurst when we did not have a 'command appointment', we officer mushrooms in the middle are as ignorant of what is going on as the most junior soldier. We wait or we trudge, trusting that the Colonel knows what he is doing.

I note how often men peel off. They drop their trousers and take an urgent dump – a strange sight in the clear, frosted, moonlit tundra. General Frost's 2 Para book also mentions it, but puts it down to a 'reaction' to the last meal in Fitzroy.

David is more prosaic when I ask if there's a medical problem: 'After Goose Green they know what's coming. Some of them are, literally, shitting themselves.'

I believe it was Field Marshal Sir William Slim (successful commander of the Fourteenth Army in Burma) who, in his 1957 book *Courage and Other Broadcasts*, distinguished between different types of courage; comparing the 'true', quiet courage of men who know fear and overcome it, as against the sometimes suicidal courage of the Japanese; a more brittle courage, he believed, that is more easily broken.

I mentally doff my cap to these Paras. How would I feel going into battle for the second time, knowing what they now know? How did the soldiers in the First and Second World Wars keep doing this day after day, year after year, knowing what they undoubtedly knew?

Let's see how I manage first time around.

'It was now that I realised that I was out of my depth with these guys. The first few hours were no problem: downhill or flat; then we began to climb and I began to seriously and dangerously overheat. It then occurred that I was carrying more than most of the tough paras and so I asked David Benest if he would lug the radio for a bit. Thankfully he did and I was saved. He is a charming chap and was to look after me from an infantry sense for the next few days. Since I had not played grunts since Sandhurst I did not know the tricks of the trade that save valuable time and effort – he saved me here. He seemed to be able to produce a cup of coffee in 2 minutes, me in 12. Not much use when it is a 10 minute rest.'

It later turned out that I was not being as big a wuss as I feared at the time. General Frost's book says of the march from Mount Kent: 'Some of the more heavily laden soldiers such as medics and signallers [that's me with my radio and five batteries] were beginning to get tired . . .' I for one am getting very tired indeed, but I'm delighted to read all these years later that I was not the only one.

My first shell is a 155mm, a big bastard, although I am not yet enough of a connoisseur of shellfire to size it accurately. A scream as it heads towards us. Towards me, more to the point.

I dive to the ground and start worming my way into the frozen peat. The last time – and the first for that matter! – I had taken such urgent, life-saving, avoiding action was when a gun went off in Belfast and I tried to meld myself into a concrete kerb whilst trying to work out just what was going on. I even managed to say those immortal words – at least for a wannabe combat soldier – 'Contact. Wait out' (meaning that I am under fire) before realizing that said shots were coming from the other side of the school I was at that moment vacating. Cue much subsequent piss-taking from my fellow officers. But gentle piss-taking – guns going off nearby in the streets of West Belfast tended not to be harbingers of glad tidings . . .

Here, none of the Paras breaks stride.

The shell lands a couple of hundred yards off to the left. It explodes, throwing up a vertical gout of black, sodden peat.

Harmless.

A few guffaws and insults from the old Goose Green hands, 'Crap hat' prominent amongst them.

I get up, semi-sodden.

A sympathetic smile from David. 'You'll learn,' he says.

A few more shells head our way – we remain under fire, sometimes sporadic other times more intense, for the rest of the march – and, clever, brave boy me, I now keep marching, as do the others. I'm getting the hang of this. I'm already becoming an old hand.

Another shell. Much louder, this time. I'm no coward. I'm not having the Paras laugh at The Blues and Royals again. I keep walking.

Too late. Everyone around me is hitting the earth. I follow, but too slow had that shell landed any closer. More like 50m away, this one. I'm only saved by the fact that it has, like the rest, buried itself deep into the soft peat before exploding upwards, throwing no shrapnel sideways as such.

Now the bold, bad Paras look at me as if I'm the idiot.

'You'll learn,' says David. And I do.

3 Para's battle for Mount Longdon is going on ahead of us and off to our right. David and I have no idea what is happening, but sometimes the fighting seems close, streams of tracer fire starting to head towards us but then burning out, still some distance away; the thump of shellfire; the sense that we are getting so close that we might find ourselves being called to go into the attack. At other times the fighting recedes. Now it has nothing to do with us.

'Finally, around 0200 we stopped. Sleep whilst you can we were told. It was, however, far too cold to sleep. I put on everything I had to Michelin man proportions and lay on top of my webbing and radio to get me off the ground. Despite only 3 hours kip in the last 24 hours, sleep was impossible. My feet were the real problem [my boots were soaking]; in fact frostbite was a near possibility.'

Front line soldiers are probably one of the few groups who still find themselves truly at the mercy of the elements. Since man first pushed into a cave and discovered fire, humans have been sheltering from the elements, grouping together at night, keeping warm, seeing out the dark hours until the sun returns. The Inuit dig igloos and Siberian reindeer herders living in -40° cold retreat to their warm, snug yurts. High Alpine ski instructors and piste machine operators return from a day in the snow and ice to their implausibly warm homes, where they wear flip-flops and T-shirts. On Sennybridge in the Welsh mountains, after days under snow, the DS declare an exercise paused, call in a helicopter, build a fire and issue us with rum when some of our Sandhurst course start collapsing with hypothermia. The next morning, partially dried out, we start soldiering again.

But not combat soldiers. It is our lot to suck up the pain and endure. To control the night we must go out into the dark, regardless of conditions. Much of our training revolves around this; learning to fight as the rest of the world sleeps or hides from the cold and dark.

It's usually colder at night. Even on a June night in England it can be surprisingly cold, especially if there is no cloud cover. We learn to understand cloud cover. Clouds are good because they retain the heat of the day; they act like a big blanket keeping the warmth in. A cloudy night is usually a much warmer night. Summer and winter. We like that. Less to degrade us as we march and stand watch and fight.

But clouds also bring rain. Get wet, and we get cold. Wet clothes leach the warmth off our bodies as our skin tries to warm the sodden material to skin temperature. That drops our core body temperature. So, we like some clouds, but not others.

We love warm, sunny, clear days. But come sundown, without cloud cover, the day's warmth evaporates into the heavens. In winter those are the ground-frost nights. The nights we literally freeze as the temperature plummets.

Tonight is such a night; crystal sharp and clear. No clouds in the sky. The earth freezes and turns white. Every other human and animal on this benighted island is hunkered down in its shelter, keeping as warm as it can, surviving as best as it can, until daylight returns.

We soldiers lie on the frozen ground. Waiting. This is what we must do. We have no alternative. Nowhere else to go. Nobody to say, 'Build a bonfire. Here's some rum.' The Colonel will be as cold as the most junior private. This is war.

Two hours later, we are off again, relieved to be moving, getting warm again as we march. We tab till daylight and cross the Murrell Bridge. Ten minutes later, the area around it is blown to pieces. Somehow the Argentines must have detected our movement and alerted their batteries. In our double Airborne Snake we make an easy target if they get lucky and drop their shells right on top of us.

'**Argentine artillery was not directed. Thank God. They had a large number of worked out DFs [pre-set Defensive Fire locations] and when their OPs (Observations Posts) reported movement in an area they DF'ed those pre-ranged in spots. If you were there you dipped out. If you were a couple of hundred yards away you were okay. The secret was to try to remember where the shells landed last time and try and avoid that area and hope that the DF did not shift at all.**'

Finally, after about fourteen hours of marching, although with frequent halts, we reach our objective: Furze Bush Pass. This is a rocky outcrop behind and under which two companies and Battalion HQ shelter. The third company digs in on the far side of a broad valley.

Digging in on the 'reverse' slope means that the shells – sporadic but constant now – either land harmlessly on top of the outcrop or fly on a couple of hundred yards too far. There is the occasional airburst – sending shrapnel down over a wide area – but the Argies set the fuses wrong and they cause us no trouble. Thank God. Had they got them 'right' they could have exploded them above us and entirely wrecked our day. Nevertheless, **'with shells whizzing around every few minutes I needed no encouragement to dig. We had just had breakfast when shells landed 50–150 metres away – we dug in rapidly.'**

General Frost was clearly not as impressed with my infantry skills as I was when I wrote up my diary:

> But to some, digging was a novel experience. Captain Roger Field was introduced to the art, with moderate success. He later confessed to the CO, 'When I left Sandhurst, I swore I would never again march, dig a trench, or blacken my face, but within twenty-four hours you have managed to get me doing all three.' He had discovered that there is quite a considerable difference between living, eating and sleeping from a nice warm tank, and doing so with the 'grunts'.

Too right, General Frost, too right . . .

The day passes in a blur of digging and cleaning kit and cooking and listening to falling shells, some close, others further off, but all aimed at Furze Bush Pass. We will be attacking Wireless Ridge tonight.

Evening arrives and with it 3 Troop, laden down with as much ammunition as they can carry. It turns out, Robin tells me, that the REME loaded their Samson (a repair vehicle equivalent to our Scorpions and Scimitars, with the same aluminium armour) with so much ammo that, when they drove over the Murrell Bridge, they collapsed it. The Sampson is on its side in the river – nobody injured, thank God – but the bridge is now broken, making the track impassable to anything other than soldiers on foot.

Only helicopters will be now able to fly up more ammo. This will be in short supply if we have to fight a couple of battles over the next few days.

3 Troop forward dumps the excess ammo they brought with them under the rocky outcrop. When the time comes for re-ammoing the vehicles tomorrow, they will have less far to travel to collect it.

'O Gp. 1800hrs . . .'

Chapter 15

Berets on, Helmets off – The Fog of War

Hazel O'Connor's soulful *Will You?*, and David Bowie's zany *Kooks* were perfect tracks for running round and round and round *QE2*. But not for going into battle. I am now singing and humming to myself to stay sane, to stay focused, to keep up with these tireless Paras. Exploding shells replace pounding feet as the background drum beat. Now I want music that is more primal, more martial.

'Throughout this period I had been humming an IRA song to myself, the chorus of which was, "Tis better to die 'neath an Irish sky" – rather a mournful lilt.'

Words that resonate hard with the Southern Cross constellation and a myriad stars I have never seen before, shining bright in the ice-clear sky above me, an insignificant soldier ant, tabbing beneath an Antarctic sky.

Its haunting melody plays to my somewhat Celtic soul. Written in the 1800s, *The Foggy Dew* is from the first record I ever bought, aged eleven, encouraged by my mother and an Irish aunt: *Irish Songs of Rebellion* by the Clancy Brothers and Tommy Makem. It has no shortage of apposite lines:

> 'While Britannia's sons [that's us!] with their long-range guns came in from the foggy dew . . .
> And the world did gaze, in deep amaze, at those fearless men, but few Who bore the fight that freedom's light might shine through the foggy dew.'

That song could have been written for us on this dank, frozen island: 10,000-plus pissed-off Argentines and all their heavy weaponry, dug in, waiting for us a mile or two away. Although it most certainly was not – the writers were Irish, freedom-seeking Brit-haters, *The Foggy Dew* an anthem to fighting the ancient enemy.

Interestingly, and it shows the extra depths of dislike three decades of murder and mayhem instilled in the Province, more modern versions of that record I bought refer not to 'Britannia's sons', but 'Britannia's Huns.' Hmm . . . clever songsters, those Irish.

* * *

'1800hrs – O Group. Night's attack plans laid out. I was at this stage informed that I was not to go with Tac Main but with Tac 1, i.e. the C.O. and a couple of advisors. In fact the same bunch who got themselves killed at Goose Green. This certainly induced feelings of trepidation.'

The shellfire has stopped and the Colonel holds the O Group for tonight's attack up on the bluff above our trench positions. He indicates Wireless Ridge and key features such as Mounts Longdon and Tumbledown off to our right, although we cannot really see much from here. It is all rising hills and mountains. Which we are going to have to assault.

3 Para are on Mount Longdon, which they captured last night. We will attack due south, across their front. If anyone thinks the Argies are giving up, then the 3 Para casualty list puts that one to bed: seventeen killed and forty wounded. Although the very fact that they defeated such a sizeable defending force tells us that they are there for the taking.

Off to their right is Mount Tumbledown. The Scots Guards and the Gurkhas will assault it tonight. We need to be aware that, in the dark, if we both push through our objectives we could end up shooting at each other.

It turns out that Colonel David only got briefed for tonight's attack about half an hour ago and his plans are a bit sketchy. Halfway through the O Group there is a sudden message – 'Boundary change'. Boundaries denote where your next door friendly forces are and the line on the ground – the boundary – which they will not cross. Stray across the agreed boundary and you risk getting shot by your own side.

'C.O. thinks for five minutes and starts on a new plan.

With the O Group at the [final] "Any questions?" stage: new message.

CANCEL [in my 'battle notebook' I underline CANCEL twice – relief, I suppose]

The reason? Glorious 5 Brigade is not ready for its attack on Mount Tumbledown. Well, everyone groaned and laughed and said "typical". Which it is.

Luckily, since RHG/D [Royal Horse Guards/Dragoons] were there I slipped into the gunner's seat of Robin's vehicle, was given a shot of port. Listened to his boogie pack and collapsed exhausted. I was not only very, very tired but feeling deep down cold.'

Robin and his crew must have slept in their tent which fixes to the side of the vehicle. They have sleeping mats to get them off the ground – camp beds, even; there's plenty of room to store stuff on an armoured car.

With my sleeping bag back at Mount Kent, just getting out of the wind and off the frozen peat is an unlooked-for luxury. I later read that it was so cold many Paras were unable to sleep. Some stomped up and down, even doing drill (Paras hate drill) to stop their feet from freezing up in their useless army-issue boots.

'Apart from being awoken by a bomb and a few shells which landed nearby I slept incredibly well.'

A near cloudless day dawns on 13 June, the sun sharp and bright. The wind drops, and it is so warm – Falkland Islands midwinter 'warm', that is, a degree or three above freezing – that we strip off our combat jackets, lay them on rocks to dry, and sit, much like lizards, absorbing every last bit of warmth.

There is a new O Group and there are new plans.

The battalion is busy. The Colonel helicopters to 3 Brigade HQ while the majors try to recce the advance to Wireless Ridge. The soldiers rehearse for tonight's attack and prepare their kit; oil rifles; jump up and down to make sure that what we carry is not clanking; the basic infantry drills I learned at Brigade Squad and Sandhurst.

Soon there is little for me to do except wait. I think it is David Benest, the signals officer I am sharing my trench with, who briefs me on how it will work with me, the Colonel, the vehicles and the radios. Certainly, I have no memory of a separate briefing with the Colonel. He is far too busy getting yet more new orders from Brigade and preparing his battalion for battle.

Nobody has used an Armoured LO to 'fire in' attacking infantry from armoured cars before, which means there is no rule book. For me, or the Colonel, or David. We'll make it up as we go along which suits me. I prefer 'surprise' parties. They tend to allow for more initiative and free thinking. I give David my ideas in return.

I will be with the Colonel, and my radio will be tuned in to the troop 'chatter' net. This is the radio net used only by the four vehicles – and now me – hence they/we can 'chatter' to one another far more informally, although without breaching security by talking 'in clear'. In turn, this means that my conversations with the armoured vehicles do not clog up the 2 Para 'command' net, which the Colonel uses to talk to his company commanders and sundry others.

Furthermore, the Colonel can tell me exactly what he wants doing – or he can grab the mic himself. I can give him instant results as I will be able to see what he sees.

The Artillery Battery commander, Major Rice, is also with the Colonel in Tac 1 and does just this – relays the Colonel's requirements to his guns. This is as taught at Sandhurst and Staff College. However, nobody has thought to do this with armoured vehicles before. At least not since Lord alone knows when. The Korean War? The Second World War? It is so blinking obvious when you think about it but, with no wars to fight, what would these Armoured LO captains do otherwise? Answer, they would be surplus to requirements. I guess I just happen to be in the right place at the right time and unexpectedly 'available'. I wonder if anybody has taken on this LO role in any wars since?

I am an outsider, and an officer, so the Para soldiers are hardly going to confide in me, but sitting there in the sun, enjoying a hot brew, I learn that Colonel H might not have been quite the Boy's Own inspirational hero I, and all of us at 5 Brigade, assume him to have been. Nobody, but nobody, questions his bravery, but some clearly think that he should not have been where he was, in that gorse gulley at the very tip of the battalion attack, let alone got himself killed in the way he did, 'leading' a lone charge with only a couple of men following.

Sandhurst teaches us that each level of officer should be one 'tactical bound' behind the soldiers he commands. A tactical bound computes as, roughly, the range of the opposing forces' infantry weapons. The Argies, like us, carry SLR's. It will be night when we attack, so that's probably 100–200 yards minimum; by day it is more like 300–400 yards. Terrain will further dictate 'best' tactical spacing, as a commander has to see what is going on, even if that pulls him much closer to the fighting. Which it will at times.

As the lead platoons hit the enemy positions, the company commanders (majors) should be a tactical bound behind the lieutenants so they can command them without getting shot at by enemy grunts with rifles.

The 'Rear' HQ, commanded by the company 2i/c, a captain, plus mortars, medics and others, should be one tactical bound behind the major's Forward HQ. So if the company commander is hit, the 2i/c moves up and takes over. He should not be pinned down, or knocked out, by whatever has done for the major.

A tactical bound behind the lead companies is the Colonel with his Tac 1 (that's, er, now me); close enough to see and understand the overall battle and command his rifle companies, but far enough back not to be neutralized if a company runs into difficulties. A colonel cannot command the battlefield if he is stuck in a ditch (or a gorse gulley), unable to raise his head.

Finally, a further tactical bound behind Tac 1, ready to move up and take over if the Colonel is killed or wounded, is battalion HQ 'Main' run by the 2i/c, Major Keeble, with the Regimental Aid Post and all sorts of support elements.

It is, of course, rather more complex than this, because GPMGs (especially when tripod-mounted for much longer range), 'Big Fifty' .50 Browning machine guns, recoilless rifles (big bazookas on tripods), shoulder-fired missiles and bazookas, armoured cars and multi-barrelled Oerlikon 20mm and 30mm anti-aircraft guns – all of which the enemy have – can eradicate or neutralize targets three or four bounds back. Sometimes further.

But that's the lecture hall theory and it makes sense, as much as anything makes sense in battle.

In the real world, each commander will discover his own appetite for risk when the dread moment arrives. Some regiments, of course, have a general expectation of greater officer ballsiness than others, and the Paras, especially after Colonel H's actions at Goose Green, are right up there at the top of the league. The fact that his actions that day will become mired in controversy is one for the future.

What matters for me is that the Battle of Goose Green has two consequences: one indirect and ongoing; the other direct, that I only learn about researching this book.

The indirect consequence: Goose Green was a battle fought by inferior numbers of attackers against a well dug-in defence with a full range of modern weapons, including aircraft. From that moment on we, the rest of the Task Force – whilst fully accepting that the Paras are especially tough soldiers – believe that we are better than the Argentines; that we can beat them. In a 1996 newspaper interview, Colonel Hew Pike – Commanding Officer, 3 Para, and a man who truly knows of what he speaks – said that 2 Para's victory at Goose Green gave the rest of us a 'moral ascendancy' over the Argentines.

The direct consequence: Colonel Chaundler, I later read, studies the battle. He concludes that things would have gone very differently had Colonel H used the 'direct fire' weapon systems available, especially The Blues and Royals, whom nobody thought to invite along. They could have suppressed or killed those trenches that caused such loss of life from 1,500 metres to 2km back – and had plenty of ammo left over for follow-up targets.

Colonel Chaundler asks Brigadier Thompson for a troop. Whether other battalion colonels also request a troop, I have no idea. But he really, really wants one. He is determined not to repeat Goose Green.

So, when Chris Keeble takes me to meet him at Fitzroy – me really angry by now that no senior bastard can be bothered to listen to me – and I spout ranges and strengths and weaknesses at him, I am pushing at an already open door. He grabs me, takes me with him, wants to learn how best to use us.

Which is why I am now here, enjoying a cup of coffee in the weak sunlight and watching the peat gout in festive fountains as the enemy shells try but fail to find us.

The Colonel seems a thoroughly sensible chap, but I rather doubt that many Para colonels are shrinking violets when it comes to guns. I wonder if he feels the need to emulate, or even surpass, Colonel H's heroics. I'll be running around beside him tonight. Having come this far I cannot imagine not following him if he decides to charge Argie trenches should push come to bang. But how can anyone know how they will behave should such a moment come?

I fall back on the mantra that has stood me well in the march from Mount Kent to Furze Bush Pass: 'No Para is ever going to be able to say that a Blue and Royal could not hack the pace.' That'll have to do for now. Tonight will bring what it will. I just don't want to let anybody down.

So I, too, oil my rifle; unload and reload my magazines; check there is no dirt on the bullets; put on more cam cream; jump up and down whilst David makes sure I do not clank or clink.

Only a couple of days ago I was cursing about dying of boredom at Brigade. 'Be very, very careful,' I think to myself, 'what you wish for . . .'

'AIRCRAFT!!'

Bloody hell! Where did they come from?

Three Skyhawks crest the col just in front of us and roar overhead, due west, then down the valley towards Mount Kent.

I don't even have time to run to my trench and grab my rifle before they are disappearing into the distance. I'd have loved to have got off a shot at them. But nobody else does.

In training, or on exercise, not to have your rifle always, literally, to hand is THE cardinal sin. Fail to put it in your sleeping bag at night, fail to hold on to it even as you have a crap, and the DS will snatch it. And then you are in big trouble.

But not at Furze Bush Pass. We are too tired, our hands too frozen and damaged, for anybody to be so petty as to bollock us for not keeping our rifles to hand. We are at war, not playing at soldiers. My SLR is propped up against a rock to keep it off the ground. A loaded magazine is clipped in place. I only need to grab it, cock it and fire. It is just not close enough. Dammit!

There's a chap with a Blowpipe surface-to-air missile and he's cursing as his mates jeer at him. By the time he's set up and ready to fire, the aircraft have long gone.

At Sandhurst the army was very excited about Blowpipe, which has recently entered service. I remember the gunner sergeant who taught us about it almost bouncing on his toes as he explained that one of the problems with the current generation of shoulder-mounted anti-aircraft missiles is that they are designed to fire at planes heading away from (or across) you. This, however, means they have dumped their ordnance on you before you can retaliate with a missile up their afterburners. That makes sense, I suppose.

So, the clever folk with pointy heads, white coats and bottle-thick spectacles invented a cunning missile which will engage aircraft coming at you. *Before* they drop their nasty shit on you!

We all look suitably impressed. Failure to do so would have meant twenty-five press-ups and a bollocking. Minimum.

The firer uses his thumb on a miniature joy stick, which talks to the missile and guides it to the target. Super-brilliant when your fingers and thumb can barely move for the cold but, moving swiftly on . . .

And here it is – abracadabra! – Blowpipe. Slight trouble, he concedes, it takes 20 seconds minimum to power up before it can be fired. But who is arguing? It's brilliant. It's the future.

I seem to remember I got to fire a simulator (the live missiles cost far too much to waste on officer cadets) but missed, not being of the miniature joystick/arcade games-playing generation. However, I wondered, even back at Sandhurst, how often a soldier might have the luxury in war of seeing aircraft 20-plus seconds out coming towards him.

The answer, as I have just witnessed, is almost never.

Brigadier Thompson, I now read, described Blowpipe's performance in the Falklands as like 'trying to shoot pheasants with a drainpipe'. It is scrapped soon after – although we continued to sell them to anyone who wants one. (There is a corollary to this sorry tale. Our canny arms dealers did manage to persuade the Argentines to buy them, and they – unlike us – do power them up in time and manage to knock an aircraft down with one. Shame it's a Harrier.)

I feel particularly sorry for that Blowpipe operator. The whole assembly weighs almost 50lbs. Although I have little doubt that his mates helped him hump it here – much as my mates helped me carry the GPMG back on Brigade Squad – he's been responsible for that thing on top of all the other kit he needs to carry just to stay alive. No wonder his mates give him such public 'stick' when he fails to fire it. It is what your chums are for.

There are a couple of ominous-sounding booms from back down the valley. Somebody's copped something – 3 Brigade HQ, it later turns out, although, miraculously, with no casualties.

I make a big mental note to myself. Those Skyhawks can only have come from Port Stanley, which means the airfield is operational. Come tomorrow, by which time I hope our vehicles will have caused mayhem, those planes will be looking for them. They will be a top priority target.

'AIRCRAFT!!'

Well, bugger me sidewise! Those Skyhawks are coming straight back at us.

I rush to grab my rifle. Again.

Blowpipe man stops, turns, rushes to where he will get a clean shot, turning on machine as he does so. He starts to power up.

And they're gone. Back towards Stanley and a nice rum cocktail. They were just too fast and low and came up on us too quickly. Oh how the Paras jeer as dejected Blowpipe man returns to his trench.

It's all change. Again. '**What was thought to be 3 Para on one ridge were in fact enemy – so plan changed for third time.**'

There's going to be a new and, hopefully, final O Group shortly.

David Benest is with the Colonel working out the signals plan. He is part of HQ Main, which is moving with all its heavy kit to a rear position down on the Murrell River, out of sight, hopefully, of the Argie artillery spotters. We say goodbye.

When a Wessex helicopter touches down 50 or so yards from my trench and disgorges a tall, rather lost-looking civilian – as well as our beloved Bergens with our sleeping bags – I wave him over.

'I've got a spare slot in this trench if you want it.'

Perhaps alerted by the sound of the helicopter, a shell lands at that moment, and this chap joins me pretty smartly. '**In late evening joined by Max Hastings, a very charming correspondent and apparently a very successful one. We became chums when the Argies finally found our range and shells started thudding around us. He offered me a cigar and I decided that now was no bad time to start smoking again.**'

Cigars drawing nicely, I pull the Laphroaig from my Bergen. As the sun sets, Max tells me about a book he has written about Bomber Command in the Second World War. I tell him about my university dissertation on late fifteenth century arms and armour, as used in the Wars of the Roses, which my examiners suggested I try to get published. If it weren't for the shells, and the encroaching cold, and a sudden snow storm, and the fast approaching night terrors, it would be a thoroughly civilized evening and, I reflect to myself as we savour a final shot of malt, incontrovertible evidence of the value of a degree in Medieval History to the modern army officer.

Chapter 16

The Battle of Wireless Ridge

And gentlemen in England now a-bed Shall think themselves accursed they were not here, And hold their manhoods cheap whiles any speaks That fought with us upon Saint Crispin's day.
   King Henry V's speech, before the Battle of Agincourt, 1415. *Henry V*, Act IV, Scene III

The Colonel yet again gives his O Group for the attack on Wireless Ridge, this time with no interruptions or changes. Cryptic notes tell me the 'highlights', if you can describe them as such, include:

- 'G' Squadron SAS, now their sneaky-beaky scouting role, has become redundant with Port Stanley awaiting us just beyond Wireless Ridge, have formed as a squadron and will attack, as a squadron, on our left flank. A waterborne, surprise attack of some sort.
  This, I later hear, is a very damp squib, which rather amuses we 'lesser' soldiers. Sorry, SAS . . .
- Brigade Intelligence believes the enemy is in regimental strength. Hmm . . .
- Tonight is going to be much like Goose Green and Mount Longdon. With us, it follows, suffering similar numbers of casualties.
  General Frost's book says that General Menendez (commander Argentine forces) tells the 2 Para officer he surrenders to the next day that we fought their 1ˢᵗ Parachute Battalion. Wiki says 7ᵗʰ Infantry Regiment and 10ᵗʰ Cavalry Squadron. Another example, to this day, of the 'fog of war' . . . All I know, as I sit and listen and take occasional notes and keep my face as impassive as the battle-hardened warriors around me, is that there will be as many of them as us.
- We've spotted minefields – plural. I'll wager mine is not the only sphincter that tightens as the Colonel utters that dread word. Lurking

killer, or leg-removing traps, hidden in the earth; the stuff of a soldier's nightmares, not least as they are so random and arbitrary.
Mines bring on the most unchristian and unofficer-like of thoughts: 'I hope the poor bugger in front of me steps on it before I do . . .'
- **'Minefields marked orange wire ankle height.'**
It's pitch black. Weather worsening. I wonder how we will spot that wire. Wait for someone to go bang, I suppose . . .
- Last and very much not least: **'3573** [that's a grid square, 1km x 1 km] **Panhard Squadron'**, says Colonel David.

Nobody here seems unduly concerned. Much, I suppose, as 5 Brigade at Fitzroy were stunned and surprised by the shock and power of the Argie air force, these infanteers seem to have little understanding what armoured vehicles are capable of. Stands to reason, I suppose. If the bosses had got their brains around that they'd have used us in every battle so far, including Mount Longdon last night. Instead, we've hardly been used at all.

I have no idea how 4 Troop is faring down south with 5 Brigade, although I very much doubt the benighted Brigadier has had a sudden epiphany. This is not good news, though. A squadron has sixteen-plus vehicles against our four. Poor odds.

Worse, we will be attacking over open ground. If they know their business – and why wouldn't they? – the enemy will be 'hull-down' behind cover with only the tops of their turrets showing, making them tiny targets for our boys to fire at.

The first we'll know that they are there is when they open fire. And when they do they should know the exact ranges to our various approaches and likely fire positions. Back on our firing ranges our gunnery instructors would 'cheat' and learn the ranges to the targets. Then they would tell us so that, come the gunnery tests, our vehicles will be better able to hit their targets first shot – and get higher scores. Which burnishes the regiment's credentials and the Commanding Officer's Annual Report. There's going to be none of that peacetime cheating here . . .

Or think of those Hollywood films, where the cunning defenders – that is if they have commanders with brains – put piles of whitewashed stones every hundred yards to mark out the range for their archers, or infantry, or cannons, or trebuchets. Whether they are redcoats defending Isandlwana against the Zulus, or Crusaders trying to stop Saladin capturing Jerusalem, the theory remains unchanged. That is what I would do if I were in charge of those Panhards defending Wireless Ridge.

Conversely, we attackers will have to 'guesstimate' ranges for our opening shots. Once we get the range we will be away. However, our vehicles don't carry ranging equipment, and the human eye, even a trained human eye, they teach us at Gunnery School, tends to be about 20 per cent out when making an initial range guesstimate. That gives the enemy a massive initial advantage and is yet another reason why the military rule books stipulate a 3-1 superiority in attackers over defenders if the attack is going to have any confidence of success.

What's more, they've had two and a half months to prepare for tonight. If that were T23 defending that ridge, I have no doubt there would be four bangs from four carefully concealed armoured vehicles and four blazing hulks. Game over.

However, we are – hallelujah! – attacking at night. And we have one thing they do not: our light-intensifying gunner's night sight.

Without night sights, and back on Chieftains, which have huge searchlights mounted on the side of their turrets, we needed overhead illumination – flares, mortars, Schermuly rockets, Verey pistols, even Royal Artillery and Naval guns (we have them all on call tonight) – to 'see' our targets.

Likewise, those Panhards will need overhead illumination to 'see' and shoot at us.

Our light-intensifying sights are the latest technology, turning black into grainy, speckled green. They are primitive compared to the gizmos that today's shoot-'em-up films depict as turning night into sharply defined green day. Nevertheless, they are complete game-changers. On the island of the blind at night, the one-grainy-green-eyed man is king.

However, and it is a rapidly worsening however, our sights need ambient moon or starlight to intensify. The longer the range, the worse the degradation, and tonight is getting ever blacker as the weather worsens.

Oh well, look on the bright side. If we cannot see them, how will they see us?

'**Tac 1 will move out at 2030 local**', which time I will use from here on in. Using Z – London time – makes it far more difficult to understand what is happening as it bears little resemblance to when it is night and day on the Falklands. If it is still confusing me as I write this – which it is, and I am using my contemporaneous Z-timed notes and books – then it will certainly confuse the reader.

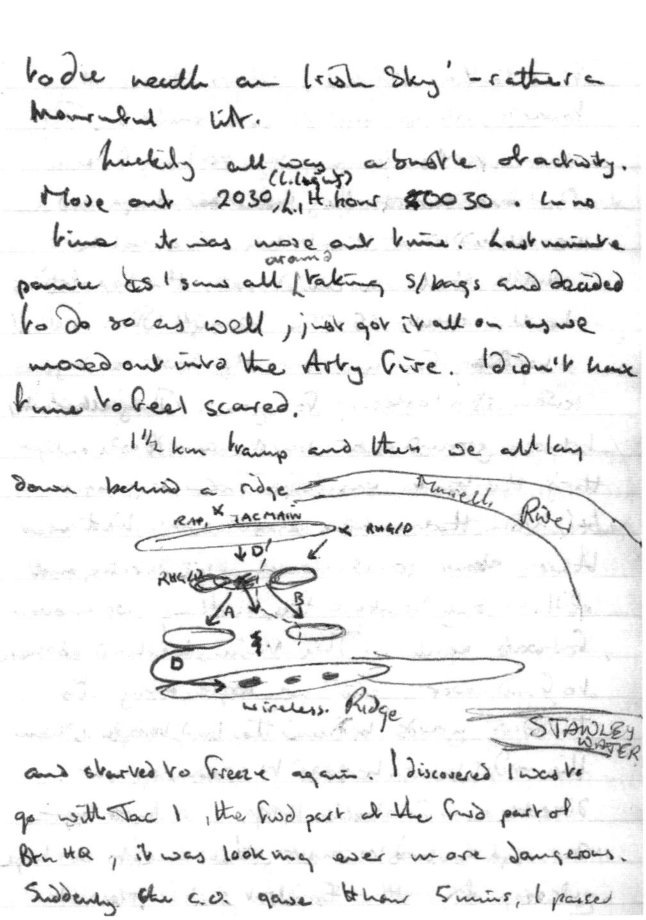

to die neath an Irish Sky' – rather a mournful lilt.

Luckily all way a bustle of activity. Move out 2030, L.1 H hour, 0030. So no time it was move out time. Last minute panic as I saw all around taking S/bags and decided to do so as well, just got it all on as we moved out into the Arty fire. I didn't have time to feel scared.

1½ km tramp and then we all lay down behind a ridge

and started to freeze again. I discovered I was to go with Tac 1, the fwd part of the fwd part of Bn HQ, it was looking ever more dangerous. Suddenly the C.O. gave H hour 5 mins, I passed

Back to my trench for a last sort-out. A Para pops over. Private Francis Slough came to visit when I was at the O Group, he tells me. Slough hasn't been able to make it before because he is dug in on the far side of the valley, but hearing that The Blues and Royals are in town and that I am here as well, he marched alone through the shellfire that is pummelling the valley floor to say hello. Slough was in my troop when I was stationed with the Junior Leaders Regiment for a year in 1980 (we took 'likely' sixteen-year-olds for two years and turned them into future NCOs). He impressed me and my DS immediately, and we promoted him quickly. However, he later decided the cavalry – or was he badged RMP? I no longer remember – was not for him and transferred to the Paras. Thinking about it, he could easily have been RMP, as they were often academically brighter, and Slough was a very bright lad – a definite cut above his fellows. Slough said to tell me that he is sorry to have missed me and will catch up with me tomorrow.

And I am sorry to have missed him. I am also very touched that he walked through shellfire to say hello. It will be good to see a friendly face tomorrow; do a bit of 'cavalry' reminiscing for a change, even if he has become a warry Para.

My radio sparks into life: **'Call sign 23 spotted an armoured car. Could he fire?**

2 Para agrees.

Two rounds fired and then a freak snowstorm intervenes. That sums up the weather.

Move out 2030 [last light 17.30 local time].

H-Hour 0030 [21.30 local].

Last minute panic as I saw all around [disobeying orders and] taking sleeping bags and decided to do so as well. Just got all my kit on as we moved out into the artillery fire. I didn't have time to feel scared.

One and a half kilometre tramp and then we all lay down behind a ridge and started to freeze again.

Suddenly the C.O. gave "H-Hour 5 minutes".

Passed it on to the vehicles.

Our group moved off, towards where gunfire now sounded.'

First the Royal Artillery and the Navy blast the ridge. Then it is my turn. I am on the troop chatter net: '3' – that's Robin, the troop leader; 'Alpha' – Corporal of Horse Thompson; 'Bravo' – Lance Corporal of Horse Dunkeley; and 'Charlie' – Lance Corporal of Horse Fisher.

I think I designated myself 'Nine' – which is a control call sign.

It is very simple, very direct and very effective. Colonel David and I can see our vehicles firing; they are liberally blasting anything they see shooting at us from the far ridgeline. Filthy weather notwithstanding, the night sights have no problems whatsoever in picking out and 'intensifying' the vivid flashes from the ends of the Argies' gun barrels as they fire at us. 'Spitting flame' is the corny comic-book expression used by myriad lazy war writers, but that is pretty much what it looks like in a night sight: white spits of flame.

D Company under Major Neame attacks first. It is the position Colonel David was initially told was 3 Para.

At some point his men are getting too close to our fire. He radioes the Colonel on the battalion net and says he needs our vehicles to shift their fire 50 metres to the left.

I'm right beside the Colonel – this is where he wants me to stay from here on in. He tells me what D Company wants.

'Hello 3, this is 9, shift fire 50 meters left. Getting too close. Over.'

'Three, Wilco. Out.'

Fire shifts left. Paras now out of danger. It's that simple.

Or, a position is giving them a problem. D Company describes where it is, using whatever features are available – streams of fire, even 'Watch my Gimpy burst,' or 'Watch my Very cartridge.' Bang! Up it goes.

I relay this to Robin, and he details off who is to attack. D Company radioes in when the problem is solved. Paras move forward. Nice and quick and informal.

We fight 'our' armoured battle on our own radio net, whilst the Colonel talks to all his other arms and subordinates without us further jamming up his airwaves. It takes us moments to eradicate any problems.

On occasion all four vehicles pour their fire on to a single position, streams of 7.62mm tracer and the more occasional 30mm and 76mm main armament rounds smashing into whatever is causing the hold-up and neutralizing or killing it; overwhelming it, in fact. No other weapon system achieves anything similar. We are the 'support arms' stars of tonight's *son et lumière* spectacular, as General Frost subsequently makes clear in the very first line of this book: 'If any particular group deserves special praise for what was done that night, then it must be the tanks of The Blues and Royals.' Although, for the fiftieth blinking time, General, they are not tanks, they are armoured cars . . .

And, military theorists and non-theorists, note my use of the term 'Support Arms' because, whilst we may be blasting the defending Argies to Valhalla, only Para boots on the ground can secure the Ridge itself. Armoured vehicles, however nasty, cannot do that. The Paras have to get into those enemy trenches and sangars and clear them. Only then can we, and they, move on.

Not that we are having it all our own way.

'**The main problem for us was artillery fire. On one occasion they found our range and we all huddled at the bottom of a bank whilst shells screamed into the top of the bank about 15–25m away. When a shell is heading for you it really howls and you know it is looking** for you. They alternated between ground and air burst and it was only that the bank was so prominent, about four feet high, that no one was hurt.'

The shells land on us so suddenly that Colonel David and I dive behind the bank together. His two close protection snipers, plus Major Rice and his signaller, are about 10–15 yards further along the bank. We two lie facing each other on the semi-sodden, semi-frozen ground, the wet beginning to seep up and into me. We cannot move. It is Colonel David who flicks the first bit of mud at me – sorry, Colonel! – scoring a direct hit on my face.

He grins. 'Got you!'

As I take aim and prepare to return fire I think back to the stern look on my Company Commander's face at Sandhurst as he gave me my 'half-term' report and told me that I must learn to take life far more seriously if I am to succeed in the army. Even as I nodded earnestly and told him I would do so from here on in, part of me was wondering why – if he too took the army so seriously – his chums called him 'Pissy'.

And here I am, as near to death as I have ever been, just been hit in the face by a naughty schoolboy Colonel, each of us with a huge grin on his face. In spite of that long ago reprimand, it is much as I have always imagined it would be: imminent death is far too serious to be taken seriously. Die with a smile on your face, or feeling miserable? No choice.

'Gotcha!' Direct hit by me.

The Colonel prepares to retaliate . . .

'We stayed there about 10–15 minutes until, during one of the breaks in the shelling, we moved forward again. This time we had nowhere to find cover and we were only a few hundred yards behind the lead troops. When the odd tracer [round] began to come in our direction and shells began to burst we again had to move, this time to a large outcrop of rock.

Excellent shelter; reasonable view of the battle, but an obvious enemy DF. And so it turned out to be.

Shells suddenly came at us, straight at us. One landed the opposite side of the rock I was behind. So near that I could smell the cordite, even with my cold.'

I nearly lose my hearing. The shell hits that rock so hard and so loud and so close that my ears are literally ringing. Another hackneyed term, but how else to describe the overwhelming effects of such a near miss?

But all is going well with D Company, who capture their objective within an hour and a half. Far, far quicker than anticipated; and with far, far fewer casualties.

'I had been leaping in and out of the mud, convinced that my original Sandhurst view of life was utterly correct, namely, that anybody doing what I was doing now when they could be in a nice warm armoured car must be mad.'

If they taught me this trick at Sandhurst, I have forgotten it. Diving into the frozen peat as yet another barrage lands, I get some mud stuck in the flash suppressor at the end of my barrel. Some of the Paras are using condoms taped to the end of their rifles to ensure they stay clean; others are using masking tape. Fire a high-velocity round with even a speck of mud inside the barrel and there is a goodly risk of the barrel 'bananaing ', or exploding. However, I don't think the regimental history books will look kindly on me, were I, a Blue and Royal – an apparently hopelessly effete so-called 'Piccadilly Cowboy' – to have said to a hairy-arsed, Village People-moustachioed Para, 'Might I borrow a condom? Please . . .'

And now I need to clean that mud out fast; with the attack developing as it is, I may need my SLR.

Colonel David is being thoroughly sensible. He is observing his tactical bounds; keeping back and controlling his overall battle whilst letting his company commanders control theirs. But are the Argentines following the Sandhurst rulebook? We are in a maelstrom of blackness and confusion, a kaleidoscope of exploding shells and illuminants; bright white one moment, deep dark the next; walls of light and shadow that move across the battlefield as flares light up high in the sky and then float to the ground on their mini-parachutes. Streams of tracer, ours and theirs, arc in and out and, just as quickly, disappear. We could easily happen into an Argentine position, or Argentine soldiers into us. I need my rifle.

I scrub away at my flash suppressor using a cotton handkerchief and spittle. The DS solution would doubtless be to break the rifle open and run a square of cotton down the barrel. But not now. First, I don't know if I have time. We could be up and running to a new position at any moment. Second, I'm crawling around in so much filth that there's a strong risk I could introduce even more dirt into the weapon. I do the best I can and hope that I don't have to find out the hard way whether I have succeeded. I am cross with myself. My infantry instructors would be pissed off with me. All that training. I'm meant to be better than this. I'll bet none of the Paras have mud in the ends of their rifles. Then again, these Paras could not operate an armoured car. Each to his own speciality.

Worse, my radio is as good as dead. My batteries having been going flat at the rate of more than one an hour. A couple do not even work when I replace them. Each should last many hours. I felt rather guilty when my first battery packed up in very short order, as I suspected that using the radio (plus attached battery) as a sort of metal mattress to keep me off the ground during that short rest break on the frozen march to Furze Bush Pass might have killed it – cold and damp being the last things a battery wants. But I'm probably blaming myself unnecessarily, since each fresh one I clip on pegs out just as quickly.

David's view when I tell him about this afterwards is that, while the batteries were checked and were working before they were issued to me, my appearance was so last-minute that they gave me what they had left, and these last ones doubtless had the least charge (they are recharged on a petrol-powered generator, all of which takes time). Adding to that the extreme cold, and what little power some had in them to start with, and it meant that mine lasted no time at all. They did the best they could; it is what it is.

When my last battery also fails, I tell the Colonel. He deems what I am doing so vital that he gives me priority on the brigade rear link radio which one of his signallers carries.

I keep at it, manoeuvring the vehicles forward on the Colonel's command and passing on his direct fire requirements.

And then it's all change. Yet again.

At about 0230 (2330 local) call sign T23B, a Scimitar, comes up on the air and reports that L/CoH Dunkeley, the vehicle commander, has been knocked unconscious. He's been smashed over the head by the turret hatch – suffering 'hatch rash', as it's known as.

What I need to do next is obvious. Without Corporal Dunkeley to command the vehicle and load the guns the Colonel has just lost 25 per cent of the firepower that is having such electrifying effects. 2 Para needs me in that vehicle and the troop back to full strength as quickly as possible.

'**I volunteered my services to the C.O. instantly; who smiled and said, "Certainly. You've been waiting for this, haven't you?"**

I most certainly had.'

T23B is told to drive back to the RAP (Regimental Aid Post) with Tac Main down on the Murrell River. I will walk back and meet it there.

'I was only scared twice during the campaign [the first time under that table at Fitzroy with the Skyhawks zeroing in]. This second time was different. I was to move back *alone* [contemporary emphasis], about 2 kilometres, over ground that which was being continually shelled. My fear was of being hit and dying alone, with nobody even realising I was missing [because, apart from the C.O., a trifle occupied in fighting his battle, nobody else was even aware that I was there]. And, since I was not even with my own regiment, no-one even terribly bothered. The only thing I could do was radio in and tell the RAP I would be returning alone; not to shoot me and, if I did not appear, report me missing.

And with that off I went.'

Perhaps it is only the secret agent, the saboteur, who truly appreciates what it is like going off into the killing fields on his own. Everything I have ever done throughout my training – my schooling, even – involves teamwork. We soldiers do everything together. Every lesson is, in some way, about looking after each other. Even when we do something as basic as sentry duty, we do it in pairs, one supporting the other.

The very heart of the regimental system is that you know that your soldiers will go way beyond the extra mile to get you home – just as you would for them; even if it is only your body that they collect, although within reason. We don't glory in talking about 'leaving no man behind' as some armies do, but I know it all the same. My 'The Blues and Royals' cap badge really does mean something – but only to fellow Blues and Royals.

From the moment I joined the Paras I have known I am on my own. They don't know me. They don't owe me anything. I doubt if anybody would feel compelled to rush forward and risk their life to help me if I were wounded. Why should they? Writing this, I wonder how far I would risk myself for one of them.

That said, I do have a slender bond, I hope, with one man: the Colonel. He invited me along. He knows who I am. I hope he now sees me as one of 'his'. But, apart from David who is back with Tac Main, he's the only one.

This next bit is going to be something altogether different again. From here on, until I reach Tac Main, I really am on my own.

The night is now bright and sharp, the ground bleached white with a deep frost that covers even the rocks. Those earlier sleet and snow flurries were yesterday's weather. Map reading is now far easier. This is not somewhere I want to get lost, or even go slightly astray, lest I bump into soldiers who are not expecting to see me, who have no idea who I am and who, jumpy already with the sheer quantity of ordnance flying in both directions, might shoot first and ask questions afterwards, as the hackneyed but all too accurate phrase has it. Walking a battlefield alone has to be one of the better ways of getting yourself shot in error.

And I am trusting – hoping, more like – that this moonlight will give me a far better chance of spotting any of those ankle-height wires that the Colonel told us the Argies use to mark their dratted minefields. Not that I've seen any so far.[1] Bullets and shells coming at me are a clear and present danger, a threat I have so far been handling mentally. Mines are psychological horrors, hidden, waiting, wanting to kill or maim you as if from nowhere – H.G Wells' terrifying Morlocks, rising from beneath the ground to drag you under.

I continue my lonely trudge. Illuminants arc up into the sky, dangle high in the air, pierce the battlefield with a harsh overhead light and then, just as suddenly, dim and die. We are taught to close one eye the moment we see or hear a flare being fired. Our instructors explain that it takes 20 minutes of continual darkness for our eyes to reach peak efficiency. A second of bright light is all it takes to 'blind' us. Then we need to start all over again. I'm good at this. Brigade Squad and Sandhurst were relentless in training us to protect our night vision.

Lines of tracer fly back and forth. Guns boom and shells go bang. We're killing each other out here, although it is difficult to get my brain around this very simple fact. Just keep moving . . .

I crest a low ridge. As I do so, the moonlight that is helping me find my way back towards the Murrell River must betray me to a hidden artillery spotter, because, no more than some thirty seconds later as I walk down the reverse slope, silently thanking whatever gods might be looking out for me tonight that I am at last safely into 'dead ground' and out of direct fire from Wireless Ridge in the distance, I hear artillery shells reaching out for me. I don't hesitate as I dive to the ground. Flatten myself. I know

---

1. On a Veterans' 25th Anniversary visit I re-walked Wireless Ridge. And, oh Mummy! I was shown some minefields, each neatly surrounded by a substantial, multi-strand barbed wire fence with skull and crossbones and 'Beware Mines' warning signs. A couple are close to where I had walked. The Argentines, it subsequently turned out, were not much given to marking their minefields, if at all . . .

exactly what is coming next. If I felt alone on my solitary journey so far, I feel very, very alone as I prepare to receive 'incoming'.

The shells burst along 'my' ridge. Airbursts. Each explosion flings shrapnel over a wide area. Airburst is designed to kill and maim infantry out in the open and is far more lethal to me than those ground-burst shells which disappear into the peat before erupting upwards in a huge gout of earth. **'Shell bursts overhead. Something thumps into the ground beside me. Every time there was a gap in the firing I made a dash; the air full of artillery. When I finally reached the RAP, frantically flashing my torch, it was to find them under fire as well. But here at least were other humans.'**

Time to find call sign Bravo, the Scimitar I teamed up with back in Fitzroy when it developed a gearbox fault. It's turned pitch black again and, whilst I can hear its engine ticking over quietly, out there in the darkness, I cannot see it. Then a rumble – they must have been looking around to find the RAP – and, suddenly, there she is. Stretcher-bearers help L/CoH Dunkeley out of the turret. He has two shell dressings on his head, soaked with blood. He rallies for a moment, demands to carry on, then lapses back into unconsciousness. He will be put on the next available helicopter – 656 Squadron are flying ammunition up and casualties back through the shelling – and taken to the nearest Medical Station. From there he is taken to SS *Uganda*, the hospital ship – and he makes a full recovery.

'Then followed a treasured moment.

I popped my head into the turret. A startled white face looked at me and then split into the hugest grin I had seen in years.

"Oh, Sir. Thank God you're here," said Trooper Ford, the gunner. He then, in a small, frightened, voice,[2] told me how they had finally managed to find their way to the RAP, under shellfire part of the time, some of it very close. They were lost and had had to tell the troop leader what they could see; who had then told them where to go.

---

2. Trooper Ford went on to become a Corporal Major and a very formidable soldier. Back in 1982 he was a young trooper who had just witnessed his vehicle commander being smashed into unconsciousness in the middle of his first battle. I think we can allow him that small moment of weakness, immediately shoved aside. But this is what I wrote about him a couple of days later, with that picture of him fresh in my mind.

Within seconds fear turned to bravado. Trooper Round, the driver, appeared and in no time I had two cheeky and cheerful troopers on my hands.

I was back with the Regiment.

Guffaws and wisecracks. Accusations of "Grunt" when they lifted the incredible weight of my webbing onto the turret and took in my cam-creamed face and tin helmet. They pointed out that I could be thrown out of the Regiment for this type of behaviour.'

Tin helmet off. Blue beret back on. Thank God.

'I climbed in and asked for a five minute refresher on 30mm drills. This amused Ford immensely as, he pointed out, it was me who had taught him gunnery in the first place, even reminding me of some of the jokes I had cracked during my lectures. [I decide to skip the refresher!]'

I check the ammunition position; plenty remaining. Ford points out some new 30mm rounds they had been given with black-tipped heads. I haven't seen this type before.

'Depleted uranium,' he explains. 'They're new and we're trying them out. They're not on general issue yet.'

I understand the concept. This solid bullet (no explosive in it) is much heavier than normal steel and, when it hits, it either smashes a neat hole through the target or, if the armour is too thick, then the kinetic energy generated will turn the strike area into a molten furnace, melting anybody inside. They will be lethal against the Panhards, but of almost zero use against anything else. They will drill straight through and out the other side of a soft-skinned vehicle, like a huge bullet. Hit a sangar with one and it will smash up that rock like any bullet, but nothing more. They exist for one purpose only: killing Panhards.

Time to rejoin the battle. I am, I realize, feeling quietly homicidal. I've never considered myself a killer. Preferred to think of myself as more of a pacifist; in the army for the skiing, the sailing and the fun, even though I love playing with things that go bang.

However, that somewhat happy-go-lucky me was another victim of our bloody tour of Northern Ireland. I spent the rest of that tour being impeccably, coldly, polite. I once forced my boys to help me push-start an IRA bomber's stalled car – we'd stopped her at our VCP and we knew exactly who she was. They didn't like it, but they did as I asked.

I called her by her name – 'Miss X' – as I offered to do so. I wanted to psych her out as I showed her that we were not the SS stormtroopers of IRA propaganda. However, even as I pushed, her ancient battery sparked into life and she drove off with a backwards 'Fuck you!', I was itching for her – or any terrorist, for that matter – to point a weapon at me. She'd have got a 7.62 round straight back. No hesitation. The least I owed my dead boys.

And here I am again. The Argentines have spent much of the last six days trying to kill me. I don't hate them as such. In fact I feel nothing for them as individuals. But, as a nation, they have been killing our soldiers, people I know (I still assume they killed Mike Forge), bombing and shelling me in a very focused and personal way. I've experienced some very near misses tonight. Now, at last, it is my turn. Payback time – I can think of no better expression.

'It was a bright moonlit night, with a deep, deep frost as we moved back to the battle – quite eerie with the distant chatter of machine guns and bursting illuminants. The only movement was that of small groups of stretcher bearers, dark against the white carpet, carrying their sad loads. Exhausted, they put down their stretchers to exchange a brief word of greeting as we passed. It was as one imagined a First World War battlefield, not one of the 1980s. The constant whine of artillery shells, the harsh back drop, small groups of men huddled together for shelter and warmth, others moving gently forward for the next attack. Modern technology was not apparent on Wireless Ridge.'

I ask Ford what happened to Corporal Dunkeley.

'We were manoeuvring forwards,' he tells me. 'He had his head out of the turret to try and see where we were going.'

Which was not much when the vehicle dropped into a huge 155mm shell hole. The catch that holds the commander's hatch in place on top of the turret failed when they hit the bottom. WHAM! The heavy lump of aluminium broke free and, pivoting on its hinges, smashed down on his head. Despite wearing his protective 'bone dome', he was knocked unconscious.

'Do you want his helmet, Sir?'

Ford hands it over.

The regiment was issued with these fairly recently. They have integral radio earphones and will protect my head against a repeat hatch strike. Had Dunkeley not been wearing his, I suspect the blow could have killed him. I look inside. Full of blood. That and the fact that I'm 'old school', have never worn anything other than my beret in the turret, means I decide not to wear his blood-soaked helmet. I'll just have to make sure that the now damaged hatch does not strike twice.

The commander's sight and vision periscopes are useless at night. Normally I would snap the hatch back into position and peer over the top of the commander's cupola so I can best see what is going on. However, that is exactly what Dunkeley was doing when the hatch hit him.

I've listened to lectures about the Arab-Israeli tank battles. Apparently, lots of Israeli tank commanders were killed not by enemy tank fire but by snipers or stray shrapnel as they stuck their heads out of their turrets, desperate to see where they were going. Getting my head drilled through by one of the mass of bits of flying steel that is turning Wireless Ridge into a demonic laser show is not how I plan to exit the island.

But I have to see, because Trooper Round, down below turret level in his driver's seat, has very limited vision. Even during the day he needs help. At night, with his hatch closed to keep the bullets and shrapnel out, he cannot see what is right in front of him. He needs me to tell him where to steer.

The inside of my hatch has a thick, padded, plastic-covered interior cushion. My solution, as we head back into the gunfire, is to rest the hatch on my head. As I guessed it would, it bounces up and down on the top of my skull as the vehicle lurches up and down through the the pot holes. But, as long as it doesn't bounce too high before thumping back down, it's not doing me too much damage.

We motor back towards the fighting, as I peer through the narrow gap between the bottom of the hatch and top of the turret ring, telling Round exactly where to steer and hoping not to get my head shot off or my brain stove in – my own DS solution.

'I was exhilarated at doing battle with my Regiment in an environment I knew; delighted to be off my feet and back with my own men; cracking jokes; listening to their war stories; shouting at the driver when he went the wrong way, and getting back into the swing of things [being an armoured soldier].'

It takes me mere moments to solve what I think of as the *Zulu* dilemma. In the 1964 film – to which I and generations of small boys thrilled – Stanley Baker's Royal Engineers Lieutenant Chard takes overall command of the missionary station when he asks Michael Caine's Lieutenant Bromhead, 24th (2nd Warwickshire) Regiment of Foot – and not the *Men*

The Battle of Wireless Ridge 141

of Harlech-singing Welsh Borderers – what his army number is. Every soldier is given a number when he joins, one following on from the other. Chard then tells Bromhead that he is senior to him by dint of having a lower number and, hey presto, he is in charge. Bromhead does not argue and, in the film at least, as good as surrenders command of his own men.

Any Blue and Royal would tell a similarly ranked non-Blue and Royal pulling such a stunt to, in polite terms, 'Go rotate'.

This, however, is very different. I am a captain in The Blues and Royals, Robin a lieutenant. I am way senior to him. And more experienced.

But, but, but . . .

I am very impressed with the way he is commanding the troop. Their drills are super-slick. Moreover, I was A squadron before joining Regimental HQ. These guys are B. I hardly know the NCOs – they have never served with me, or under me – and I don't know some of the troopers at all.

Nor do they know me. Turning up in the middle of a full-on battle, telling them I am taking control, might be the action of a thrusting keeno or a Hollywood hero, but it does not feel right to me. Don't mess with something when it is working so well; my mission is to help, not cause confusion.

'Hello 23, this is 23 Bravo. Rejoining you. Where do you want me? Over.'

That tells everyone what I am doing without spelling it out.

'23. Take the extreme left. Over.'

'23 Bravo. Wilco out.'

No one has ever asked me since why I didn't claim seniority and take command. I must have hit on the correct DS solution, without ever being taught it . . .

As I drive up a track on to a ridge I spot two of the other vehicles. The third is some way over to my right. We ease forward to find a good fire position, then I spot some men in the way. They turn out to be machine-gun platoon. I warn them to move off to a side as, if I fire over their heads I might damage their eardrums. They move behind a rock, off to my right, where they **'spend a restless evening waiting for me to hit their rock by mistake.**

Call sign 23A seemed to be playing a little game. A short burst of GPMG fire; the Argentineans usually fired back. The cars hit the source of the enemy tracer; that particular position would not fire again.'

Then someone fires at us from Wireless Ridge and we go into action.

We fire for about 2–3 hours in all, but time telescopes and only certain incidents stand out clearly; what actual order they happen in I cannot remember, even when I came to write up the battle three days later.

'Ford staring down the night sight, spotting movement.

'Got something . . . Fire'

Half a box of GPMG later, [Ford] gives them a couple of 30mm [rounds].'

At night, unlike daytime when the commander controls every aspect of the shoot using his powerful commander's sight, only the gunner can see what is going on through his night sight.

As the commander is blind, the sequence of giving 'fire orders' is reversed: the gunner reports a target; the commander loads the guns – both the 30mm Rarden cannon and the 7.62 GPMG; he tells the gunner when the guns are loaded and ready to fire; the gunner tells the commander that he is firing.

The only partial control the commander has at night is, first, telling the gunner he is good to fire; second, perhaps choosing a priority target if there is a choice; and finally, deciding what type of ammunition to load. But, once again, given that he is entirely reliant on the gunner to tell him what he will be firing at, the type of target pretty much dictates what ammunition he selects.

'My fingers are so broken and sore at the ends [from where dirt and grunge has compacted under my fingernails which are beginning to fester] that I find difficulty in loading as fast as I would like. However [my loading] gets very fast by the end [as the blood pumps through my fingers and the pain disappears in the excitement.]

I spot the flash of a gun. "Traverse left."

"Got it."

"Fire."

Other vehicles have also spotted it. Whoever that was will not shoot again in a hurry.'

A burst of three anti-aircraft shells streak over the top of the turret. They wink like devil fireworks as the trace element in their tails burns towards and then past us in long, festive-looking lines before exploding in star clusters that will rip us apart if they connect. They seem horribly low. How low, I'm not certain. I've never before tried to calculate the height of shells coming straight at me.

Another burst of Triple A. I look carefully. They are coming from way, way over to my left. Trouble is, these Triple A's have a super-long range for engaging distant aircraft, far longer range than my own 30mm Rarden cannon. There is no chance of me engaging it. They obviously haven't got night sights or we'd be dead already, but I need to confuse its aim. Time to 'jockey' – shift to a new position.

'Driver reverse.'

'I can't, Sir. The accelerator pedal has broken.'

'Well, bodge it,' I tell him.

'I am.'

'What with?'

'Black masking tape . . .'

Round later tells me that he was already on his stomach, head-first on the floor, desperately wrapping tape around the broken-off pedal when I tell him to get moving 'Now!' as we are about to have our turret blown off.

Nothing for it but to hold our nerve and hope those shells don't find our range.

'Ready, Sir!' says Round.

At last.

I stick my head and shoulders right out of the turret, regardless of the risk of getting them shot off. I have to direct him as he reverses. I am also very aware of the Paras dug in all around us. The Colonel has even joined us with his Tac 1.

We reverse. Then we drive off to one side before, finally, moving forward again to take up a new fire position about 100 yards to the right. In theory, we should 'jockey' every time we fire a few rounds, lest somebody is lining up on us. Every time we jockey they have to re-find us and line up on us all over again.

In reality, and especially in the dark, there are very few alternative fire positions to move to on this short stretch of ridge. Furthermore, every time I move I risk squashing some poor Para. So I don't. Until, that is, something nasty happens, like that AA gun zeroing in on us. Then I need to jockey double quick-sticks, and I'll leave it to the Paras to get out of our way.

For some reason the Triple A stops as suddenly as it started. I have no idea why. I am just mightily relieved.

We get back to our work. Inevitably perhaps, the GPMG stops firing – I later discover that, by the end of the night, only two out of the six tripod-mounted 'SF' (sustained fire) GPMGs used by 2 Para's Machine

Gun Platoon are still functioning. Misfire drills, taught at Gunnery School, dictate that if the Gimpy stops we should wait a standard 10 minutes in case a round in the red hot breech of the gun 'cooks off'. This works fine on the range. There we put up a red flag to show we have a misfire and sneak a quick cup of coffee whilst we wait out the required time. But not here. Not tonight. '**I turn my face away as [Ford fires] so that, if there is a breach explosion, it doesn't damage me too much. Not taught like that at Lulworth.**

Another stoppage. [This time it looks to be my fault as I cannot see any belt and rounds in the GPMG. That means I must have allowed it to run out of ammo].

I play safe [this time].

My God.

An obstruction [in the gun] with only 3 rounds left [in the belt, which is why I assume it has run out of ammo].

Cautions wins as I hold the working parts back [and clear the obstruction], otherwise [had I just loaded a new belt without checking I would have "fired" a new live round into the back of the bullet currently stuck in the breach]. There would have been a drama [perhaps a breach explosion, with bits of deadly ammunition flying around the inside of the turret].'

Something else they don't teach me at Lulworth is that I need to lever off the tops of all the metal 7.62mm ammunition boxes. Some come off quick and easy. Others are a bastard to remove, especially with my swollen and painful hands and fingers. There just isn't time to frig around with a jammed lid when I need to get the Gimpy reloaded and pour a load of unpleasantness back at the Ridge in double quick time.

I teach myself another trick. As soon as one box of 200 rounds is half empty I take the end of that half-used belt and clip it to the first round of a fresh belt. That way I should always have about 300 rounds ready to fire if need be. What is more, I won't have to cock and reload the gun at the end of each belt we've fired.

We are blasting through our 30mm main armament as well. I also use any 'quiet' moments – relatively speaking – to reposition the clips of three rounds nearest to where my hand will naturally drop as I grab the next clip. I am only using HE (High Explosive) and APSE (Armour Piercing Secondary Effects) to wreck their rock sangars and force their heads down in their trenches. I store the depleted uranium rounds off to one side, ready for those Panhards should they come out and play.

We are firing amazing numbers of Gimpy rounds. '**The rate one gets through it is incredible.**'

We learn, both at infantry school and at Lulworth Gunnery School, that a Gimpy 'ranging burst' should be about 2–3 rounds of trace – tracer rounds are used every other round – so each ranging burst uses 4–6 rounds. This is how it is meant to go:

> Spot target. Ranging burst. Adjust fire. Another ranging burst. Hit it. 'Target!' Now the gunner has your confirmation that he is hitting the target.
>
> Perhaps 8–12 rounds used establishing the range to the target. Maybe less, maybe more. Depends on how many ranging bursts the gunner takes to hit the target. Of course, once Ford has the range to one trench then, should another open fire nearby, he remembers his 'sight picture' as it is called and hits that next trench with his first burst. That's what good gunners do. And Ford is a bloody good gunner.
>
> Once the gunner has ranged in and hit the target, his next burst will be a 'killing burst'. A maximum, as taught, 5–10 trace rounds.

Not on Wireless Ridge. Not tonight. At least not in call sign 23B. Once Ford acquires the target, I tell him to 'Give it welly.' Fifty-round killing bursts, 100 rounds even. The reason for only using shortish killing bursts, apart from the constant peacetime need for ammunition conservation, is to stop the Gimpy from overheating and breaking. Sod that. We are firing such long, concentrated bursts that the barrel glows red hot. So what? We have a spare. And, for once, no officious mini-Hitler gunnery instructor is going to bollock me if I burn out the first barrel. Kick on . . .

We are firing to kill, but also to suppress or neutralize – choose your expression. It takes the unkillable hero of a Hollywood action film to stick his head above his trench and fire back when continuous, accurate bursts, each of 50–100 rounds, are smacking into the top of it. Any sane mortal lies at the bottom of his trench – much as I and those bold, brave Paras lay under that bank and behind that rock when the shells were smashing into it – keeping out of the direct line of fire and praying not to be hit by shrapnel or a ricochet.

As the Argentines try to stay alive under our sustained fire, 2 Para moves up on them unmolested. We stop firing. By the time they lift their heads it is too late. The Paras are all over them. That is called 'winning the firefight'.

What's more, even if they fire back at us with their rifles they are not going to hurt us behind our armour. Had it not been for the past few days, I might even have felt sorry for them. But they and their chums have been pouring near-constant shit on to a defenceless me, and I don't suppose they felt any remorse as they did so. Now, nor do I.

'Gunner spots someone lighting a cigarette.

50 rounds later.

"He didn't finish that one", says Ford.'

Then I do worry. Fast-flying metal parts need plenty of oil lest they seize up, and our Gimpy is working overtime. Grab long-nozzled oil can; liberally squirt oil; pray the gun is not so hot the oil catches fire; keep shooting. We blast through thousands of rounds.

'Fire arcs over us, it goes over my turret. We zap it back, silence from that [machine gun] nest. We cheerfully think it is a 7.62 machine gun, only later [when we drive past the position the next morning] do we discover it is a .50 with armour-piercing rounds. If they had hit us that would have opened us up.

They then start firing at us with anti-aircraft guns but again high. We are not unduly worried.

By now [we are] well into the second sandbag of empty GPMG [rounds] and we are beginning to run a bit short.

"Oh, look. Twelve of them running away," shouts Ford. A very, very long burst of fire.

"They all fell down," says a delighted Ford, looking like the murderous fiend he is when behind a gun.

"Oh, dear. I think a couple might try and get up again."

I fire the GPMG. It makes me more aware of what I am ordering the others to do. The fact that we are all loving it is irrelevant; I am now as guilty of causing death as they are. How does one explain that on theological and moral grounds?'

I blame my Catholic education. My first school – a Dickensian horror called Ladycross – might have thrashed religion out of me, but the monks at Downside, my senior school, nevertheless managed to imbue me with elements of their morality – or, at the very least, made me think about it – when it comes to profound philosophical matters such as justifying killing. Whilst I haven't 'found' God in any trenches tonight, although He's had plenty of opportunities to do a meet-and-greet, that does not prove He does not exist. I've been issuing fire orders, loading guns, telling Ford who to kill and where for hours now. What if I find myself facing St Peter at the Pearly Gates? Discover there *is* a God and a Heaven and a Hell? Facing eternal damnation, I wager I'll plead the Nuremberg Defence[3] . . . 'I never pulled the trigger.'

If Ford is to be condemned for tonight, then so should I be.

There is an override firing lever on the left side of the GPMG. I tell Ford what I am going to do, but not why. This is not the moment for a theological debate about the ethics of justifiable homicide.

He aims.

I fire.

'Fifty rounds later Ford grins: "I think that's the lot."

He is delighted.'

I am complicit.

'**They begin to learn. They cease daring to fire.**

More and more are running away.

D Company is now into the rocks and we hear their battle through the position on our radios as they move from rock to rock.

Rather them than me. I like fighting from my vehicle.

Green Verey lights show the forward edge of their positions. Every time a Verey light goes up from the Argentinean positions it is greeted by a few rounds of main armament from us.

Then it is all over.

Most Argies have run away from our fire and the artillery bombardment. Most who stayed are dead.

We pull back. I meet [Major Chris Keeble] the second in command. "Enjoy that did you, cavalryman?" he asks.

I grin.'

---

3. Used by many Nazis at the 1945/6 Nuremberg War Crimes Trials: 'But . . . I was only following orders. I never actually killed anyone.'

Chapter 17

The Fog of Victory

The opening sentences of my Journal:

16 June. Well, they surrendered at 2100hrs (Z) 14 June. At least they signed some sort of ceasefire agreement which was subsequently ratified. There was a fear, and to my mind a very valid one, that this might be an elaborate trap. Luckily we had knocked the stuffing out of them and it really was all over.

What then of my part in the great scheme? Having trogged 8,000 miles I finally got into battle. Let me regress . . .

It is 14 June. The Argies may have run, but the vast majority of their troops are down there in Port Stanley, as are those Panhards: sixteen to our current four, or eight when 4 Troop joins us.

However, it is now day, and the huge advantage our night sights gave us is gone. It will be their 90mm guns, plus turret-mounted GPMG's – identical to ours – versus our 76mm and 30mms. My map shows that Port Stanley has metalled roads. Our tracks will give us no advantages over their wheels on the tarmac.

Worse, if it can get any worse, when we drive down the reverse slope of Wireless Ridge, which we will have to, I doubt there will be much cover for us. We will make easy targets as they will be able to see most of our vehicles as we come down the hill.

Most of our 7.62mm Gimpy ammo is gone. I've fired off well over half of our main armament rounds. All the vehicles need an ammo replen. The Paras are also desperate for more ammo.

I lead 23A back to the RAP at HQ Main down on the Murrell River where last night, the Colonel tells us, 656 Squadron has been flying up and forward dumping our spare ammo. Flying the ammo in and taking the casualties out; hovering a couple of feet off the ground as shells burst all around them. These army pilots cannot be any relation to that RAF pilot (sorry RAF, but . . .) who on Day One pulled a U-turn and refused to fly us forward when he heard rumour of shooting up ahead. Although I didn't know it at the time, I was witnessing Captain Greenhalgh AAC winning his much-deserved DFC (Distinguished Flying Cross).

It takes us a couple of hours to load it all up, and it is full light, approximately 0930, before we are done. **'We stuff it everywhere; into the vehicles and onto the vehicles, anywhere it can be tied. T23A [CoH Thompson] has so much inside that he cannot get into the turret.'**

I can, just, but I am still perched on stacks of 7.62mm boxes and 30mm shells, with much of my body outside the turret. The whole top of the front of the vehicle's hull is layered in boxes of 7.62, further obstructing Round's already restricted line of sight. This is totally in breach of every rule ever invented, but we need to get as much ammo back to our vehicles and the Paras as we can possibly carry. As far as I am concerned, last night's attack was a warm-up exercise. The main encounter of the campaign, the Battle of Port Stanley, is about to begin.

What's more, those Skyhawks that surprised us at Furze Bush Pass are presumably still in Stanley. They'll be out looking for us this morning and, after last night, we have to be a top priority target. It will only take one aimed bomb, unlucky shell or even chance bullet, for my ammo-laden Scimitar to go bang, with a wallop that will be felt for miles. We have become, in essence, massive mobile bombs.

I tell CoH Thompson to keep a good couple of hundred yards away. No point us both blowing up.

We meet up midway with 23 and 23C, who have also pulled back. They refill their vehicles from ours. We 'forward' dump the remainder of the main armament here so we can pull back and get to it easily if we burn through this next load. The remaining boxes of 7.62mm we will share with the Paras.

'In our absence [they tell us] 2 Para beat off a mini counter-attack and Ts23 and 23C go on a foray. They try to shoot at aircraft at 3500m range and, not surprisingly, fall short. 23C manages to hit a house, which explodes – an ammo dump we think.'

I spot a long, lanky figure I recognize from my trench last night. Wearing an old fashioned Para 'smock' – he told me he was once in the

Para TA (Territorial Army) – Max Hastings is clearly determined not to miss out on the action. He comes over and I offer him a lift. He'll have to cling on to the back of my turret but, as I once did just this on a schoolboy visit to The Blues and Royals, aged seventeen, for twelve hours in a thunderstorm for part of the time (rip out your hair in outrage, Health and Safety inspectors), I feel sure he will manage.

Max ends up winning 'Journalist of the Year' for his coverage of the war. As he put in his award-winning *Evening Standard* article, which is subsequently re-published in the *Spectator* magazine:

'Do you want a lift?' called Roger Field of The Blues and Royals. One of the most pleasant parts of this war was that, after so many weeks together, so many people know each other. I climbed clumsily on to his Scimitar, and clung fervently to the smoke projector as we bucketed across the hillside.

'Max jumps onto our vehicle.'

We spot a large enemy position and go and inspect it.

'We see some of their anti-armour weapons [.50 Browning machine guns – like ours – and recoilless rifles on large, deadly-looking, fixed tripods] and are shocked. We had been luckier than we had guessed.'

They would have ripped us apart had they hit us last night.

Someone opens an Argie ration pack. 'They've got small bottles of whisky in them!'

I 'liberate' a bottle, as we all do, of 'Breeder's Choice' whisky, with three bull's heads on it. I pop it in my pocket rather than drinking it (it is still beside me, unopened, in my desk drawer as I write) since I still have some of the much finer malt in my hip flask.

As we head back we spot a body, undoubtedly British with its distinctive waterproof over DMS boots, covered in a green poncho. His rifle and helmet are laid on top of him as if in a scene from the First World War. A terribly lonely figure in that huge, open, empty, frost-bound amphitheatre.

'In no time [an artillery] DF brought down onto us; back into the vehicles very quickly.'

Max has acquired an Argie Stirling SMG (British-supplied of course). He must have 'liberated' it from one of the trenches. I wonder for a naughty moment about NUJ rules on reporters carrying weapons but

I have no issue with it. One of those Argentine 'stay-behinds' who so exercised Brigadier Wilson in what now seems a parallel universe could appear at any moment and start shooting at us. Having Max on the outside, able to return fire instantly, can only be a good thing. The more weapons the merrier, say I.

'I see the Second in Command who says thanks, and that not only did we save many Para lives but we were instrumental in causing the enemy to flee. This was a message I was to get from many in the next few days.

From the soldiers it was: "Wow. What a demo. Those guns are incredible. It really did an incredible amount for our morale to see the enemy being zapped as we went in."

From officers it was an appreciation of our ability to stand off and take out KPs (Key Points) which would otherwise cause large casualties. All agreed that Goose Green would have been a very different story if we had been there. A Tango c/s [an armoured car] could have easily done from 1500 metres what H lost his life doing.

On to Wireless Ridge. 2 Para press forward, us with them, covering them at every point.'

Up to the top and over. A rocky ridgeline which we spent last night blasting. A natural defence line. But not against Scorpions and Scimitars. Below us is Moody Brook – the single-storey Royal Marine barracks the Argentines attacked all that time ago, on 2 April. It is a burnt-out wreck, but just seeing it tells me we are almost there. Back where it all began. I'm beginning to get a good feeling about this.

We are ordered to wait. The news from elsewhere is good. The Scots Guards took Tumbledown last night. The enemy are in full retreat. Nevertheless, there are far too few of us to start heading down that hill.

It is about 1100 local time, 14 June.

'We see soldiers in the distance chucking down their guns. We are told that they have surrendered. By now we are north of Stanley Harbour, covering the town, spoiling for a fight.

Suddenly it was all over, the Argentines had surrendered. Our initial reaction was of disappointment, adrenalin was flowing. We were looking forward to a really good punch-up.'

Wireless Ridge was just the taster. Our real battle, The Blues and Royals' armoured battle against the Panhards, is about to begin.

Except it isn't. It really is over.

'This was followed moments later by an immense surge of relief and delight; we had survived.'

'Endex!' an anonymous wag says over the radio. 'Endex' means exercise over.

Everyone laughs at that. Colonel and majors too. No officious 'Watch your radio procedure. Who was that?' bollocks. I guess everyone, from the most senior to most junior, is realizing what I am just beginning to. I've fought. I've survived. I'm going home. Who gives a damn about those Panhards?

It is huge smiles all round. Nods of appreciation. No hugs. Not even any handshakes or 'Well dones'. We are British. Not American. Just huge, huge smiles. Of delight. Of relief. Yes. Mainly relief. I really am going to live.

And then it is steel helmets off and red berets on as the Paras prepare to march on Stanley, now desperate to be first in and to grab the bragging rights that will go with it. The Milan team, weighed down with their heavy launchers and rockets (which I don't think they needed to use last night, with us giving it 'welly') clamber up on to the front of our vehicles. Huge smiles and thumbs up from them. They are only too glad to use us as taxis. And we are only too happy to oblige.

We drive down to Moody Brook, the old Royal Marine barracks, smashed up and gutted by fire. Trooper Round can hardly see anything now, but who cares? I tell him where to steer. We're all still grinning and chattering away to one another. Max climbs back on board, I seem to remember.

At Moody Brook we get on to the metalled road that then follows the south side of the harbour; Port Stanley is a couple of miles ahead. We're flanked by marching Paras. We stop and start and stop.

Then it starts getting tense. Have they really surrendered? All of them? Might somebody take a shot at us? We are an easy target strung along this road, one vehicle behind the other. We're so keen to be first in that we've forgotten our basic drills.

We pause beside the race course whilst the Colonel finds out what is happening. Beside me, on my right hand side, a 'bush' gets to its feet.

'Hello, Rog,' it says.

Having recovered from shock I lean over the side of my turret: 'Hello, Chris. How long have you been here?'

'Oh, a couple of days.'

Then his radio starts squawking. 'Must go. Catch you later.'

And off trots Chris Brown – 'Gunner Brown' as we called him at Sandhurst, and a chum. Turns out later – sadly I don't see him again for many years – that he is working as a Royal Marine Commando FOO (Artillery Forward Observation Officer). He has been sneaky-beakying around the Islands, calling in Naval Artillery and thoroughly wrecking various Argentines' lives, for months now. Small place, the Falklands War. Chris goes on to make three-star General. He's one of the genuinely good guys.

Corporal of Horse Thompson, in 23A, produces a Regimental flag, which he ties to his antennae pole. Ford rummages around in an outside bin and pulls out a Union Jack, which we attach to ours.

With us halted and Stanley lying there, waiting for the scooping, Max decides his moment has come to go it alone. His *Spectator* account records:

> It was simply too good an opportunity to miss. Pulling off my web equipment and camouflage jacket, I handed them up to Roger Field, in his Scimitar, now parked in the middle of the road with a large Union Jack.

I remember it very slightly differently.

We have moved slightly beyond the racecourse and are stopped at the War Memorial to the victims of the 1914 naval 'Battle of the Falklands' – the most southerly Great War memorial in the world, I later read. Max has been off doing his journalist thing with 2 Para. He clambers back up on to my Scimitar. We armoured cars are the very lead point of the 2 Para advance; all our weapons are cocked and loaded, ready to pour a storm of fire at any Argies who might decide they are not surrendering after all.

It is absolutely flat, and we get the best view from up here on our turrets. Apart from Government House off to our front and right, there are no houses, nowhere to hide, just this long, exposed road along the south side of the bay. Coarse, tussocky grass stretches off to our right; open 'tank' country – for them and us. At the far end of the road, half a mile or so away, are the first, rather uninspiring, wiggly tin houses that are Port Stanley.

'I want to go in,' Max says, or words to this effect. 'Is that all right with you?'

My answer would have that Colonel of PR I clashed with back in Fitzroy reaching for his Court Martial manual. The charge doubtless: 'fraternizing with the press'. Or, put another way: 'failing to control the press'.[1]

'You're a civilian. I don't have any authority over you. Your decision.'

Which, I still happen to believe, is the correct 'legal' answer (a few years later, I qualified as a lawyer). And, it occurs now, writing this, had I said, 'No you can't,' Max would have doubtless given me two fingers and gone anyway. What was I going to do? Arrest him?

As I answer, I distinctly remember thinking that he might not be a soldier but he has an outsize pair of *cojones*, not least as we still don't know what is going on with this surrender. Or is it only a temporary ceasefire? I hear different terminology being used. All I know for certain is that we've been ordered to stop here because, if we push on into Stanley, those who do know what is going on are worried that we may piss the Argies off and they may start shooting.

And we'd fire back. And there are upwards of 11,000 of them about half a mile away with all their heavy weapons, and about 500 of us – and our four armoured cars.

Rather Max than me, walking into that.

'I'm going,' he says.

I look him over. He is wearing an out-of-date Para smock. He has a military webbing belt with pouches for his kit and, slung from his shoulder, that 'liberated' SMG.

'Not like that, I wouldn't. You'll look like a soldier to any pissed-off Argie sniper hiding in those far buildings.'

He hands me the SMG, webbing and combat smock, which I store away for him. He's still wearing cam cream but, with his big spectacles and unarmed, he now looks pretty harmless. Still rather him than me, but he clearly senses that fame awaits – as it does – and off he goes.

I am mighty relieved when no shots are fired and he disappears into the town to get his 'Journalist of the Year' scoop. The *Evening Standard* of the

---

1. That Colonel would have been semi-right in this instance. And I most certainly in the wrong. I later learn that 'Divisional' orders were that no journalists should get to Stanley ahead of British troops. Nobody told me . . . But – and here is the old conundrum, at least before they started making journos sign contracts – what right does Divisional HQ have to order around journalists?

next day, 15 June, carries the front page headline: 'Max Hastings Leads the Way: THE FIRST MAN INTO STANLEY'. I even get a couple of nice mentions, although I only see the article when I get back home.

Whatever is causing the hold-up is, apparently, sorted, and it is our turn to follow.

'Then confusion. Followed by surrender. Tremendous pride and elation. The only thing missing – the people.'

I did not expect a repetition of the liberation of Brussels or Paris in 1944: pretty girls, bottles of champagne, flowers. But I imagined a bit more than this. A couple of ragged-looking Islanders standing by the side of the road waving. And that is it, our Victory Parade. Oh well.

'Into the town.

No, there is no peace.

"Stop."

We stop.

We look around. It begins to rain.

We waited. One by one the heads disappeared, the hatches closed, the troop slept, exhausted, drained, woken only by the chill of a late afternoon, and a sense of great anti-climax.'

And, when we wake, it really is all over. The Argies are pulling back to the airfield, some two miles beyond the far side of town. My memories of what happens next and in what order are pretty vague. I leave the troop at this point as my presence will cause friction with Robin. He is their troop leader and I am not. If I stay I will have to take command, but what is there for me to do? Nothing really. Anyway, I have no idea how long I will be able to stay here before HQ 5 Brigade grabs me back. As they are bound to do. Better to let the troop get on with their tasks: gunners cleaning guns, drivers their engine maintenance. I have had my moment and I am now surplus to requirements.

It's dark when I wander into Government House – or at least I am pretty sure it is Government House. Someone has a big fire going. I don't think they were officers and they make a space for me; we Blues and Royals can do little wrong with 2 Para after last night. I stretch my legs towards the fire to warm my frozen feet. As the heat hits, jolts of pain shoot up my legs. My feet have been 'seizing up' all day, and I have been hobbling slightly when I walk.

Someone tells me to haul off my boots.

Bloody hell. My feet are doughy-white underneath. The skin looks almost dead, deep black lines running through and across it.

'First-stage trench foot,' says one of the interested group of foot specialists. Nods from the others on the medical committee.

'We've all had it,' says another. 'Get your feet dry. Get some dry socks on. You'll be fine.'

I stay there for an hour or so, until I feel warm; the first time in many days. I put on my spare dry pair of socks. I am soon walking fine. But another couple of days out in the elements with sodden, frozen feet? Trench foot, almost for certain. Not exactly impressive. Then again, these guys train to keep their feet working. I'm an expert on Scimitars. Each to his own.

I walk over to the Upland Goose hotel and pub. It is packed full of soldiers and journalists, drinking hard. I spot some of the journos I mixed with at Fitzroy. Max, although I did not know it until later, has been to the pub, claimed his 'First Brit to arrive' double whisky and is already on his way back to San Carlos to file his award-winning dispatch for tomorrow's newspapers. One of the journos I befriended at Fitzroy buys me a pint of beer. I am on the fringe of his group, though. I'm not going to start talking about last night, and they don't ask, so I appear to have nothing interesting to offer. I don't really know them, and they don't know me. This is an extraordinary night, one best shared with friends. I leave him to it.

The soldiers are in their huddles, as would I be had I served and fought alongside someone for the past three months. The advantage of being a 'butterfly' is that I have flitted from job to job, experienced such very different things. The disadvantage is that the only place I actually belong is back at HQ 5 Brigade with my fellow watchkeepers. The last place I want to be.

I've never been one to be a wallflower at a party. I drift into the night to find somewhere dry to lay my sleeping bag. '**Exhausted. Night in potting shed.**'

Chapter 18

The Spoils of War

'16 June
   Day of idle "looting". To airfield by motorbike. My booty:

   1x 7.62 FAL (with folding butt)
      1x 9mm Squirt gun
      3 x bayonets
      1x Machete
      1x Pistol holster' [which I still use for fancy dress parties when I go as a 'cowboy'. The former officer owner really was a bit of a cowboy. It has a thong to tie the holster to my leg, above the knee, just like a gunslinger in a Western.]

With little else to occupy us we turn into weapons collectors.
   'Find ourselves a comfortable house and get stuck into being victors.'

* * *

Next morning, 15 June, I make my way to where 2 Para has set up its HQ in a house – or was it a shop? Port Stanley is a shit hole. Or, more to the point, the Argentines have turned it into a shit hole. Piles of rubbish burn in the street. The Argies obviously thought it a good idea to add live rounds to these smouldering bonfires, and every so often bullets cook off and fire into the air. Bloody great. I survive what I did, and then to get killed like this . . .

We are warned about booby traps. The wankers have left them for us. I hear that someone rigged an abandoned Panhard to blow. What fun if an inquisitive child had crawled in to take a look instead of a cautious Para. I also read of a rigged hand grenade left in the school – true or false, I have no idea, but we are coming to believe it of them. I later learn that they leave about 30,000 mines, mostly in unmarked minefields. These will blight the Islands and threaten the lives of the locals – human, animal and marine – for generations.

I'm sorry, Argies. You had a once in a generation opportunity to impress. You shout to us and the world that '*Las Malvinas son Argentinas!*' But, when you grab them, instead of respecting the land, showing the locals how you will look after them, you crap all over the place. No wonder they don't ever want to see you again.

I spot Colonel David and explain my dilemma. He's happy to oblige. He'll shelter me here, not ask for the return of his Education Officer; but, he warns me, 5 Brigade are bound to come looking. I 'belong' to them and not to him.

I know that. I just want to avoid them for as long as possible.

Someone runs in to the HQ. 'They're fucking fighting!'

Turns out that either a Marine or a Para said, 'Crap hat', or a 2 Para asked a Marine, 'What took you so long to get here?' – and off it kicked. The Marines walked (I only learn the word 'yomp' from the newspapers after the war) the entire length of the Island, whilst 2 Para got helicopter lifts – as well as tabbing – and beat them here. The Bootnecks are not taking it well. And, with no Argies left to fight, well . . .

Some senior Paras rush out of HQ to stop it before it escalates.

The Colonel tells me there is to be a Service of Thanksgiving that afternoon at the Cathedral. The Blues and Royals are invited. It is a lovely sunny afternoon, warm almost, as we march proudly to the church. It is filmed, and it is those TV shots that my parents see and discover I am alive.

David Cooper, 2 Para's inspiring Padre, gives the sermon. It's all over now, he tells us, 'But what did you really think of when you were going to *die*? Was it your wife . . . your girlfriend . . . or even your dog?' Much laughter from masses of much-relieved warriors.

Me? I now know I sing IRA songs to myself to try to contain the fear. And I picture the chaos at my funeral as various ex- and semi-current girlfriends meet up in a welter of confusion and recrimination. That scene kept me smiling when things looked bleak.

The boys find a furnished house – it belongs to someone called Robin Pitaluga – and I join them. It's luxury: a proper bath, sheets on my bed and lovely and warm. The previous occupants, it turns out, were Argentine Air Force officers, and they, unlike so many of their compatriots, looked after the house beautifully, even going so far as to store the family's possessions in cupboards, sealing the doors so nothing got stolen. In fact, I suspect, they were far tidier than we are.

We inspect the Panhards. We soon have three lined up outside our house. Another five (I seem to remember) are in the centre of town, which means they only ever had eight – two troops, just like us. And most have broken down in any event. Thank God.

We soon get bored. I go to Government House, where there is a ship's container of Argentine 'goodies'. Whole sides of beef hang in there, rotting. Someone said they were short of supplies. Not from where I am standing. It has been well picked over by our boys, because all I find are a couple of pairs of white cotton socks. Perfect for tennis. If I ever get off this blasted island, that is. Which is already beginning to consume my thinking.

As I emerge from my 'shopping trip' I am surprised to see a couple of Argies outside. What they are doing here I have no idea. I thought they were all up on the airfield. A couple of our boys must have been detailed off to keep an eye on these two, because they are happily chatting with them. Stanley is rapidly filling with our troops. Maybe these guys were not combatants – plenty did not see any front line action, as is the case in any war – but this unsettles me. Were our boys being rude to them I would intervene and put a stop to it. But friendly? Only two days ago we were killing them, and they us. Icy politeness is my approach. Not chums.

The Welsh Guards have a prisoner-of-war problem, I later learn. They guard the *St Edmund*, a Sealink Harwich to Hook of Holland passenger and vehicle ferry when she sails the PoWs home. Heavily outnumbered, they are mighty worried lest the prisoners try to pull off a 'Hornblower' or an 'Aubrey' (Patrick O'Brian) by overcoming their guards and sailing the captured ferry home. Argentine heroes, prisoners no longer.

The Argie officers request a meeting. 'Can we have our pistols?' they ask.

'You've got to be bloody joking' is the answer.

The Argentines explain. The soldiers are so angry at what has happened to them, the way some officers treated them up to and during the fighting, that they are in genuine fear of their lives. They need those pistols to keep their own men under control. Stop them from dropping them overboard.

The Welsh Guards officers confer. Their soldiers have reported back on the depth of anger towards their officers from some of the prisoners and agree that they might do just that.

A compromise solution is reached. The officers can keep their pistols, but unloaded. As they are issued with Colt .45 automatics – the bullets contained in a magazine in the grip – the soldiers will not be able to see that they are not loaded. It worked, and they all sailed safely back to Argentina.

Mark Coreth appears with 4 Troop and I learn what happened to them. In retrospect I am little surprised, especially given how little that entirely uninterested Brigadier ever understood about armoured vehicles.

He attaches them to the Scots Guards for the assault on Tumbledown.

4 Troop is assigned to a 'diversionary attack', designed to make the Argies think the main attack was coming from the south and thus draw off their forces from the main objective.

Commanding Officer's 'O' Group over, Mark goes to some high ground and, using his binoculars, pre-recces the ground as best he can. He is dismayed to see what looks to be masses of empty boxes for mines littering the ground up ahead, ground he will be driving over in the dark. They appear to be both anti-personnel and, far more worryingly, anti-tank mines. If this is not bad enough, the minefield is unmarked, so he has no idea where it begins and ends. Nothing new there, then; it was the same on Wireless Ridge and elsewhere across the Islands. He is, however, out of time to do anything about it.

While the Scots Guards' attack is starting, 4 Troop drive up a track towards their firing point and into a very accurate artillery DF, shells landing literally yards from them. A direct hit, and that would certainly have been that, especially a hit on the very thin top armour (tanks/armoured cars have their thickest armour on the front, facing the enemy; their thinnest is on the top of the vehicle, where there is least chance of a strike).

The empty mine boxes he had seen earlier are off to either side of the track, but he now spots a massive crater blocking the track in front of him, something he had not seen earlier. He stops and thinks. He reckons that if the hole was caused by an artillery shell then it is random and there is little reason not to drive around it. However, if it is a deliberately blown culvert, then it is probably designed to push anyone coming up the track off it and into that minefield. Whichever it is, they are going to have to go round it if they are going to get to their designated firing positions. He knows he has to kick on.

Mark is leading, as is his wont – no sending the junior vehicle first to get knocked out first, as is established military doctrine.

He tosses a mental coin; left or right? He goes left.

The explosion blasts Mark's Scorpion three feet into the air when it hits a dug-in bar mine (a large anti-tank mine).

That certainly got the Argies looking in their direction.

However, 25 per cent of the Scots Guards armoured support has just been destroyed.

Mark and the crew have, miraculously almost, survived. Back in England I am shown the hull of Mark's Scorpion which has been repatriated to the Alvis factory where it was made. It has a huge, domed, concave bulge in the bottom where the armour has 'stretched' and, mercifully, not broken. The only possible reason, an engineer explains, is that a Scorpion, at a mere 8 tons, is so light. That bar mine is immense and designed to destroy heavy main battle tanks which, instead of flying into the air as Mark's vehicle did, allowing the blast to dissipate sideways as it did so, would have remained sitting solid on the ground, allowing the full force of the blast to focus and blow upwards, destroying everything.

Unable to move his surviving vehicles around the hole lest they hit more mines – he counted fifty-seven around them the next morning – Mark does the next best thing; albeit now with a massive headache! Regardless of the shells thudding all around them, he first sends his two crewmen back. He then moves the next vehicle up to the crater and directs their long range fire onto the nearest Argentine positions from outside the turret, jumping off the vehicle and burying himself in a ditch beside the track as and when he hears a shell heading towards him 'danger-close'.

When that first vehicle runs out of main armament ammunition he sends it back and the next one takes over. And again with the last one, Mark still directing their fire from the outside.

Huge personal bravery from all the troop – Mark is awarded a much-deserved Mention in Despatches – but, to my mind, of precious little tactical effect; no direct fire role as they were too far away to bring their guns to bear. A sad waste of what was a battle-winning, life-saving asset. And all because HQ 5 Brigade could not be bothered to spare so much as half an hour to learn how to best deploy them.

Down a Scorpion, Mark helps himself to a spare Panhard. He's operational again.

'17 June: 5 Brigade search for and find me.

18 June – Fitzroy: Festering muddy hole. Here I am back on watch at 5 Brigade. I have had my war and, surprisingly, I enjoyed it thoroughly.'

I am back to sleeping in the filthy sheep pens. No more baths. Welcome to the relentless cold and tedium of four-hour watches.

Not that I am going quietly. Nor is Adam. He and I are awaiting the arrival of our suitcases and, with them, our shotguns: it turns out he's brought one too. There's plenty of fresh, tasty meat flying around overhead, but how to knock it down in the meantime? Time for a shoot.

We spot some tasty-looking geese foraging behind the Brigade HQ house. We organize a gun line, and with a promise of payment in fresh meat we send some bored soldiers round the back to flush the geese over the house – we want sporting shots – and over our guns.

Over they come. It is like Fitzroy and those Skyhawks all over again.

With the same result.

I switch my now swapped-back Stirling SMG to automatic and give a full-speed goose a full magazine: 30 rounds.

SLRs, pistols, SMGs . . . it's a wall of gunfire.

The geese fly safely through, not even a feather disturbed.

The Brigadier goes berserk; convinced HQ is being attacked by one of those pesky Argie 'stay-behinds' he has been obsessing over since Day One.

I seem to remember Brendan finding it difficult to keep a straight face when he duly bollocks we obvious 'ringleaders'.

Even the Padre was in the gun line; shocked at shooting at something 'alive'.

'Thank God I missed', he tells me. 'Never again!'

The Brigadier decrees that there is to be no more shooting in Fitzroy, and I suppose – all these years later – he has a point. In the army we rightly obsess over 'range safety'. Clever people with slide rules – this was long before pocket calculators became commonplace– did complex mathematics to work out exactly where and in what direction it was safe to fire our weapons. Before we even start firing on a designated range we are taken through our safety drills. Again and again; all to help prevent accidents, which tend to be lethal with high velocity rounds. However, we gung-ho, bored bandits have been 'weapons-free' since we arrived on the Islands and are still in that same, weapons-free frame of mind. Our shoot could, in retrospect, have been catastrophic, although not to the geese. But we thought it hilarious and the Brigadier's adverse reaction typical 'spoilsport' HQ bullshit . . .

Finally, our shotguns do arrive with our suitcases, and Adam and I go into the meat-marketing business. We first do a deal with 656 Squadron:

the only time I have been able to 'afford' to go helicopter shooting in my life. They fly us around to look for teal and geese. When we spot them near a pond they drop us off and then return to pick us up a few hours later. Price per return flight: one goose or two teal. Bargain!

We shoot the birds. We pay our helicopter taxi drivers. We eat some. We sell the rest. Price, five tins of beer – we have no money – or six tins for 'oven ready'. We subcontract the plucking and gutting for a tin of beer a bird. It gets me out and about. It keeps me sane. I perfect 'Duck *à la pêche*' as my signature dish – using army tinned peaches.

'22 June' tells me that I am, '**Established as Squadron Leader RHG/D, or CRACFI**' (Commander Royal Armoured Corps Falkland Islands.) This is the most important command appointment I ever have in my army career. A very proud moment.

Also the shortest appointment I ever have as, next day, I am flown into Stanley, where The Blues and Royals are loaded on to HMS *Fearless* – Mark astride his captured Panhard, towing a second, spare, for good measure. One ends up outside the Household Cavalry Museum at Combermere Barracks, Windsor, the other is given to the Tank Museum, Bovington.

As they drive aboard I become the ex-Squadron Leader of The Blues and Royals as I no longer have anything to command. I feel thoroughly depressed as I smile and wave the boys *bon voyage*. I have no idea how long it will be before I see them again.

Back at Fitzroy, I start going quietly bonkers. I suppose I should just be grateful that I got to fight, didn't 'just' sit on those radios. But all those who did fight are already either on their way home or will be shortly. And here I am, stuck here in this festering hole, back on watchkeeping duty.

The boys somehow get hold of that promised bottle of champagne as I 'saw action' and won the 'bet'. We thoroughly enjoy drinking it, but there is no mention of return dates. Months, we suspect, as the huge clear-up operation is yet to begin. Much as Colonel James prophesied.

Then, an opportunity. Flights are beginning to arrive from Ascension Island – although they involve two rather hairy-sounding mid-air refuellings. Brendan tells us that 5 Brigade doesn't need all six of us any longer. Two of us can go home. We can decide who amongst ourselves.

Two of the guys are married – neither from our *QE2* room, though. 'You'll let us go first, won't you? We've got wives . . .'

I think they genuinely believe we will go with that.

'Fuck off' is the unanimous and immediate response from us four bachelors. 'Getting married is your problem, not ours.'

We agree on drawing cards. This will decide our order of return, from one to six, from here on in.

'Aces high?' I ask as my heart sort of sinks. I never win anything. I just don't. Ever.

'Yes. Aces high.'

'Pulled ace in draw to go home. So first out. Not getting too excited – wary.'

It's beret on as I am allocated a flight two days hence. Only me, as there's now only one spare seat. Then it's beret off again as a massive snowstorm hits us that morning and word is that the flight is cancelled. But back on again as the worst of it blows out to sea as rapidly as it arrived. The flight is a 'go'.

I say farewell to my fellow watchkeepers. We will all keep in touch – although I'm not sure the married two are feeling quite that same depth of brotherly love at that moment. But we will. This sort of friendship, forged in these sorts of experiences, last for life. Don't they?

And off I go (**'In a snowstorm'**), half-expecting the flight to be cancelled again or for someone more important to be allocated my space or for Brigade to change their minds and decide they need me after all. Only finally believing I really am going home when the wheels leave the tarmac.

After almost 36 hours of near-continuous flying, much of it in the nylon, plastic parachute jump seat of a very slow, propeller-driven Hercules, the lavatory a hole in the floor with a curtain around it, I finally land at RAF Brize Norton in the soft warmth of a perfect English summer night.

It's 3 July. I've not even been away two full months. I cannot begin to get my brain around the fact that I am standing here in Gloucestershire, let alone what has happened to me.

I see Paddy Tabor, a chum from my regiment, coming to meet me. I really don't know what I'm going to say to him. It's all so very simple, and yet so very confusing.

Chapter 19

Windsor

'I wonder what the army has to offer now . . .?'

The concluding sentence of my 'Falklands War Journal', written on 17 June, the day 5 Brigade finally tracks me down and orders me back to the grot and grunge and tedium of Fitzroy.

That cryptic final question is far more prescient than I realized when I wrote it . . .

* * *

I beat the Task Force home by over a week. Which makes me almost the first home and a sort of travelling freak show.

That first week, apart from jottings in my normal, social diary about meeting up with various chums, female and otherwise, is a complete memory blank. Were it not for those cryptic entries I could not tell you that I meet with a couple of army bigwigs, including the Minister of Defence, John Nott.

I hold our government culpable for the whole shebang. Still do. What were MI6 doing? How could they miss an entire invasion force being assembled? Pretty punk if you ask me, but I suppose Maggie T knows that if she kicks Nott under the bus, where he rightly belongs, she is next in line for the blame bullet. I suspect she keeps him in place to take the incoming that she deserves. Although I doubt I tell him that when we meet.

Anyway, no danger of that. The country has gone Task Force-crazy.

In the absence of anyone else to quiz, I am as near as it gets to an oracle. I mind my Ps and Qs and tell my superiors what they want to hear. After all, there is no shortage of great things to tell them in the limited time-slots I am given. What is more, the much more senior soldiers I meet have seen proper action themselves. I can have a sensible conversation with them.

Not in my regiment, though.

If you are a Para, a Marine, a Scots or Welsh Guard and you missed the trip 'down south' then, in the absence of any other wars to fight, that omission will probably colour the rest of your military life. Condemned to explain why you weren't able to go when almost everyone else in your regiment did. And how pissed off you are. But never, however solid the reason, able to get past that one simple fact: you either went; or you did not.

Conversely, very few of the rest of the British Army even got a sniff of a chance to go, although most would have grabbed it if they could. I have little doubt there were majors who would have taken a demotion to get a captain's watchkeeper slot. Anything to get on one of those ships because, once aboard, anything was possible. Furthermore, every army thruster knows to the very bottom of his khaki-camouflaged heart that he would have performed every bit as well as we who went. Doubtless far better, their gleaming upwards promotion paths and glowing Annual Reports incontrovertible proof of their military excellence – if only they had been given the chance. As for my chums – doubtless slightly jealous, but far too decent to give any hint of it – they have little idea what to say to me about how I spent my summer, or I to them about how they spent theirs.

So it is that, back in the Officers' Mess at Windsor, it's not quite Fawlty Towers and 'Don't mention the war', but it feels that way. One day, just as I am leaving the army, I forget my rule of silence. A couple of the lieutenants ask me something about the Falklands at a boozy dinner, and I answer. A contemporary overhears and, with much grog inside him, explodes, 'I'd have done every bit as well as you!' before realizing what a dick he sounds and storming off; still furious but now also shame-faced. He is a genuinely all right guy and a vague chum, however he's trained for war all his adult life and now cannot get his head around the fact that he missed out whilst I 'got lucky'.

Bizarrely, an element of this attitude continues to this day. A couple of years ago, a very fine London club holds a Falklands Dinner. A non-military chum, promising me the finest of wines and food – he was not exaggerating – asks me as his guest. I know I am there to be a carnation in his lapel, but I am an unashamed tart when it comes to fine wines and food shared with amusing folk in luxurious surroundings. I am introduced to a member who is talking Falklands at the bar before dinner. He's got the medal, he tells me to the evident admiration of his chums.

'Which regiment?' I ask, always delighted to meet one of our small band of brothers.

He names a Scottish regiment, but it is not the Scots Guards. Nor do I recall him being on board. 'We were ready to go down on the *QE2*,' he explains, 'but X Guards (I cannot remember which) went instead. We were much better trained and prepared . . .'

'Here we go again,' I think as I listen to this 'we would have done it better' sentiment. Instead I ask, genuinely puzzled, 'But how come you got the medal after the war was over?'

'We replaced you lot immediately afterwards. There was still an imminent threat of re-invasion by Argentina, so we got the medal as well.'

'And the three bears . . .' think I. Threat? We didn't feel remotely threatened post-war. Except the Brigadier, who was clearly still fretting about 'stay-behinds' and felt hugely threatened when we let rip at those geese.

Peacetime boy-scouting more like, although with loaded rifles and unmarked minefields; left to clear up the – literal – crap whilst earning none of the glory. Rather him than me.

There is no level on which he and I can have any sort of meaningful Falklands War discussion. You were either on the Islands as the guns sounded, or you were not. End of. That said, I ask him all about his time there and he's happy to oblige. Saves me having to sing for my supper, and he's a member after all. I don't want to risk giving offence, at least not until we have finished the port.

It transpires that there are four 'proper' Falklands veterans at that dinner. One is a chum. He knows another, and by the end of the evening we four have come together. By three in the morning we are the only ones left. We've sucked down all the hooch we can find and finally, throats drying, our conversation falters. Time to go home.

I walk miles across London to where I am staying; enjoying the feeling of stretching my legs; remembering the sheer exultation, back on the morning of 14 June, of realizing I was going to live; savouring the good memories for a change. Although I do puzzle over one oddity as I walk. Once we watchkeepers were all back, Adam invited us to a hugely jolly dinner at his house in London. As we say our well-watered farewells we are all convinced this will be the first of many. Sadly, I have never seen any of them since.

Normally, though, my thoughts are more conflicted. Ever since Wireless Ridge I've been chewing over a couple of things and finding no answers. I still haven't to this day and, short another war, never will.

I know I did okay, did my job, but in my mind's eye I see those bold, brave Paras literally shitting themselves on the frozen march from Mount Kent to Furze Bush Pass. They had already fought one desperate battle. They knew what was coming next and had the balls to do it all over again. No whingeing, no hesitations. But, as David Benest told me when I remarked on it at the time, some were still shitting themselves.

I know I was wired up the morning after Wireless Ridge; itching to take on those Panhards and storm Stanley. But was that brave, like 2 Para were brave, when I had had such a relatively easy night of it? Wireless Ridge was not exactly a cakewalk; four dead – including, heart-wrenchingly, Francis Slough, who I will never get to shoot the breeze with about the good old days when I commanded him at Junior Leaders – and eleven wounded, but almost nothing compared to what my regiment went through in, say, the 1944 Normandy campaign. I find myself questioning how ballsy I would have felt, how keen to 'Driver advance!' if I had just seen one (or two, or three) of our vehicles blown apart beside me, knowing I was next? Not quite so gung-ho, I suspect.

The other issue is the polar opposite. Like Adam in the Garden of Eden eating that apple from the Tree of Knowledge, I have dined at the Tree of Combat. I know the thrill, the adrenalin surge of bundling up all the fear of imminent death and then hurling it back at my tormentors. Like a predator that tastes human flesh, I discover I like the flavour.

I have never felt as alive as when I was facing death. I want more.

My diary for July shows a long list of dates with various girls – these are the 'Dark Ages', long before mobile phones. We write 'dates' into our diaries and turn up at the time and place agreed perhaps weeks earlier.

Trouble is, I am struggling to relate to 'civvies'. Not that it's their fault. It was much the same when I came back from Northern Ireland. Back then, I just stuck the whole thing in a box and tried to forget about it. Nobody was much interested anyway. It was truly a 'forgotten' war, and that suited me.

Now I am being lionized. Friends naturally want a bit of it, of me. I'm okay with 'Was it cold? Did you see any penguins?' – the obvious questions which tend to open most Falklands conversations. Answers to which are: 'very' and 'no'. Which is where I'd rather close the discussion. I certainly get very uneasy when I see the dreaded, 'Did you . . .?' question coming along the conversational road. I clam up or change the topic. I cannot be easy company.

The 21-year-old I had such high hopes for and had invited out the night before I boarded the *QE2* sends a rather limp letter that finally makes landfall in post-war, muddy, depressing Fitzroy. In its dreary way it is worse than the ones from the bank; she obviously made the right decision when saying goodbye to me the night before I left. Six days after landing back at Brize, it is the Regiment's Summer Dance. I invite someone else I really like who was away travelling when I left. One problem: she has taken to calling me her 'hero', and this grates. Badly.

Nevertheless, I could do with some affection, and she's gorgeous. We have a sort of understanding. I am driving her back to her flat in London afterwards. Things are going great until the band lets off some sort of banger as we dance.

Bang! Puff of smoke. Whoops and cheers from the writhing dancers, hands on hips, imagining themselves Mick Jaggers and Marianne Faithfulls, all hoping to get some 'Satisfaction'.

'Cool!'

I am on the floor. In the drum kit. Skyhawks overhead, bombs and shells falling.

'Ho, ho! Look at the war veteran!' Laughter from my fellows as the band stops playing.

I just feel like a twit. And deeply unsettled, sharply aware all too suddenly of those who aren't here; who would love to be here; who will never be anywhere ever again.

Next, it's irritation as I leave the dance floor amid smirks. The guests are mainly soldiers and their girls. Lots of Guards and cavalrymen. How many, if any I wonder, have ever been under fire?

My friend is very understanding, and kind. Thankfully.

Colonel H's brother has been invited by the Colonel to the dance. He would love to meet me, the Colonel says. It is a request and not one I can disrespect. My photos are just back, including some I took of the still-smouldering gorse gulley beside which H was killed, and others of Wireless Ridge. I spend time with him, don't hurry him, talk him through them. It is the least I can do. I am alive; his brother is not. I spend far too long doing it, though.

By then my head is not where it should be, and the dance seems flat. My friend has been left hanging around waiting, and she's tired; all the excitement of the early part of the evening is gone. We agree that she should head back to London with a friend. **'Dance not a great success'**, says my diary. I feel a confused failure. I have no memory of seeing her again.

Today we know this for what it is. But not in 1982. Had someone mentioned the need to 'decompress' after a combat tour – and I am not joking here – I'd have thought they were referencing scuba diving.

These days, the psychologist's mantra is to 'share our feelings' and 'let it all out', so that our wartime experiences do not fester and poison our present and future lives. While that was not the military way back in the 1980s, I think these things are far more nuanced. For example, I am forever hearing people talk about their parents' and grandparents' generations that went through the Second World War. 'They never mentioned the war', they say, as if it is a badge of honour, this stiff British upper lip of ours.

But I wonder.

What I do know about reminiscing is this: give me a comrade in arms and a few drinks – one invariably comes with the other – say goodnight to our wives, and we barely draw breath as we refight old battles; inevitably making light of things; laughing as we remember the idiotic whilst treading warily around the demons. Much like the children's toys in *Toy Story*, or the exhibits in the film *A Night at the Museum*, as soon as the non-combatants go to bed we become our younger selves once again. As soon as a 'grown-up' appears to check that we are still alive, silence descends and the war is no longer mentioned.

I would wager that most of that Second War generation did discuss the war. Endlessly. But only with each other. Just as, I would also wager, endless generations of combatants have done before us. This, though, is all in the future for me.

A couple of months later, I can no longer avoid the issue and experience my Damascene moment. I am on a three-week exercise in Germany. My experience of 5 Brigade is troubling me. I would not want to go into combat with an organization like that again.

I accept that the Falklands War was an aberration, unlikely to be repeated. So, what next? What am I training for and dedicating my working life to if I stay in the army? Where are the threats? *Are* there any genuine threats apart from our old, ever-reliable Cold War enemy, Russia.

The Blues and Royals will return to Germany in 1984/5 for five years where their NATO role is to face down the Soviets. I did a stint there when I first joined the Regiment and hated it. It felt little different to being back at boarding school, except that we had cars, and money in our wallets. However, we're as good as confined to camp as there are few, if any, places nearby worth driving to come the end of the working day. Many of the older locals don't much care for us, and the younger generation, the ones I'd like to meet, object so strongly to our presence – 'occupation' as far as they're concerned – that some have taken to lobbing cans of paint on to our tanks as we drive under their bridges.

In the Mess there's a strict school-style hierarchy which is impossible to escape. This is long before Ryanair was even a twinkle in its creator's eye, which means our girlfriends are a full day's drive and a long Channel crossing away. Few relationships last under these conditions, and the Mess is filled with bored, frustrated, unmarried officers. After three glorious years of freedom at university, finding myself locked back up in the equivalent of a unisex school drove me near demented in very short order. I soon realize that I'm not a 'good' regimental officer.

Windsor is, by comparison, a blast. Come 4.30 and knocking off time, I shed my uniform, drive to London and become a civilian; a 'normal' human being. I probably spend no more than nine or ten nights sleeping in my room at Windsor in the couple of years I am stationed there, and each time I do, there is a specific reason for it: a Dinner Night or going on exercise early the next morning. Otherwise I live in London. What is more, soldiering in Windsor, being ready for immediate worldwide deployment – which is how we found ourselves on the Falkland Islands – is as exciting and fulfilling as being ready to face down the Russian menace on the inner German Border is repetitious and dull. Some love the pure khakiism of Germany, a working world almost devoid of civilians. But not I.

As 1984 and our return starts to draw closer, I decide I will not go back to that bizarre existence. Certainly not as a bachelor and, my way of thinking tells me, probably not as a married officer either. My reasoning is this: I cannot imagine subjecting someone I love to that khaki-bound, status-obsessed world, where the wives as good as wear their husband's rank. And flipping this concept on its head, I cannot imagine being happily married to someone who would enjoy being part of that world. As she would have to. Or, at the very least, pretend to if I am to have a worthwhile career in the army. A wife's attitude can damage or help a soldier's military career as much as his own competence.

Just as bad, I now know that our military role in Germany, our *raison d'être*, is semi-sacrificial, semi-suicidal. Our mission is to hold off the

Soviet tank hordes long enough for the politicians to talk; to try to prevent MAD: Mutually Assured Destruction. Although, sacrifice made, we front-line Blues and Royals won't be alive for the peace celebrations. Which seems a bit of a bummer of a concept to build a lifetime's career on.

If I failed to properly buy into our mission in Germany first time around, there is zero chance now. I've seen war at first hand. I know what these casually tossed around concepts – first strike, deterrence, air power, artillery DFs – actually mean. I'll commit to a war we might win but I've little appetite to train for a war we're almost certain to lose. Not that I believe any longer that the Russians will be coming. They've had thirty-seven years to attack and haven't. Why do so now?

That said, I concede that it is vital that NATO continues to be seen to deter. If it looks as if there's nobody there to stop them, the Russians might just wander in. Because they can – much as they have done recently in Georgia, the Crimea, and literally, as I write this, Ukraine.

But this is 1983. The Cold War is already almost forty years in the waging and does not look as if it is going away any time soon. On the northern tank plains of Germany glittering military careers are being forged by those who must really believe in this future war; officers who genuinely enjoy training constantly for this appalling possibility. But that's no longer me, if it ever was. NATO, I conclude, will have to manage without me.

This autumn 1983 exercise in Germany is great fun; normal Blue and Royal work hard, play even harder. But it is also a useful reminder that there are only so many near-identical conversations I can have with my fellow officers before I need a break. What's more, I'm back to playing at soldiers again.

Cue my Damascene moment.

'We're under artillery attack,' shouts an RHQ signaller one sunny afternoon.

'Run! Run! Get under cover!' shouts the Adjutant, all urgency and keenness, when a couple of us dawdle as we scatter.

But my heart is just not in it. I just can't get enthusiastic about 'playing' artillery so soon after living for so long under it. What's more, it's not as if we're even doing this properly. The only way to survive artillery is in a trench. And nobody in the cavalry digs trenches. Yes, I'll dig a trench, enthusiastically even, but only if someone is shooting at me. Otherwise I've got better things to do with my life. War, I realize, has spoiled peacetime soldiering, and that has consequences for my future.

Back in Windsor, the government announces a 'London Victory Parade of 1982' through the City of London. Our Scorpions and Scimitars will take part, but as I was not a troop leader, or even a member of the troops, I will be a spectator.

Major Brian Keeling, Director of Music of the Mounted Band of The Blues and Royals, is selecting the music for when the band ride past the saluting dais outside Mansion House.

'How about Rod Stewart's *Sailing?*' he asks me over a morning cup of coffee and a custard cream or seven in the Officers' Mess. 'The news said it was the troops' favourite as you headed home.'

I tell him about *QE2* leaving the dock as the bands joined together and played. I tell him that, as far as I am concerned, only two pieces of music sum up what the war was about; the sacrifices made, and the long British fighting tradition that the Falklands War encapsulates: *Land of Hope and Glory*, or *Rule Britannia*. His choice. In comparison, *Sailing* would verge on the tawdry.

He follows my advice, although I can no longer remember which one they played. Sorry, Sir Rod . . .

We are permitted one final burst of glory before we put the Falklands War behind us. On 1 December 1982 the Household Division holds the 'Presentation of the South Atlantic Campaign Medals Parade' in the rear gardens of Buckingham Palace. As 'Senior Detachment Commander, The Blues and Royals' and thus the senior officer of the senior regiment on parade, I will lead off the whole parade at the end of the ceremony.

Furthermore, as 'Senior Detachment Commander', The Duke of Edinburgh will present me with my medal. A huge honour.

A former Guards Depot, Pirbright 'Drill Pig' (he's done the Guards Drill Course and taught trainee Guardsmen at Pirbright: terrifying folk) is unearthed at Windsor and we practise our drill. Unlike the Foot Guards, who do public duties and who are forever marching and stamping their feet, we armoured lot don't do much of this, so we are rusty. The Corporal of Horse (sergeant) drills us, but he doesn't dare beast us. We Falklands boys have attained a certain status within the Regiment.

This culminates in a 'final rehearsal' at Buckingham Palace. Regimental Sergeant Major 'Wolfman' (our Sandhurst nickname for him) MacKenzie, Scots Guards, who greeted me back in May at the top of the gangplank on *QE2*, is directing proceedings. Whether he has to control his eyebrows from hitting his gleaming peaked cap when he sees who is in the lead and will give some orders, he manages to keep to himself. Actually, whilst I was a general menace with an 'attitude problem' when he trained me at Sandhurst, I was always pretty sharp at drill as I had previously trained as a squaddie at Pirbright before becoming an officer. Not that he will remember that.

At the end of the parade I will order everyone to 'Quick march!' before leading them along the back of Buck House. I will then order The Blues and Royals detachment to 'Saluting to the Right . . . Salute!' as we march past the saluting dais at the top of the steps into the Palace.

My major concern, apart from making my voice carry right across the gardens – grass is not great for acoustics and sound-travel – is keeping time as I march, on my lonesome onesome, across the grass. Nobody in front of me. Everyone else behind, keeping time with me. No crunching of boots on gravel to help me keep in step.

I've never marched on grass before. Nor, for that matter, have I ever led two battalions of Foot Guards and their massed bands before, and I'm very conscious that, if I get anything wrong, I will not only mess up the entire parade, but do so in a massively public way. There will be 2,000 spectators and about 1,200 men on parade. I am trying to stop a certain part of my anatomy from puckering up and going 'sixpence – half a crown, sixpence – half a crown' (as the old army expression goes).

It is now the last part of the rehearsal. My moment comes: 'Parade will turn to the Right . . . Right Turn!'

My voice carries. Everyone turns. So far, so good.

'Quick . . . MARCH!' I bellow.

Pause, two, three (say it to yourself, that is the exact pause).

I then step off with my left foot at exactly the same moment that the big drum will go 'thump!'

And the Massed Bands join in. And off we will all go. In perfect step, arms all swinging together, all perpendicular to the ground . . . 'Or I'll rip it off and hit you with the soggy end!' as the Drill Pigs love to scream at us

Just as you see every June at the Queen's Birthday Parade on Horse Guards.

Except it doesn't work. Not today. Everyone steps off at different times. Mayhem. The drum and I are way out of synch.

'STOOOOP!!!!'

We all come to a sort of halt.

Wolfman heads towards me, face contorted like a demonic dervish. I can read it. I've been here before with him. 'Fucking Field! Again! Fucking Household Cavalry! Can't march for toffees . . .'

Here we go. Immediately banished. I've no idea what has gone wrong, or why. But it's not me, and I'm not taking any shit from him.

'What went wrong, Mr Mackenzie?'

That stops him, and he backs down slightly. He explains. 'You stepped off too soon . . . Sorr.'

'No I didn't. My timing was perfect.'

All credit to him, he doesn't argue. He looks across the garden. He assesses distances. He thinks. 'I reckon I know what's happened . . . It's the distance. Across the grass . . . The sound is taking twice as long to carry . . . This time I want you to count a double pause before you step off. I'll brief everyone. Wait for my command.'

And off he goes and briefs the Scots and Welsh Guards Colonels and the Massed Band on the very far side of the garden. He signals.

Same orders. Except when I bellow, 'Quick March!' I go . . . pause, two. three . . . pause, two, three (try saying it again). Then I step off.

That's the time it takes for my voice to cross Buckingham Palace gardens and register with the drummer on the far side. Who hits his drum.

Thump!

The sound travels back to me and I step off in time with the drum, after six beats instead of three.

The men in the middle step off after the normal pause. Wolfman's solution works.

My friend Anna is there on the day. It was she who got me into the Stranger's Gallery for the Saturday morning Falklands War debate in the House of Commons that was, although I didn't realize it at the time, the start of my adventures. As is Paddy Watson, friend, soldier and (usually) good-natured butt of any number of my infantile jokes. And, of course, my parents.

Prince Philip gives me a smile as he hangs the medal on my chest and we discuss my article in *The Guards Magazine*.

Chest out, new medal gleaming, I salute as I lead the parade past the Duke of Edinburgh and the spectators. Then out across the front of Buckingham Palace to Wellington Barrack, crowds watching, 1,200 pairs of steel-heeled boots crunching in perfect time on the tarmac behind me. I will never experience a moment like this again.

'Parade . . . Parade . . . Dismiss!' Everyone turns smartly to the left. And it is parade over.

The Scots and Welsh Guards mill about, chatting to one another, enjoying the moment. Tonight, all over London town, in smart restaurants and beer-filled pubs, they will be celebrating with family and friends and comrades; savouring a very special day; reflecting on what we achieved, and lost, in that already receding war.

However, for us twenty-five Blues and Royals this is another day in the British Army and not a Hollywood film. No happy ending for us. Time is tight. We get straight back on to the coach that brought us here from Windsor. It sets off immediately, destination Castlemartin Ranges in the far west of wet and windy Wales, where Annual Gunnery Camp has already started.

I settle down and close my eyes. I do what soldiers usually do when there is nothing else to do. I sleep. We've a long trip ahead.

Postscript

The Falklands War coloured my subsequent working life. On a macro level it changed how I thought about myself and what I expected from others. How I saw the world. It certainly made me far less tolerant; far ballsier, too, I'd like to think. Although it is my nature to avoid confrontation, I no longer cared what people thought as long as I was trying to do good and go about things in the right way.

On a micro level, every CV I wrote after leaving the army included a sentence which, I knew, would single me out from everyone else: 'Saw active service in the Falkland Islands'. Employers were invariably intrigued, and it always got me to the first interview; although some who hired me soon discovered that that statement carried with it rather more nuance and 'attitude' than they might have bargained for. Others were delighted with their rather unconventional new hiring.

'Do you miss the army?' people used to ask me. Some still do.

My stock answer was and still is: 'On a fine summer's night, out under the stars, or firing guns on the ranges, or about to set off ski-racing or sailing – absolutely. When it's pissing with rain and the wind is howling, and I'm settled down in front of a blazing fire with a drink in my hand – absolutely not.'

The army is a young man's game, an older man's profession.

There are Falklands War anniversaries, some of which I get invited to – along with sundry Majors, Colonels, Admirals and Generals – because on the army lists of those who went down there, mine is sometimes the first name: senior officer of the senior Regiment. On the tenth anniversary, on *Canberra*, I at last get to sample one of their First Class cabins, but it does not begin to match my *QE2* stateroom. Maggie Thatcher is the guest of honour. She is no longer PM but she moves around the room as if she is the queen of her domain, surrounded by a Praetorian Guard of gurning, grinning Admirals and Generals; they are loving it, and her.

I am unsure what I will say should I meet her. I am not on any list to be introduced, but it is a small space and I might easily bump into her. Luckily I don't, as I still blame her and her government for allowing it to happen in the first place. I am half-minded to tell her so. Being hugely proud of having been there and not wanting to have missed it for the world doesn't change that fact.

Brigadier Wilson is as good as written out of the history books. Brigadier Thompson is awarded the CB (Companion of the Order of the Bath) and promoted to Major General. He is, quite rightly, one of the heroes of the hour. Brigadier Wilson receives nothing. He is nowhere to be seen. Six months later, in January 1983, he leaves the Army and moves to America. The British Army looks to have cold-shouldered and then dumped him.

On the 25th Anniversary, the MoD invites me to spend ten days on the Islands. In return, I am to be available to talk to the media who are descending on the place en masse. It is February 2007, the Falklands summer. All sorts of 'big' names are here: the Marine photographed setting off for Stanley with a tiny Union Jack flying from his antenna; the pilot of Vulcan 607 – cue much piss-taking from us lot: 'All that way and you missed!'

'No we didn't.'

'Oh yes you did.' Give us some beer and we army boys revert to the playground in an instant.

'What do you want to do?' A delightful Falkland Islander asks me on the first day in the Media Centre. 'We're here to help.' The Islanders really have *not* forgotten 1982.

'Three things,' I say. 'Revisit Wireless Ridge and walk my battle. Catch a sea trout behind Wireless Ridge [I've brought fly rods and tackle]. Finally, I'd love to have a cabby [a "go"] on the latest infantry weapons . . . Please.'

'Leave it to us.'

I end up fishing for four days. It is perhaps the most 'Zen', calming thing I ever do: catching a fish on the Murrell Sound, just below 2 Para 'HQ Main', behind Wireless Ridge. The last time I was here I was waving my torch frantically, worried that someone was going to shoot me by mistake, whilst Corporal Dunkeley was hauled, slipping in and out of consciousness, to a waiting helicopter, as the artillery rounds fell. I recorded my emotions later in this poem:

Fish
(The River Murrell under Wireless Ridge, February 2007)

Peace: a sea trout on a river which once knew death.
Understanding: a hook that sweeps the river to snare a fish,
where bullets once churned the water to snare a life.
Victory: a fish for supper,
not a body for the pit.
That is healing
Twenty-five years later.
Pity, perhaps, the fish.

From *Heroes: 100 Poems from the New Generation of War Poets*, edited by John Jeffcock, Ebury Press, 2011.

Now there is no sound to be heard. Even the wind has dropped. It is grey and overcast. Perfect fishing weather. A seal pops his head up and has a look.

'You'll not catch a fish here today. Not with him here,' says Nick Bonner, the best guide on the islands. Only the best is good enough for us 1982 boys. When I leave, Nick refuses to be paid, or tipped, or anything. It is his privilege, he tells me. It is all I can manage to get him to keep a few of the flies I brought out as a present.

He has already taken me to the 'best' fishing spots and I have been catching fish. But I want a fish from behind Wireless Ridge. I don't know if doing so will help, but I somehow sense that doing so might, perhaps, salve something in me.

I persist. The seal must have swum off because, not long after, I land a 3lb-plus sea trout. Not huge, but big enough for four of us to enjoy a superb dinner that night. It is somehow a profound moment; eating that magnificent fish from that very personal place. I hope I am beginning to find my own catharsis and silence my ghosts. It is only later that I learn that there is a clear and present danger for veterans who visit the Islands. Whilst it helps most, it can open boxes best left alone for others. We are taken to the 'Memorial Wood 1982' in Port Stanley. The Islanders have planted a tree for each member of the Task Force KIA (Killed in Action). Their children have each been given a tree to tend and care for. And the children have been doing so. Back in Britain, this may be fast becoming a long-ago war, but out here, a tiny, lonely island in the South Atlantic, Argentina a still uneasy and massive neighbour, they've forgotten nothing.

That wood, those trees, the palpable sense of gratitude and remembrance are exceptionally moving.

Then comes a shocker. I am shown an 'Annex' to the garden: a tree for each serviceman who has taken his life since the war. There are already more trees in the Suicides side than the KIA side. That was 2007. There have been more trees planted there since.

The following day, Nick and I drive to Furze Bush Pass and then on to Wireless Ridge. We retrace my route through the battle. I expect to get all stirred up, but do not. Perhaps that fishing moment yesterday really did excise some demons. I am shocked, though, when he points out some minefields, all marked now. Bloody hell! I walked right beside these. Perhaps even through one or more of them. Small margins . . .

For the first time ever I tell someone about Wireless Ridge. In detail. From position to position as we get to each one. He wasn't a fellow warrior but he is, as Izaak Walton (1593–1683) would have described him, a 'Brother of the Angle', a fellow fisherman. We have hardly mentioned the war over the four long summer days we have been fishing together. Most talk has been about how best to catch fish; the sheer focus on the water required to hoodwink and catch these wily and powerful prey a palliative, an antidote, to less happy thoughts.

He listens, he doesn't ask. And he is an excellent listener. Up on Wireless Ridge, the sun beaming down, I amuse him with my story of the accelerator falling off as the AA gun opens up on us, threatening to knock our turret off, Trooper Round 'bodging' like a maniac.

'From where?' he asks.

We are where I was that night. I picture it 25 years ago with the shells zipping in clusters just over my head. I point way over to my left: 'Over there'.

'There weren't any AA guns over there.'

I tell him I can still see it right now, but he is emphatic. There is a sophisticated Battlefield Tour industry on the Islands that caters for tourists, he explains. It amuses returning veterans, because the local guides often far know more about 'their' battles than they do. After all, the soldiers 'only' saw the fighting from their own trenches. It isn't that he doesn't believe me, but . . . 'If there was a gun way over there we'd know about it.'

'Happy to take a look?' I ask.

We're not fishing today and we've time to kill before ITN films me for my big 'Leading the attack on Port Stanley' TV moment, which will end up headlining *News at Ten*.

We mark the spot and drive over in his old Land Rover. A good three kilometres or so, I reckon. And there, exactly where I said it would be, is a cluster of nearly perfectly round shell holes; one with bits of shattered, rusted-out metal scattered around it. No wonder that gun stopped firing so soon after it started. Some clever Gunner dropped a shell right on top of it.

About 30 yards away I spot an intact 20mm five-round ammunition tray. It is beside me now, balanced on an unruly stack of manuscripts in my study as I type this.

The Army arranges a shoot on Onion Ranges for interested veterans. Four of us go. We have, excuse the pun, a complete blast on that old warrior still in service, the GPMG, as well as 'newbies' like the Minimi machine gun and the 5.62mm rifle that replaced our SLRs. They give us stacks of ammo, and we four happily turn live rounds into empty cases. I am still that schoolboy who wanted to join the army because he loved adventure and sport and shooting things that go 'bang!' Never doubted it, though.

We are beautifully looked after by a platoon from the Mercian Regiment who are also using the range today. A young private is designated to 'assist' me – keep a careful eye on me, more like; make sure I don't kill myself or anybody else!

He tells me that they are here on the Falklands doing live 'work-up' training for a tour of Afghanistan. This is 2007, and that war is in its full-on, explosive horror. They came back not long ago from a nasty tour of Iraq. This platoon is an example of the British Army, in the words of General Lord Dannatt, 'running hot'.

The private looks painfully young. I am reminded of 3 Troop when we went to Belfast all those years ago, little knowing what awaited us. Aged twenty-three, I was the fourth oldest among us. His, however, is an army generation that is bred for war. His army has been properly combat-ready since the First Gulf War in 1990 and fighting hard since 9/11. My two turning-up campaign medals turned heads and looked pretty cool back in the 1980s. I now meet guys with two rows of medals. That private as good as confirms this. He is not at all 'fazed' to be going to Afghanistan so soon after Iraq; in fact he wants to. War is what he signed up for. A total contrast to my skiing and sailing peacetime army, with our sometimes haphazard approach to warfare and training. The Mercians are war-trained. We, in comparison, were playing. But then we never expected to fight a proper war. This lot know they will.

As we talk I reflect that 'the moral majority', the people who decry how 'soft' the younger generation have become, ought to meet these guys. How little they know.

At some point I say, and no, I am not blowing smoke up his fundament, that I am in awe of what he and his mates are doing; the sheer relentlessness of it, month-in, month-out. Tour after tour. He really is a combat soldier. After all, I think to myself, I was in and out and diving into a drum kit all in less than two months.

He is almost sheepish as he answers me: perhaps I don't understand what an honour it is for him to help me with the weapons today. He and his mates look up to us and what we did. To them we are, to put it simply, legends.

I feel very humbled.

In 2012, on the 30th Anniversary, at a 'Commanders' dinner, Admiral Sir Jonathon Band, former First Sea Lord, gives a speech saying much the same, but from the geopolitical, strategic viewpoint: 'What you guys did down there changed the course of British history in the latter part of the twentieth century'.

The Falklands War, he tells us, halted Britain's perceived decline as a world power; underlined the validity of Britain's seat on the Security Council of the UN; played a key role in convincing Russia that when Britain said something she not only meant it but was capable of following it up, helping to lead to the end of the Cold War.

Powerful, humbling stuff. Although, given a choice, I'd take the words of that delightful private in the Mercians for my epitaph any day. I just hope he made it back home.

Appendix

The Guards Magazine
(Summer 1982 edition)

A Vignette of The Falklands as A Watchkeeper, Infanteer and Car Commander

BY CAPTAIN R.A.K. FIELD, *The Blues and Royals*

It was with a great sense of finality that the *QE2* slipped out of Southampton. After weeks of uncertainty, the feeling that the Argentines would surrender any day, the mad dash to get hold of Arctic Equipment, endless shopping trips to prepare myself for a potential six-month sojourn in the Falklands, and many farewells, we were at last off. It was a tremendously moving occasion. On one level with friends and family on the dock, and on another with the thousands of well-wishers who could be seen cramming the beaches like so many black dots, long after Southampton had disappeared. It was brought home to us the meaning of 'England expects' and we realised that we truly carried a nation's hopes.

Six of us had been attached, all from different Regiments, to Headquarters 5th Infantry Brigade as watchkeepers. As I and the three others who shared our stateroom settled in, we tried to convince ourselves we were in fact off to war and not a pleasure cruise. A glance at our well stocked refrigerator and opulent surroundings made this difficult. As we cruised down through the tropics this sense of unreality persisted. Not really involved at that stage in the working of the headquarters, and having nobody to train but ourselves, we were left by and large to our own devices. Brigade operation procedures were read, criticised and revised. Webbing, unworn since Sandhurst, was put together, and we began to run enthusiastically. Bergens were packed, were discovered to be so heavy as to be unliftable, and were constantly repacked. The miniature tape recorder was taken out and the bottle of 12-year-old malt most definitely left in. The unreality of life on our deck, 'Mirage' deck as it came to be known, was only checked by the furious training taking place on the lower decks, on 'Exocet' and 'Tigerfish' decks. One threaded one's way to a signals lecture through lines of blindfolded men stripping and assembling weapons, practising Emergency Stations and First Aid. We ate excellently and the weather was kind.

Suddenly, overnight, the weather turned cold and it was announced that South Georgia was only a couple of days away. The ship had been blacked out at night, and now .50 MGs appeared on the bridge. Sightings of icebergs were reported, the incessant pounding of feet stopped. Outside it was now very cold and windy.

We awoke one morning to be overawed by the majestic and startling beauty of Grytviken, where during the course of 27 May we transferred to the *Canberra*. Reality was here at last. Not only had the camembert run out days before and the last bottle of champagne drunk on *QE2*, but Canberra was announced to be a dry ship.

Once aboard, it was with a real sense of urgency that we practised air attack and 'abandon ship' drills. Sipping soup in the dining room whilst one's waiter cheerfully regaled the company with tales of Mirages swooping in below bridge height not only gave one indigestion but dispelled the cruise atmosphere remarkably quickly. The weather also decided to let us know what the South Atlantic could produce in the way of waves. Conscious that I had been booked that week for a cruise to Cherbourg on *Gladeye* [the Household Division yacht], I took to my bed feeling exceptionally seasick.

On a very overcast 1 June we landed at San Carlos, delighted to be at last on dry land. Captain Schrayne, 13/18 Royal Hussars, a fellow watchkeeper, and I instantly went into our recce role and found a deserted Marine trench. The other four watchkeepers joined us, and with the rain gently falling we were lulled to sleep by the sound of Brigade Headquarters digging in around us.

The next day saw us at Darwin, the battlefield a wreck, still smouldering after the attack by 2nd Battalion, The Parachute Regiment. Two 1000lb UXBs [unexploded bombs], one 'friendly' and the other 'enemy', both apparently made in Britain, and the sight of cartloads of Argentine dead still being brought in for burial, indicated that we were at last catching up with the war. Any worries about the unexploded bombs were dispelled when a gargantuan pig gamely tried to eat one; both bomb and pig survived.

We got into the watchkeeper routine, three on, three off, eight hours on, eight hours off. I was fortunately on the 'G' (Operations) desk, either on the forward net to the battalions or the rear net to HQ LFFI (Land Forces Falkland Islands). This was a necessary but frustrating job, hearing about other people's actions but stuck oneself to a handset. Theoretically we were not meant to make decisions, only monitor the net. All too often, the only answer we could give was the infuriatingly familiar 'Wait Out'. Luckily we found a house, so life was not too bad. But when, later, we were living outside, the eight hours off was never long enough to eat, wash, do some personal admin, and sleep.

Since I was to advise the Brigade on the correct deployment and use of the two troops of The Blues and Royals armoured recce who had come under command of 5 Brigade, I was, on 6 June, sent with the Brigade step up to Fitzroy. The two troops had driven over the mountains from Teal Inlet on their own. Brigade reckoned it might take two days; they made it in about six hours. The exceptional cross-country performance of CVR(T) in the hands of experienced drivers had scored its first major success.

Each troop, both from 'B' Squadron The Blues and Royals, consisted of four vehicles: two Scorpions (76mm main armament and co-axially mounted 7.62mm MG) and two Scimitars (30mm gun and similar MG). I was concerned they be used correctly, standing off to use their excellent guns, rather than be jeopardised at close quarters.

Higher command was beginning to recognise their value. Lt Coreth, Troop Leader 4th Troop (Callsign 4), had given invaluable support to 3 Para on an earlier attack on Mount Longdon. 2 Para, after their experience of Darwin/Goose Green, wanted a troop badly. They had had to use Milan and 84mm [anti-tank weapons] to knock out Argentinian MG posts and they had run out of these with obvious results. The vehicles had also proved themselves in the anti-aircraft role, claiming hits at both San Carlos and on the tragic 8 June at Fitzroy. It seemed that whilst British soldiers dived into trenches, the interested inhabitants of Fitzroy watched 3 Troop firing back. A group of excited civilians all agreed that a 30mm shell had knocked a chunk out of an attacking aircraft.

On 11 June, whilst I was with Major C. Keeble, 2 i/c 2 Para who had 3 Troop under command, to advise on ranges and deployment, he suggested that I might like to join them as armoured LO. I was delighted.

Two hours later I was with 2 Para in a helicopter bound for Mount Kent. There we dumped our Bergens and sleeping bags and got into belt order for an overnight march to the Murrell River. This involved carrying only food, water, and ammo; all else was dispensed with. We were the reserve for

3 Para and the Commandos in their attacks that night, and as we marched, the fighting would get near and then recede again as the Argentines were pushed back.

By morning we were under shell fire ourselves. Some 14 hours later we arrived at our destination. The Argentines seem only to have had predicted artillery targets and did not have the ability to adjust their fire. This was a relief to us, since we must have presented an excellent target as the double line of Paras threaded their way through the frozen countryside.

Dug in, in comparative safety, in a ravine, that evening we watched 3 Troop, under Lt Innes Ker, join us. With the incredible logistics problems of trying to get helicopters to fly up ammo, especially under fire as we were, the vehicles had as much aboard as they could carry. We were due to attack that night, but with our 'O' Group at the 'Any Questions?' stage, we were told to cancel. We attacked the following night, our objective being Wireless Ridge from the north. The Blues and Royals were to sit on the ridge lines and fire in the Paras. They were to soften up the enemy in conjunction with our artillery and then provide very direct support when the latter had to stop.

The Troop moved out before last night. I was in Tac 1 with Commanding Officer 2 Para, with a radio on the Troop Chatter Net – a net without which the troop could not have worked so effectively. Callsign 23 spotted an armoured vehicle. 'Could he fire?' 2 Para agreed. Two rounds fired. A freak snowstorm intervened. That sums up the weather.

At 2030 hours, local time, on 13 June, the attack started on some features leading to the main part of Wireless Ridge. It was over by about 2200 hours with the position captured. The Troop blasted Argentine positions using their night-sight capability. Meanwhile, I had been leaping in and out of the mud with Tac 1, convinced that my original Sandhurst view of life was utterly correct, namely that anybody doing what I was doing now when they could be in a nice warm armoured car must be mad. At this moment it came over the air that L/CoH Dunkeley, the commander of Callsign 23B, a Scimitar, had been knocked unconscious. The CO of 2 Para accepted my offer to take command of the vehicle.

Trying to remember where the artillery DFs had been on the way up, I picked my way gingerly back to the RAP. I arrived safely and asked the gunner, Tpr Ford, for a quick revision of 30mm misfire drills; he pointed out that it was I who had taught him gunnery in the first place. If Callsign 23B's gunnery was not good, I had only myself to blame!

It was a bright moonlit night, with a deep, deep frost as we moved back to the battle – quite eerie, with the distant chatter of machine guns and bursting illuminants. The only movement was that of small groups of stretcher-bearers, dark against the white carpet, carrying their loads. Exhausted, they put down their stretchers to exchange a brief word of greeting as we passed. It was as one imagined a First World War battlefield, not one of the 1980s. The constant whine of artillery shells, the harsh backdrop, small groups of men huddled together for shelter and warmth, others moving gently forward for the next attack. Modern technology was not apparent on Wireless Ridge.

We moved from the ridge line to join in the shoot onto the main part of Wireless Ridge. The Troop was doing a good job. Callsign 23A seemed to be playing a little game. A short burst of GPMG fire; the Argentines usually fired back. The cars would hit the source of the enemy tracer. That position would not fire again. Anything that moved or fired at us was 'zapped', and the real star was the Rarden 30mm gun. The Rarden with its flat trajectory, its 6-shot capability and incredible accuracy could neutralise a target very quickly. The HE (High Explosive) and APSE (Armour Piercing Secondary Effects) rounds were used.

We were stood off at about 800m from the enemy and with our GPMGs were able to put sustained bursts of fire into their positions. Trooper Round, my driver, when not on the ground trying to replace the accelerator pedal which had decided this was an excellent moment to fall off, played a crucial part in target acquisition. The prize, though, must go in this respect to the incredible night sight.

Fire Orders changed, even before 2 Para's attack, from 'Maggie (MG) traverse left' to 'Running Argentines'. Tracer rounds floated over our heads from, it turned out, .50s firing Armour Piercing rounds. We also came under intermittent fire from 20mm anti aircraft guns. None of the vehicles was hit. This was in contrast to Lt Coreth, 4 Troop, fighting a similar action in support of 2nd Battalion Scots Guards who ran over an anti-tank mine. His vehicle was blown up. However, despite the headaches, all were unharmed, and Lt Coreth continued to direct his troops from the outside of C/S 24A.

'D' Company, 2 Para, successfully attacked the Ridge and suffered few casualties, a fact possibly due to the support of The Blues and Royals. Daybreak, after a brief ammo replenishment, saw us moving on Stanley, from ridge line to ridge line. Morale was sky-high after the previous night, and there was much discussion about Panhards and what was soon to happen to them.

Suddenly it was all over; the Argentines had surrendered. Our initial reaction was one of disappointment, adrenalin was flowing, we had been looking forward to a really good punch-up. This was followed moments later by an immense surge of relief and delight; we had survived.

With the Milan Platoon loaded onto our vehicles, the dash for Stanley began. The vehicles, surrounded and covered by members of 2 Para, The Blues and Royals flag proudly flying, we drove into Stanley. We were exuberant. We reached the War Memorial on the outskirts, in the lead by now, where we were told to stop. I hoisted the Union Jack from the antenna of my vehicle, and we waited. One by one the heads disappeared, the hatches closed, the Troop slept, exhausted, drained, woken only by the chill of a late afternoon and a feeling of great anti-climax.

3 Troop moved next day into a comfortable house and captured masses of trophies, including two Panhard armoured vehicles. 4 Troop moved up after a few days from Fitzroy to join 3 Troop and go aboard HMS *Fearless*. Their full story has yet to be told,

Having established myself for two days as CRACFI (Commander Royal Armoured Corps Falkland Islands) I waved goodbye to the two troops as they boarded HMS *Fearless*. I returned to the mud hole that is Fitzroy and the duties of a watchkeeper once again.

Life was dull in the extreme, only saved by the wildfowling opportunities. Captain Drummond, Grenadier Guards, and I had brought out shotguns and we went into the Goose Marketing business – five tins of beer a goose, six tins 'oven-ready'.

A week later, I pulled an ace in a draw for the next flight back to the UK. For a few days I was stunned by the transition from the Falklands to England. Just over a week later it is beginning to fade and, if it were not for my photographs, I would find it difficult to believe it really happened.